AROUND THE WORLD IN

BLACK & WHITE

AROUND THE WORLD IN
BLACK & WHITE

TRAVELING WITH A BIRACIAL BLENDED FAMILY

Alana Best

SHE WRITES PRESS

Published 2023
Printed in the United States of America
Print ISBN: 978-1-64742-531-9
E-ISBN: 978-1-64742-532-6
Library of Congress Control Number: 2023908204

For information, address:
She Writes Press
1569 Solano Ave #546
Berkeley, CA 94707

Interior Design by Tabitha Lahr

She Writes Press is a division of SparkPoint Studio, LLC.

This book is dedicated to the greatest loves of my life, to which I owe everything—Roland, Josephine, Kymani, and Sydahlia.

&

To all those who dedicate their time and energy to make this world more inclusive and just. The world is indebted, and the future generations thank you.

"Darkness cannot drive out darkness; only light can do that. Hate cannot drive out hate; only love can do that."

—MARTIN LUTHER KING, JR.

AUTHOR'S NOTE

THIS NOVEL TAKES PLACE IN 2018, prior to George Floyd's death and the subsequent Black Lives Matter movement that stirred a wave of protests across the globe and subsequently, an awakening of social and racial consciousness.

This novel contains stories and language that may be triggering, make readers uncomfortable and may be considered offensive. The language, stories and thoughts accounted are uncensored to provide as raw and realistic account as possible. This includes the use of the N-word, which I have chosen not to write out in its full form as I do not feel appropriate for a white person to ever do.

I acknowledge that this book is written through a white woman's eyes, which includes all the biased and privileged perspectives this entails.

FOREWORD

———•◦•———

AROUND THE WORLD IN BLACK AND WHITE brilliantly weaves together the double narrative of a couple's (Alana and Roland) dream realized with the realities of anti-Black racism. They embark on a yearlong worldwide adventure. While on this once-in-a-life-time excursion, they encounter the realities of traveling as a Black and white couple.

Written from the voice of Alana, the white spouse, this memoir brings us into the emotional roller coaster of a couple taking off from their everyday professional lives to embark on a yearlong venture (with a six-week-old baby and later a young child in tow) and all the excitement and anxieties and thrill this implies, interrupted by the sobering realities of traveling while Black and white.

"I never considered the possibility of being met, constantly, with racism" encapsulates why this book is a must-read for anyone who has had similar experiences or is interested in how racism manifests itself on people attempting to live their dreams. As blinders restrict the field of vision, making it difficult to see the broader context, so does racial privilege. This book eliminates the blinders that keep racism and intolerance so soundly in place and sharpens the realization that comes when these blinders are removed. Racist encounters recounted throughout the Bests' travels reveal the global reach of the legacy of colonization, African enslavement, and the ideology of white supremacy. These events also forced Alana's blinders off so that through love, proximity, and the draw of familial ties, she empathizes and begins to comprehend her husband's experiences with racism. The way racism infiltrates daily existence makes even a mundane walk in Beijing turn into an unpleasant event. Their hopes for a regenerative travel experience is punctuated by hyper-surveillance at some moments, overt racism and invisibility at others. As a Black woman married to a white man and rearing children with him, these experiences particularly resonated with me—but regardless of racial background it will resonate, I believe, with every reader.

Around the World in Black and White also explores not only the impact of racism on individuals but also the stresses these types of external factors put on relationships. It asks who should stand up for whom and what the impact of having to have others stand up for us is. There are clearly consequences on both sides of the ledger. Free-flowing and often humorous despite their sober moments, Best's stories pull us along to witness the human toll of racism and its manifestation not only for the person targeted but for those friends and family members who share their outcomes on a more personal level.

The context of the book is also extremely interesting, as it forces us to see the ways in which racism manifests itself in the far reaches of globe and compels us to reckon with the enduring consequences of imperialism, colonialism, and the enslavement of Africans. One might expect that places that have experienced the ravishes of colonization would be places of refuge for Black travelers; instead, the ways in which colonization co-opted various groups as part of its project has meant that anti-Black racism is a global phenomenon, one this couple and their children could not escape. No matter where they turned, it was a recurring theme of their trip. This demands that we reflect on why it is that anti-Back racism is so enduring and so global in scope.

Around the World in Black and White also forces us to ask ourselves some difficult questions. For those of us who are racialized, particularly those in the Black community, what does it mean when those closest to us do not really grasp our perspectives and our experiences? Is this the effect of self-censorship, or is it in fact the blinders of those around us?

Despite dealing with difficult topics, the book presents them with great humor and commonplace humanity that create enjoyable reading.

June Francis PhD, MBA, LLB
Cofounder of the Co-Laboratorio Project
Associate Professor of Marketing, Beedie School of Business
Director, SFU Institute for Diaspora Research and Engagement

PROLOGUE

Bangkok
2 months, 3 weeks old
March 8, 2018

"What breaks each person's heart is different—be it racial injustice, war, or animals. And when you figure out what it is that breaks yours, go toward it."

—GLENNON DOYLE

A GROUP OF YOUNG TOURISTS openly mock my husband. They cackle like hyenas, their shrieks piercing the air so erratically I momentarily question if they're sober. They feed off each other's energy, grasping one another's shoulders, their heads jerking back and forth. Two of them cover their mouths with one hand, pointing at him with the other. A short lady with a chin-length bob and thick bangs, falls to the ground, clutching her stomach.

I stand and stare in paralyzed shock, my arms clenching to our infant son strapped to my chest.

Roland turns to me, "I need to go speak with them."

My kind, loving, and tolerant husband reached his breaking point. After countless stares, requests for pictures, inappropriate comments, and an endless stream of pointing and laughing he's had enough. My naive, white bubble is bursting.

Kymani, our two-and-a-half-month-old son is curled up against my body. He is wrapped in his carrier, blissfully unaware of the scene unfolding around him. My heart breaks for him.

"I hope this world treats you better, little one," I whisper, sweeping my fingers through the soft curls on his delicate head.

I am not prepared for this. We have been in Asia for six weeks, the beginning of our yearlong trip, our adventure of a lifetime. I expected the typical challenges of travel and the added trials of bringing our infant son and a ten-year-old daughter with us. However, I never considered the possibility of being met, constantly, with racism.

HOME

Roland, Alana, and Kymani take a float plane to Vancouver

Victoria, British Columbia

0–5 weeks old

December 13, 2017–January 18, 2018

———————◆●————————

"The most effective way to do it, is to do it."

—AMELIA EARHART

MY TRANQUIL CANADIAN CITY IS suddenly filled with potential hazards and frightening possibilities. *Alana, just breathe. One step at a time. Dress the baby. Pack his diaper bag. Change him. Feed him. You got this.*

I wish Roland could come with me, but he is working. If he were here, he would be cracking jokes and cooing over our son, making my heart and the tension melt.

I cradle the back of my five-day-old boy's curly-haired head as I put him in the car seat. "You're going to be fine Kymani," I whisper trying to soothe myself as much as him. His dark brown eyes barely open before he shifts a little and falls back asleep. I adjust the straps around his chubby-yet-fragile arms and legs. After a deep breath, we walk out of the house for the first time since he was born.

Cars speed by on the street in front of our house. *Sit in the driver's seat. Start the car. Back up—SLOWLY—*

"Are you okay, Mom?"

I jump. Josephine's soft voice startles me. My intuitive ten-year old daughter gives me a concerned glance from the passenger seat.

"Yeah. I mean . . . I will be. Honestly, this is a bit harder than I thought. Thanks for coming with me."

Ten minutes later, I pull into the parking lot of the photo studio and breathe a sigh of relief. Inside, a table is set up for Kymani to lie on. A ladder stands beside it so the photographer can take his passport photos from above. I scoop Kymani from his cozy car seat and place him carefully on the table. The bright overhead lights make his complexion even paler than usual. Nadine, my beloved mother-in-law, informs me his skin will darken over the next year.

The photographer casually conveys the photo requirements. "We need a picture with his eyes open. He can't be crying, making any facial expressions, or put his hands near his face."

I resist rolling my eyes at these unrealistic demands and set about changing him to wake him up. He opens his eyes and lets out a weak cry. After a moment he calms down, but as soon as he does, he closes his eyes. This prompts the photographer to take some wet paper towel and wipe his face to arouse him.

Josephine shakes her head. "That's not a good idea."

I suppress a grin and squeeze her shoulder in thanks for saying exactly what I'm thinking.

Kymani is predictably shocked and starts wailing. His entire body constricts, and he scrunches his hands into fists beside his face. I scoop him up, rock him, and whisper apologies. After a minute he calms down, rubs his eyes, and slips back into unconsciousness.

I take control of this situation. "Alright, I'm going to pick him up and then put him back down. The movement should wake him up without upsetting him. You'll only have a moment to capture the picture with his eyes open."

The photographer nods her head and returns to her camera, assuring me she's ready.

4

I pick Kymani up. He opens his eyes and extends his arms. I place him back down. His eyes are open, and his face is calm. *Perfect.* I quickly move my hands out of the way. She adjusts her lens, fidgeting with the focus. When the *click-click* of the camera's shutter starts, Kymani is lying peacefully, eyes closed.

The photographer avoids my frustrated eyes as she scrolls sheepishly through the pictures. "Let's try it again."

I wait for her signal. Looking through her lens, she gives a subtle nod. I pick him up and place him back on the table. *Click-click-click.*

"I got it," she announces.

Relief washes over me, interrupted by the sound of Kymani pooping in his diaper. Josephine bursts into a fit of giggles. I can't help but join her.

A short while later, Kymani is clean and cocooned back in his car seat. We retrieve our hilarious, worst-baby-passport-picture-ever and twenty extra copies for all the immigration visas we'll need along the way.

When we arrive home, all in one piece, I sigh in relief. We did it. As I cuddle Kymani on the oversized blue club chair in the living room, I try to relax—but a bubbling worry builds in my stomach. Kymani's tiny sleeping face rests in my arms. This one-hour errand into town was overwhelming. In four weeks we would be leaving to travel the world, for a year. The anxiety threatens to flare into panic. *What the hell are we thinking?*

Our travel adventure began as a manageable concept. Six months into my relationship with Roland, we moved in together and could afford to put money aside as we split living expenses. We applied to our joint employer for their deferred salary leave program, which put twenty percent of our earnings into savings for four years, after which we receive a year off. Our jobs are guaranteed upon our return.

We had not initially planned on bringing an infant with us. However, as our relationship (and the pot of money) matured, the *to baby or not to baby* question came up. We wanted to grow our family, but we didn't want to give up our lifestyle or our dream travel plans. I was in my midthirties and Roland was over forty. Time was ticking.

One night, as we agonized over the discussion once again, Roland said, "picture us at seventy-five years old." I winced a little sipping my wine. "We're thinking back on our lives together."

I marinate on this thought, of the life I wanted with this man I loved so deeply.

He continued. "With the wisdom of age and the advantage of hindsight, would we regret not having a baby? Or, on the other hand, would we regret not taking a year off to travel?"

The answer to both was yes. We would be saddened if we delayed and could not conceive. And we would be disappointed if we gave up on our adventure—because who knows if we would ever have the chance again?

It was decided.

To complicate things further, we evenly split custody of Josephine with her dad. We knew it would be difficult for her to leave either parent for an extended period of time, but there was no other feasible solution. We worked out a schedule whereby she would finish the school year with her dad, then come traveling with us for six months.

To avoid anxiety-induced paralysis about leaving in a month, I resolved to leave the house every day. Each outing got easier.

✈

"WE NAMED YOU KYMANI FOR A REASON," I assure him as we wait to board the first of many planes this year. "It means 'adventurous traveler.' See, you were born to do this!"

I put the noise-cancelling headphones over his tiny two-week-old ears and walk out of the harborside terminal to the floatplane. The flight is a short thirty-minutes to Vancouver, where the French Embassy will review our European Union visa applications.

Roland, Kymani, and I cram into the small seats. I wait nervously for takeoff, a soother in one hand and a bottle in the other, but the vibration and the loud white noise of the engine put Kymani to sleep.

As the plane descends, the pilot announces that due to bad weather he is landing at a different terminal. Our appointment is in forty-five minutes, and it will take us at least that long make it downtown from this alternate airport.

On the sky train, I struggle to remove the layers of clothes required in rainy British Columbia to nurse Kymani. Increasing numbers of commuters pile in at every stop, and Roland creates a barrier with a receiving blanket. I wish I was more confident and cooler about it, but I'm sweaty, awkward, and self-conscious. People are either staring at us or trying desperately hard not to. I guess I should get used to this, there will be a lot of public nursing over the next year.

When we exit the sky train, we are ten minutes late for our appointment. Roland holds Kymani in his carrier, I throw the baby bag over my shoulder, and we start jogging the couple blocks to the embassy. Soon my lower abdomen cramps, and blood gathers in the postpartum pad. I gave birth two weeks ago; my body is not ready to be running.

We arrive at the consulate fifteen minutes late, frantic and apologetic. Despite their strict policy, they kindly honor our appointment.

On our flight back, I am exhausted but with renewed confidence. No matter how much we plan, things will go wrong on our trip. Obstacles and setbacks are inevitable. What matters is, notwithstanding the challenges today, we did well under stress. We helped each other and completed our mission.

We've got this—Bring it on, world!

Alana playing with Kymani on his first international flight

Beijing
1 month, 1 week old
January 19

———————•◦•———————

"Any problem can be solved with a little ingenuity."
—ANGUS "MAC" MACGYVER

WE ARRIVE AT THE SMALL VICTORIA airport so early there are hardly any other people in the building. Our first flight takes us to Tokyo, with a layover in Beijing. We anxiously approach the customer service agent. Roland and I booked our plane tickets separately due to a messy situation correcting Kymani's birth date and passport numbers on his ticket after he was born.

"Where are we off to today?" the attendant greets us cheerfully. As she types and checks the screen I begin my long pre-rehearsed, slightly stressed-out speech. I finish by asking if she could please, for all that is good in the world, put our seats together for all our flights. She nods with a smile, "Of course, no problem."

I shrug it off; this frenzied, stressed-out-mom routine is not me. I take a deep breath. *You'll get the hang of it. Relax and enjoy yourself.*

At the gate to our flight, Roland chats with the agents about our yearlong adventure, telling them this is the first of our fifty-six flights. Roland's positivity is infectious and uplifting. I see it so often in the faces of strangers as they speak to him and listen intently.

The agents take a picture of us standing in front of the gate with the flight number and destination on the screen behind us: the first snapshot of what will be an incredible journey.

We board the plane and find our seats easily but scramble with our bags. Lesson learned, next time I won't pack our carry-ons organized by person. Instead, I'll put everything we need at our feet in one bag, and the rest in other carry-ons to go overhead.

As we reach our flying altitude over the ocean, I recline my chair at a sloth's pace as to not disturb Kymani. I softly smile down at my boy nuzzled up to me, sleeping, and my guilt about traveling with our newborn melts away. All he wants in the world is to be close to us. To be fed, changed, and loved. We could have enjoyed this time with him in the comfort of our home in Canada, or while exploring the world—it doesn't matter to him. Home is wherever we're together.

We land in Beijing in a dreary haze. We are staying here overnight before catching our flight to Tokyo in the morning.

At the airport kiosk, that provides us with a shuttle to our free layover hotel, the agent informs us that our names are not on their list. It takes over an hour of discussions and a few phone calls before we are escorted to a van.

At the check-in desk, they cannot rectify that we want one room instead of two as our tickets were booked separately. Exacerbated, we tell him to give us both rooms, but we'll only use one. This rattles the clerk, who insists on calling the airport and airline agents. He grasps the receiver with a shaking hand, his eyes glued to the floor.

When he gets off the phone he spends fifteen minutes fidgeting at his computer without talking to us. Roland's patience wears thin. "Two vans full of guests were helped and we're still standing here. Our baby needs to sleep."

The clerk nods and picks up the receiver to call someone else.

Roland is not quick to anger, but when he does, he means business. "No. We are not waiting any longer for you to sort things out. Give us our room please."

He complies hesitantly and hands us a key.

We walk into our room and drop our bags on the bed, exhausted.

I unpack my belongings, along with my stress. "We are here, with a roof over our heads, and we're all going to get some sleep."

Roland lets out a deep sigh and nods in agreement.

I continue to decompress as I wade through Kymani's gear, finding everything he needs for bed. "Babe, do you have any diapers? I have two left in his diaper bag, and I can't find any in my backpack."

Roland puts the tangle of wires and electronics he's holding on the bed and opens his carry-on to search. "Nope, sorry."

"Fuck!" I screw my eyes shut in frustration. "They're all in the checked luggage. We won't make it through tonight and the three-hour flight tomorrow with two diapers."

Roland sighs. "I'll check the store in the hotel lobby."

✈

"THEY DON'T SELL ANY HERE AND WE are nowhere near a store," he announces fifteen minutes later when he returns. "I did find some instant noodles though. That's a win."

We smile weakly at each other as he turns on the kettle. "I got my first inaugural picture request."

I manage a slight laugh. "I am sure that won't be the last one."

"Yeah, I'm not sure they see many Black people. I wonder if Kymani will also get a lot of requests?" he bends over our son for a quick kiss.

"I guess we'll see." I grip Kymani's deliciously plump leg in my hand and turn my attention back to the task at hand.

11

I'll 'MacGyver' my way through this with some creative ingenuity. I line the diaper with a pad. In the morning when I take it out there should, in theory, be a clean diaper underneath. I lay him down in his bassinet, and hope for the best.

✈

THE MORNING LIGHT WAKES US JUST before 8 a.m. I glance over at Kymani, who is sleeping serenely beside us; instinctively his eyes open seconds after. It amazes me how babies do this.

I lean in to pick him up. *Shit.* He's soaking wet. The pad prevented the diaper from locking in the wetness at the seams, but underneath, the diaper is still clean and dry. There are more clean outfits than diapers to spare, so I try again with a thinner pad.

On the plane, we discover the thinner pad makes zero difference. We arrive in Tokyo on a chilly afternoon in mid-January, Roland and I bundled up in our usual winter jackets, and Kymani donning his last clean diaper and a blanket as a toga.

JAPAN

Alana and Roland with snow monkeys bathing in the hot springs

Tokyo & Nagano

1 month, 1 week old
January 20–27

———————◆•◆———————

"One life, one encounter."
—JAPANESE PROVERB

WE WERE WARNED TAXIS IN JAPAN are outrageously expensive and that the transit system in Tokyo is an easy venture we should rely on throughout our stay. Despite this great advice, we can't muster the mental energy with two suitcases, two backpacks, a baby bag, and Kymani in his stroller. We find the first cab big enough to fit us all, and hop in.

To our surprise, we arrive in twenty-minutes and the rate is reasonable. We are doubly grateful for the cab driver, as we did not know Japan's address system has entrances, and therefore addresses, on multiple sides of buildings. Our front entrance is hidden in what would be considered a back alley in Canada.

Our adorable studio apartment is exactly what we need: a little kitchen, two futon couches, and a double bed tucked away in the corner. I drop my bags and head straight to the bathroom, where I pause and stare at the electronically enhanced toilet in front of me.

I sit down, and immediately jump back up. The seat is warm. It takes me a second before I realize it is not because someone just spent an hour on it before me, it is equipped with a seat warmer. "This thing is more high-tech than my smartphone!" I call to Roland as I examine the remote-control panel beside me. It offers an array of interesting features including various music and spray-cleaning options. It is an exquisite experience.

Finally, after twenty-four hours of travel, we've made it to our first destination. There's no debate about what to do with our first hours in Tokyo: sleep.

✈

THE NEXT DAY WE WAKE UP EXCITED, wrap up warm, and venture outside. Our itinerary includes one major outing a day, a tactic we will stick to for the majority of our year of travel. This ensures we can enjoy the sights, but also gives the baby plenty of time to nap and us some downtime. We are conscious that this is a travel marathon, not a two-week vacation sprint. We don't want to burn out.

The Tsukiji Fish Market is a ten-minute walk from our place. The dock hauls in over 1,000 tons of fresh catch each morning to be sold and traded at auction. The reviews online insist we arrive before it gets too busy and enjoy a sushi breakfast. Since we're up early with Kymani, this suits us perfectly.

Small cartoon-like trucks and forklifts transport crates of seafood in ice around the industrial pier. The distinct smell of fish is surprisingly faint as we walk among the stalls and the hundreds of stacked containers.

The vendor and restaurant area displays rows of open stalls selling fresh packaged fish and seafood, including oysters and urchins. The market doesn't allow strollers, so Kymani is bundled and fastened to Roland in his carrier. We wander through, guessing what the deep-fried snacks contain and drooling over the sushi.

The cold January day prevents us from lingering outside for too long. Kymani is content, snuggled in warm against his dad, but he'll only last so long before wanting to eat.

We find a small sushi restaurant comprised of a fifteen-foot bar with a number of people sitting and eating. We squeeze through the narrow space between the bar stools and the knobs on the wall which hang patrons' jackets. The ultra-tight space does not comfortably accommodate our medium-sized North American bodies, which are about a third larger than the average Japanese person. The baby is not helping the situation, adding an extra foot of girth. A lady sees us struggling and graciously takes our backpack behind the counter.

We quickly order some green tea and a random selection of sushi and sashimi. We no longer have the luxury of perusing menus, contemplating our choices.

The chef elegantly piles our plates, made of giant banana leaves, with the fresh delicacies. Every move he makes is careful, deliberate, with a gentle finesse. He is so graceful in his movements, like watching a ballet. He takes his time, an extra instant of respect to everything he does including handing us our menus, pouring our tea, or plating our food. I'm reminded of a Japanese proverb, which translates as *One life, one encounter*—or, treat every moment like it's the only one. I love this reminder to be present, and I decide to honor it as best as I can on our journey.

I have never seen pieces of sashimi so plump before. I bite down and before it even touches my tongue, I'm in heaven. The texture of the tuna as my teeth glide through it makes me close my eyes, anticipating the delicate flavor to come. The clean, subtle taste fills my senses. *How can I ever go back to regular sushi after this?* This is the first day of our trip and already, I will never be the same.

We work our way through breakfast in soft moans of delight. Kymani wakes up as we are finishing. The proprietors courteously give us time to feed him a bottle of milk, pumped earlier that morning. When we clumsily exit, we are amazed to find a long lineup of patrons waiting in the cold.

Fluffy flakes of snow fall lightly on us as we finish meandering through the market. I did not anticipate this weather. As I find out, nobody did. We are in the heaviest snowfall Tokyo has had in four years.

Despite the cold, we go in search of diapers. At the first store the lady at the counter doesn't understand English, and neither does her coworker. This surprises me; Through my previous travels to other Asian countries I never experienced a language barrier like this. We leave having searched unsuccessfully ourselves.

We find a 7-Eleven a block away. The cashier, clueless to what I'm saying, points to a Free Wi-Fi sign. I download a picture of diapers and show her. She beams with that unmistakable *Ah-ha* expression that says, *I understand*. However, she follows with an apologetic shake of her head. Two more stores give us the same *sorry, no* expression. Finally, we find a minimarket selling emergency packages containing two diapers. We deplete them of their stock and head home. The snow formed a thin coat over Tokyo and continues to pour out of the morning sky.

At the apartment, we take off our cold, damp outer layers. I remove Kymani's hat, mitts, jacket, and booties. We pull on fresh socks and warm sweaters. Roland makes himself comfortable on the couch.

I stare out the white window. "I have about zero interest in going back out in this today."

Roland is relieved, grateful for the rare opportunity that I want to stay in and do nothing. "Let's call it a snow day." He sinks further into the couch, propping his feet on the coffee table and sets about editing the pictures he took this morning.

That evening, we video chat with Nadine, Roland's mom. She is eager to know how our first voyage overseas went. When we tell her about the MacGyver diaper incident, she almost falls off her chair laughing.

"We wish you were here with us; we miss you so much." I'm not giving lip service. Leaving Roland's parents for a year was a difficult decision. Nadine is an endless source of love and support for us.

In Victoria, she was at our house almost daily, and if she wasn't holding Kymani, she was helping. Although in her midseventies, she is energetic, strong, and agile. She cooked, scrubbed, hauled, wiped, and packed for hours on end, getting us ready for this trip.

We committed to frequent video chats but still, I am guilt-ridden for putting an ocean between her and Kymani.

"How's Pops doing?" Roland asks, inquiring after his dad.

Nadine's smile fades a little "Oh, good," she reassures him. "You know . . . nothing really new."

Ed's health has declined over the past few years. His short-term memory is playing games with him, coming and going as it pleases. His motivation to go to the gym and remain social is as much a mental barrier as a physical one. The charismatic, boisterous dad Roland knew growing up is changing. Worry of his health further complicated our debates about leaving for a year.

Roland turns the phone toward himself, "Give Pops a hug from us and tell him we miss him."

His entire family habitually ends conversations by sending best wishes to anyone who isn't there. It's easy to fall in love with this considerate, kind-hearted family.

✈

THE SNOW STAYS FOR ANOTHER few days, but we brave the cold. We walk through the expansive park and gardens of the Imperial Palace, a tranquil refuge in the center of Tokyo surrounded by moats and massive stone walls. We take in the cityscape at the top of the Skytree and visit Shibuya Crossing, the busiest pedestrian intersection in the world. We people-watch in cool neighborhoods like Ginza, which is like New York's Fifth Avenue meets Times Square. We push the compact stroller down crowded sidewalks and listen to a GPS-navigated tour. We marvel at the modern architecture of Ginza's flagship stores and wander through luxury boutiques, lusting after lavish merchandise.

Today, on Kymani's six-week birthday, we are on a less exciting journey. He needs his vaccination shots. We sit in the waiting room of an international clinic, next to another couple from Canada who are vaccinating their adopted Japanese daughter. She is precious, and about half the size of our hearty son, even though they're the same age. As we wait, we compare notes on sleeping and eating schedules, and being parents to newborns.

In the patient room, the doctor and nurse weigh and measure Kymani. He's in the ninety-fifth percentile for height, weight, and head circumference. He's a healthy, robust boy.

My pleasure evaporates as the nurse takes Kymani and the doctor pinches his chubby leg with his fingers. I am hot with anxiety. Kymani lets out a small cry as the first needle pierces his skin. *Okay, not so bad.* The second needle comes, and he constricts his muscles then screams his discontent. I rush over and comfort him with a cuddle, rocking him back and forth.

✈

KYMANI LOVES TO BE TOUCHED AND coddled. Often, at night, he will cry and won't go back to sleep unless he's directly on me, skin-to-skin. Usually I can coddle him to sleep and then transfer him to his bassinet, but this evening is rougher than usual, likely due to the vaccines. Every time I break contact with him, he shrieks. I'm left with no choice but to hold him all night.

The next morning I'm exhausted but I muster up the energy to get ready because today is a *big* day. We're going to a sumo wrestling tournament. I boil some water to make some instant coffee. I miss my espresso maker, badly.

The day-long event begins with the amateur matches in the morning and finishes with the highest-ranking professionals in the evening. We arrive midday; thinking six hours of spectating will be more than enough. We order some over-priced sushi and Sapporo beer from the arena vendors. Although a tad pricy, the quality is substantially better than the hotdogs I would grab at a Blue Jays game.

The workers at the arena usher us to our box seats. Unlike the North American sort, which are perched like glamorous penthouses overlooking the entertainment, these are small, square spaces close to the ring. There is enough room to sit four Japanese adults, cross-legged, on little flat red cushions. Our perimeter is defined with gold bar railings a few inches off the ground and behind it, a narrow walkway.

We squeeze into the snug box, experimenting with crossing and extending our legs while wrangling the baby gear. I tuck in our jackets and Roland ensures me our baby bag isn't spilling into our neighbor's box. We are surrounded by mostly Japanese fans, who are comfortably situated in their allotted space.

Kymani is dressed in a dark blue Kimono with black trim I picked up while on business in Vancouver, especially for this occasion. Our neighbors express their love for Kymani and his attire. "So cute!" they admire, pointing and touching his outfit. "Beautiful!" I gush over the compliments, proud that the effort is appreciated.

The rules of sumo wrestling are simple: if you are tossed out of the ring or you touch the ground with anything but the soles of your feet, you lose. The matches are entertaining and easy to follow. These gigantic men in tiny outfits exude flexibility and strength. They put on a show before the match begins, hitting their thick thighs with their white chalky hands then kicking high into the air. Once they engage, the wrestling is ruthless, quick and tough, as they jar each other with remarkable agility. Each match is over in seconds.

Despite the enthusiastic energy in the arena, I am yawning, and tired tears spill from my eyes. I wonder if I could huddle into the fetal position and nap in our box. I'm jealous of Kymani, who is sleeping in a nest of our jackets in front of us.

The crowds become thicker and more excited as the high-ranking wrestlers start appearing around 4 p.m. The last half-dozen matches get people screaming and flying banners, cheering for their favorite competitors. The vibration in the arena uplifts and reenergized me. I begin to cheer with them as the giant men collide and throw each other around the ring.

✈

AFTER TWO SUBWAY TRANSFERS, we're on the bullet train heading for the town of Nagano, 245 km north of Tokyo. Our compartment is clean, orderly, and packed with soundless people. Passengers come and go, patiently waiting their turn in line, helping each other load and unload luggage, and then sitting respectfully beside their neighbor. This brand of civility is a rarity I have only ever seen *en masse* here in Japan, where it seems everyone is treated with polite regard.

We have not had one unpleasant encounter. Not one rude remark about Kymani; no resentment aimed at us as tourists; and no exceptional treatment toward Roland, who I am sure, is the only Black person many of them have ever seen. If there is any negativity, they are too considerate and refined to show us even a hint.

This graciousness signifies a strength that is so different to the bravado North Americans often associate with power. This dignified calm and kindness are the attributes of the Nelson Mandelas and Gandhis of the world, and yet are frequently dismissed as weakness or meekness. These leaders used silence to command a room and their wisdom lied in their still deliberations.

Or I have it all wrong, and the strictness of this society is actually stifling. All I know for sure is, traveling in Japan is a pleasure.

At Nagano station we meet our Dutch tour guide, Anna. She speaks impeccable English, which is a delight after so many significant language barriers throughout our stay. She has been living in Japan for the past two years, improving her Japanese. It is thrilling to meet people like her while traveling. I am inspired by her interesting and unexpected journey through life.

When we arrive at Jigokudani Monkey Park, we cocoon Kymani in multiple layers and strap him to me in his carrier to keep him warm in the minus seven degree cold.

Our group is waiting for us at the entrance of the hiking trail. The pine trees tower over the path on either side, dwarfing us as we begin the climb uphill. Enormous wet snowflakes tumble out of the sky and create a thick layer of sticky snow that clings to the branches and trunks and covers the ground like a glistening duvet. I close my eyes and breathe in the sting of the crisp, cold air. The way it hits my lungs and bites my cheeks takes me back to my childhood in Saskatchewan, building snow forts with my siblings and gathering snow in bowls to eat with maple syrup.

There is no wind, and the only sound is the light crunch of the snow as it compacts beneath our boots. I brush the thick snowflakes that gather on Kymani's toque and peak into the carrier to make sure no snow is getting inside. His eyes are closed, and he is scrunched up in the fetal position sleeping. I cover him again and zip my jacket over top, marching upward.

At the top, there is a shelter for those who need a break. I bypass it, too eager to reach the monkeys. I exchange the quickest of glances to Roland who is thinking the same thing. Without having to say a word, we carry on.

Only a few feet away from the shelter is a troop of Japanese macaques, also known as snow monkeys. Their light gray–brown coats and vibrant red faces contrast strikingly against the white backdrop. There are forty or more peppering the landscape, along the base of a small valley and up the gently sloping ridge. Many are digging in the powdered hills, rummaging for food, while others tumble and twirl as they play and chase each other.

We continue down the path to the hot springs. They are perched on the rocks, nuzzling tenderly for warmth alongside the natural pools of warm water. The moms feed, clean, and carry their little ones on their backs with loving ease.

Roland, camera in hand and a grin on his face, crouches down to get a shot of two grown macaques hugging at the edge of a steaming pool. Then he makes his way to a higher vantage point to take a picture of another drinking water. The macaque sips delicately then lifts his head, small drops of water dripping from the fur under his mouth.

Two teenage macaques burst out of a tree in full chase. The adults turn their gaze toward the rambunctious duo, who run after each other around the pool's edge. One of them dives into the water, its arms and legs stretched outward in glee, and the second, without hesitation, follows his comrade. They swim to the other side, pull their slim, soaking wet bodies out, and after a couple of shakes, jump at each other and tear off into a snow drift. I shake my head a little at the surreal performance playing out before me.

Soon my fingers and toes are numb from the cold, and

Kymani wakes up with squawks and squirms. I leave Roland with his camera and head to the shelter, where I find a bench to sit down on and unstrap Kymani from my chest. "Thanks little man for giving us the opportunity to be here. You did awesome," I whisper as I pull out the nursing cover.

After we break for lunch, our tour continues to the tranquil Zenkō-ji Temple. Anna assiduously points out the architecture and explains the symbolic meanings of the gate, buildings, and spiritual symbols as we leisurely walk through the area. Though the Buddhist temple was built for the common people, the structures are intricately and royally decorated in crimson, forest green, and gold.

I break off to tend to Kymani. The washroom is a basic building with no heat, though the four walls and roof provide some shelter. On the floor of the entranceway there is a black rubber mat and some tiny sandals. *Oh no. Am I supposed to take off my shoes?* The cold temperatures are keeping the freshly mopped floors wet, and my feet will not fit in those sandals. "I'm sorry," I whisper to nobody and anybody I might be offending as I step past the mat and into a stall.

There is no changing table or surface I can lay Kymani on, and I fear the floor would give him instant pneumonia. "Okay buddy, we're going to get creative here." I rip off my jacket and struggle to take my three layers of pants off with the carrier still on me, moving my legs back and forth like a toddler, trying not to pee myself.

A warm trickle escapes my body. My bladder is not the same after two kids. I tear the remaining clothes off and sit on the toilet, but my underwear and first layer of pants are already wet.

Kymani cries. I'm not sure if he is mirroring my frustration or if he really needs to be changed. I stay seated on the toilet, pants around my ankles. I unstrap him from the carrier and lay him on my lap. With his diaper off, I bend down to grab a new one. Another warm trickle runs down my inner thigh. *You've got to be kidding me.* "Now *you're* peeing on me?!" I change and dress him quickly.

At least one of us is now dry and comfortable, I think, just before Kymani boisterously vocalizes his readiness to eat. *Great, I didn't want to get out of these peed-on pants anyway.* I wrangle my sweater off and add it to the stack of items balancing on my backpack, to keep as many things off the ground as possible. My jaw clamps, the muscles in my exposed legs and torso clench, and my skin shivers in the cold as I nurse.

I laugh. What a ridiculous sight I am. I laugh a little more, then irrepressibly. This is why everyone back home looked at me like I had three heads when we announced our travel plans with Kymani.

The footsteps outside the stall stop my laughter. A Japanese lady is asking me something, in a worried tone, I don't understand. She's probably wondering what on earth I'm still doing in here. Or she's heard me laughing and thinks I lost my mind. My cheeks burn red with embarrassment as I tell her I'm fine and that I'm tending to a baby. Her response fades as she walks away.

After Kymani finishes nursing, I lay him on my waterproof jacket on the ground. I take off two layers of wet pants and put them into my backpack; I'll have to survive the rest of the day with the one thin layer.

I tiptoe out of the washroom but am spotted by the Japanese lady. She inquires with a concerned and questioning expression, and when I unveil the baby from his carrier she understands instantly, smiles, and laughs. Some things are universal.

✈

WE'RE TOSSING A FRENZY OF BAGS, clothes, diapers, and gear around the room in an attempt to get organized and out the door in short order. We have an early flight to Beijing, and we've committed to taking the transit system now that we've learned how to use it.

For the fifth time, I check the clock, "We're not going to make it, we need to leave."

Roland avoids eye contact, organizing one of his bags diligently. "Why don't we take a cab, it'll be quicker and easier."

Annoyed but unwilling to start an argument, I agree. "Okay, but how do we order one?"

Roland already thought it through. "Earlier this week I saw them lined up a few blocks down on the main street. I'll run down—you can stay in the lobby with Kymani and the bags."

Hesitantly, I concede, which gives us another half hour to finish packing and tidy the flat.

In the cab, the meter rolls over yen at an expeditious rate. My downloaded map indicates that we still have another forty minutes to go.

"Roland, this is going to cost us a fortune." I do some quick math in my head. "We're $100 deep and we're only a third the way there."

In equal measures of confusion and concern Roland gasps. "How did it cost us so little on our way in?"

"It was a different airport. This one is farther away. We should have taken the metro." This shouldn't be new, bewildering information. I remind myself that because I planned all the logistics, everything is clearer in my mind. I should not have agreed to this taxi plan; I should have said something.

"Oh well," I sigh with the equivalency of a yoga *Om*, attempting to release all the tension and stress. "We can't do anything about it now. It will be whatever it is."

At the airport I hand over my credit card for the $321 mistake we just made. I try not to think about how much French wine that could have bought me in six months' time.

CHINA

Roland, Alana, and Kymani on the Great Wall of China

Beijing

1 month, 2 weeks old
January 27–February 3

———◆•◆———

"I look at an ant and I see myself: a native South African, endowed by nature with a strength much greater than my size so I might cope with the weight of a racism that crushes my spirit."

—MIRIAM MAKIBA

A GROUP OF MEN SURROUND A makeshift table made of a barrel with a piece of sturdy cardboard overtop. The men on one side raise their hands, clenching playing cards, in victory. The others clamp their fists hard to their hips in defeat. Our cab driver yells out the window to the group, who are ignoring the fact that they are blocking off the narrow *hutong* (long alleys that run between the residential courtyards of Beijing). Without a glance back, they pick up their game, moving over for the car to pass with a quarter inch of space on each side. I'm awestruck by the accuracy of their collective depth perception. In North America, where the cars are wide, but the roads are wider, we do not need to acquire this skill.

The neighborhood is packed with small convenience stores, hairdressers, and shops weaved through multi-family dwellings. The ever-narrowing alleys must have been more practical some seven hundred years ago when they were built. Our car squeezes past people hefting bags, riding bikes, and congregating outside in the bitter late-January cold.

The cab driver stops in the middle of the alley and points down a narrow corridor lined with bikes. "Orchid, your hotel."

We follow his pointed finger to a white building tucked fifty feet back with the hotel sign. As we gather our bags, our eyes meet, and we raise our eyebrows simultaneously: *This should be interesting.*

We're greeted with warm smiles at the front entrance, given a complimentary smartphone to use during our stay, and offers of help with our bags as two staff members prepare to walk us to our residence. It takes a village to travel with a baby, and instead of resisting the help I say thank you and hand over my suitcase.

The pair leads us back into the cold alley. We follow them through a labyrinth, stopping at each intersection where they point to the signs, seven feet up on the buildings' walls, suggesting we make note of how to navigate our way out again. The unique character of the neighborhood has Roland digging out his camera to take pictures along the way. We pass mattresses and other rubbish piled up in corners, a man sorting through garbage bags outside his building, a lady sweeping debris out her front door, and a young man scurrying from the communal bathrooms back to his home.

The curb appeal of our new place is . . . well . . . true to the Hutong District. A maroon steel door marks the end of the alley. A double mattress leans against the wall beside it and clothes hang from lines above. Behind me is a couch with two small dogs lying on it. There are no discernible owners to be seen. As if hearing my thoughts, the scruffy tan and white dog opens its eyes, before stretching its legs, shifting over, and going back to sleep.

Our front door is secured with a thick metal frame and bars. Inside, we're shocked at the contrast of the villa to its surroundings. The apartment is bright and clean and minimalist, with modern decor and brand-new everything. The ensuite jacuzzi is especially inviting after walking in the wind-biting cold. Upstairs, a private rooftop patio overlooks the low-level housing and winding alleys. *This will do just fine.*

✈

I SIT UP IN A STARTLED PANIC at a thump above me. "Roland, wake up," I whisper sharply, intending to convey emergency without waking up Kymani, who is in the travel bassinet beside me. "Someone is on our roof!"

Roland doesn't move a muscle. "*Roland!*" Still nothing. I shake him.

"What babe?" he murmurs, half asleep and instinctively rolling from his back to his side, assuming he's snoring.

I nudge him again. "I heard a thump on the roof. Listen!" Roland sits up and gazes toward the ceiling, the room in total darkness.

Thump. The clamor moves swiftly from above the bed to the front door.

"Shit, what is that?" Roland pulls off the bed covers to investigate.

"I don't know. Where's the phone the hotel staff gave us?" I rummage in my purse next to the bed. "Here it is, got it. Ugh! It's an Android, I don't know how to use this thing." I rub my finger along the perimeter, searching for the power button.

"Babe, come here."

I walk over, the phone still clenched in my hands. Roland peers up at the skylight with a grin on his face.

"What is it?" I follow his gaze upward. A cat's plump butt is sitting lazily against the glass.

A few seconds later another cat pounces on the roof, making the same thump as before. They both scurry off together. I roll my eyes, laughing-off my fear. "I thought for sure we were getting robbed."

As I drift off to sleep I wish Josephine were with us. She adores cats. *She would have loved this.*

✈

WE DON'T HAVE PROPER WINTER GEAR. I have three to four layers on, but they are thin, and I'm so terribly cold that my fingers and toes are stiff and turning an unhealthy shade of blue. My eyes follow the gondola up to the Great Wall, and I give my complaining head a shake. I remind myself that Roland and I grew up in the Canadian prairies, where winters are twenty to thirty degrees Celsius colder than it is here. We will survive.

As we turn the corner, a line of vendors appears. They are selling gloves and toques to ill-prepared tourists, like yours truly. I dip into a shop and over-pay for two pairs of gloves for Roland and myself. Kymani, as usual, is the warmest of us all, snuggled in layers of Canadian winter–approved gear and huddled up in the carrier strapped to my chest.

The Mutianyu Great Wall is one of the best-preserved sections, and as we walk along, looking to the horizon, I mentally travel back in time. I imagine the soldiers patrolling this same path, gazing out at the same view, centuries ago. Roland stands beside me, throwing his arm around my shoulder with a proud smile for making it here. In silence, we take in the visible length of the Wall as it meanders through trees and over hills in subtle waves and curves.

Kymani whimpers with hunger, so I leave Roland to take pictures and explore the watchtowers. I settle into a nook that offers some privacy and protection from the wind. Surrounded by the wall and the watchtower, a stream of sunshine comes through parting clouds, warming my face.

Here I feed Kymani, and gaze over the quiet, peaceful scene. I appreciate these moments he gives me. He forces me to slow down, and when I do, I take in my surroundings differently. I am submerged in the stillness. I breathe in the cool crisp air and look out onto the soaring structure across the skyline. I touch the Wall, the dust from the brick coats my hand. I wonder what this wall has witnessed, what secrets it holds. I imagine the battles it beheld, the words of love, loneliness, hope, fear, victory and defeat it has heard over the centuries.

I think of home and how our first months of Kymani's life might have been: spent cozily on the sofa with the television on in the background. A profound sense of gratitude washes over me for all the choices that brought us here, to this moment where I am breastfeeding my newborn atop one of the wonders of the world. I hold him closer and close my eyes, turning my face fully toward the sun, and breathe.

✈

BACK AT THE HOTEL, WE REPLENISH the baby supplies then go for a stroll through the neighborhood in search of a restaurant for dinner. My long, thick, dark hair is tied in a topknot behind a heavy curtain of blunt bangs giving me a local-lookalike disguise that means I go largely unnoticed—except when I'm beside Roland.

Everywhere we walk people stare and point in Roland's direction. Many people want to take a selfie with him. Parents ask if Roland will join their children in a picture. Some kids are good sports and others are apprehensive of the friendly stranger getting close to them.

The requests are endless and exhausting. I consider, with greater empathy, how this type of treatment exasperates

Hollywood celebrities. I'm in a weeklong crash course of public gawking, pointing, and picture taking, and I'm about done with it.

Kymani is also a little mini celebrity. People stare at him, touch him, ask to hold him, want pictures with him, and say things like, "Aw, he's cute. Skin like mama, face like dada." It gets said so often we soon have a running joke about it.

Tonight is the same. Two women stop us outside the restaurant. They pinch Kymani's little feet, wiggle them playfully and smile at him. The older woman turns and speaks in a hushed voice to the younger one before sharing a chuckle.

"Let us guess, he looks like his dad but has light skin like me," I say.

Their eyes bulge, "You speak Cantonese?"

"No," I laugh, "we've heard it a number of times."

The restaurant is tucked into a dim, desolate back alley. I'm a bit scared to go inside given the rugged exterior, but it was highly recommended by our hotel's owner, who is a chef from Montréal. He transformed our Beijing visit into a culinary escapade.

We step inside to discover the definition of 'diamond in the rough.' The front lobby exposes an open-air brick-paved courtyard adorned with lush plants and surrounded by glass-enclosed indoor seating.

Once we're seated I give Kymani a bottle to put him to sleep in his stroller beside us.

"Does it bother you?" I ask Roland "All the attention?"

Roland pauses, thinking about it for a moment. "If they are good-natured, I don't mind. However, when it's a negative vibe, that's different."

I pause, surprised. "I'm sure the majority are just curious."

"Alana, I wish that were the case, I really do."

"Well, sometimes when I see someone beautiful, especially if they have a unique look, I have to make a conscious effort not to stare," I suggest.

"Alana, I wish more people thought like that and saw beauty in others the way you do."

"Well, maybe they do."

His silence tells me he doesn't agree but doesn't want to engage any further. This puts me into lawyer-mode. I start building a case in my head, with examples, analogies, and facts to prove my point. I relish the opportunity for a debate because it helps me get to the heart of an issue. I'll argue a side, and not necessarily because I believe in what I'm saying or because I want to be right; often I do it because I want to draw out more from the other person.

My mind races through a slew of examples. One, when I was at an event in rural Jamaica, several children ran up to me wanting to touch my hand. They were so interested in my skin, my eyes, my painted nails, and my hair. Another similar experience occurred when Roland, Josephine, and I visited a school in a remote village in Kenya. The kids gravitated to Josephine, who was their age but whose appearance was unalike to them. In both instances, these were children. Their interest, their staring and wanting to touch, could not yet be rooted in anything negative. I believe they were simply interested in seeing something—some*one*—so different to their everyday. Couldn't that be it?

A text message interrupts my thoughts. "Ah! Emma sent us a picture of Savannah."

This puts a smile on Roland's face. Emma is a close friend from back home. She and her partner, Damian, are taking care of our dog Savannah for the year.

"Awe, our girl," Roland beams. "How's she doing?" His naturally passionate expression is one of the many reasons I love him. If you have good news, he's the first person you want to tell because you are guaranteed a genuine, heartfelt, and animated response. It's impossible not to be swept into a higher level of happiness when you're with him.

"She's great," I respond, happy yet sad because I miss her already. "She's snuggled happily on the couch."

"What a beauty." Roland adorns. "I still can't believe they agreed to take her for the entire year. Seriously, best friends ever."

✈

THE FOLLOWING DAY I CAN'T STOP thinking about our conversation from the night before. I endeavor to pay more attention to people's reactions. Between watching over Kymani and taking in the sites, perhaps I haven't noticed the negativity. Am I giving people the benefit of the doubt because I don't want to believe people are that awful?

We are in the Forbidden City no more than five minutes before Roland turns into the biggest draw at this world-famous tourist attraction. Families and tour groups point and stare, then tap the person next to them on the shoulder to make sure they also get a good look. It's like walking around with the Mona Lisa. I still can't tell if they're curious because they've never seen a Black person before or if there's a more xenophobic undertone.

Roland plays his audio guide and studies the statues perched atop the steeply sloped roof of the imperial palace. I'm sure he feels the eyes on him—it wouldn't escape him for a second. He is deliberately focusing on the crouched stone beasts, disregarding the people staring at him.

People are also looking at Kymani, and then at the two of us, putting it all together in their minds. They clearly aren't exposed to biracial couples often, and to top off their experience they can see the offspring! We are the entertainment.

I have that sinking feeling in the pit of my stomach telling me this is wrong, and that I should do something—but what? I do nothing, and I say nothing. In this moment, I am unprepared. I don't have the tools or the knowledge to take this on but acknowledge that I should. For now, I take a lesson from Roland and ignore them. I plug in my audio guide and escape into the ancient history of the palace.

After our tour, we start the forty-minute walk back to our accommodations. I'm cold and tired. However, finding a cab is basically impossible and if we do, we're likely to get ripped off or scammed in some way. So, this is easier.

On our way back, we pass by a frozen lake. Parents lovingly clutch their wobbly children, friends laugh as they glide across the ice, and young lovers hold hands and gaze into each other's eyes. People enjoying the simple things in life, in the midst of a cold winter, is uplifting.

An interruption of giggles explodes behind us. Four young women, no more than twenty years old, are staring at Roland. They are pointing with one hand and covering their mouths with the other. They are undeniably laughing at him.

Is this actually happening? I search Roland's face. He shakes his head and turns his back to the ugly side of humanity so he can enjoy the beautiful side twirling and gliding in front of us.

"I'm so sorry, babe . . ." I say. These racist ladies are being atrocious, but it is not just them. I am apologizing for being caught up in my own world, in which this would never happen, that I didn't notice what was happening. I assumed he was wrong in his assessments of strangers' behavior, and instead of caring for him, I protected myself. There is a lot more discrimination in this world than I was prepared to admit.

I shift my attention to Kymani and wonder what conversations will be required with our son that will never apply to our daughter. I'm sad the world isn't closer to the "post-racial" place I naively decided it was. I am disappointed in myself for not wondering until now how often racial-based acts of prejudice happen to Roland at home—how ignorant I have been.

How many times has he not wanted to make a big deal out of something? Held his tongue to not ruin his day or mine? Chosen not to explain things to me because I might become dismissive or defensive?

As we stand watching the skaters, the sounds of laughter still ringing behind us, all the anger, hurt, and shame I have unknowingly been working to avoid by not acknowledging the racism behind these acts is filling me up.

I want to say something to acknowledge all that I'm realizing in this moment—but the scale is overwhelming, and my thoughts are coming too thick and fast to verbalize. So instead I take his hand, and squeeze it, hoping the love I have for him is enough, for right now, of an apology.

✈

THE LAKE IS THE FIRST TIME I NOTICE the mocking, but now that my eyes are open it happens time and time again throughout our stay. People point and laugh everywhere we go: at the museum, walking to a restaurant, visiting the bell tower. Now that I am conscious of it, I'm not sure how he keeps his composure. I hope going to the Dashanzi Art District will give him a break.

Art restores my optimism by reminding me there is beauty in the world. It has no linguistic barriers and can transcend and break through cultural, ethnic, and religious differences by addressing the commonality of our human experience. It speaks to the heart.

I hope we can connect with this place and its people in a meaningful way by immersing ourselves in their art. I want to be transported from my present disappointment in humanity and remember our commonalities.

The 798 Art Zone is a funky area made up of old military factories converted into art galleries, shops, studios, cafés, and restaurants. There are not many people walking around on this cold winter day. It gives us the space to linger and enjoy the work and capture great pictures without the gawkers we've become accustomed to.

Murals, graffiti, sculptures, and installations blanket the alleys and streets. We walk leisurely through the area, stopping at three red dinosaurs in cages, a stack of chubby Buddhas grinning animatedly, statues of soldiers, a mural of the back of someone's head with a window to a blue sky in its center. We try to interpret what we're seeing and discuss what it means to us, wondering if our responses are even close to what the artist intended.

On another recommendation by the Orchid, we arrive at a lavish restaurant on the outskirts of the district. The square interior has seating along the perimeter and a tranquil garden in the center. The floors and walls are decorated in deep reds and gold, and the pillars, oriental carvings, and statues lend it a regal elegance.

Soon our table is filled with a feast of glazed pork, Peking duck, rice, and vegetables, served on delicate Chinese porcelain. We lift our glasses of wine and cheers to a wonderful day.

I'm a quarter of the way through my meal when Kymani starts fussing. Thankfully I've mastered the art of feeding him with one hand and eating with the other. I'm serving him his bottle when a short waitress shuffles her feet, delicate as a dancer, toward me. With a jubilant smile that extenuates her apple cheeks, she gestures for me to hand him over. I oblige gratefully, and, delighted, she takes him in her arms to be cooed and coddled.

At this early hour, customers are sparse, though a full complement of staff is awaiting the dinnertime patrons. Her coworkers come over to greet our little man while the waitress kindly rocks him in her arms. She holds him long enough for me to enjoy a healthy glass of wine and the majority of my meal.

I'm reminded that people can be wonderful. I'm glad we're leaving Beijing on a high note.

Alana feeding Kymani while walking the Ming Dynasty City Wall

Xi'an

1 month 3 weeks old
February 3–6

———◆●◆———

"Certainly, travel is more than the seeing of sights; it is a change that goes on, deep and permanent, in the ideas of living."

—MARY RITTER BEARD

"DID YOU KNOW HE WAS BLACK when you were meeting him online?" our guide asks as we discuss how Roland and I met through a dating site.

We're walking on top of the ancient city wall that acted as a protective shield to the old capital of China, Xi'an. The fourteenth-century structure is lined with red lanterns on both sides. A couple smiles as they ride their bikes slowly past us, making their way along the iconic monument. We walk to the edge to take in the view of the city from our high vantage point. Her shoulder-length dark hair flies with the wind as she meets my gaze with a serious, yet curious intensity.

"Oh yes, yes I knew," I turn my head to hide my shock at her question. "We both posted a number of pictures of ourselves, along with a description."

43

She's been asking me all sorts of things about our marriage all day, trying to figure out the dynamics of our relationship. Does he have money? Is he in a powerful position? Was I seduced before knowing he was Black? Do I have some sort of Black fetish?

I explain to her that no, I don't just date men of color, that my ex-husband is white, and my daughter is white. I tell her I loved his kind eyes and his sincerity, so we met for a drink and the relationship grew from there. The reason we are together is not about money or power. We are just two people who fell in love, end of story.

This is a tour guide who interacts with people from all around the world every single day. She's educated, speaks multiple languages, and is regularly exposed to foreigners. If this is how she thinks, I can only imagine what the gawkers, the pointers, and the laughers must have going on in their prehistoric thought patterns.

I am grateful she is comfortable enough to ask me all these questions, despite how uncomfortable it is. I remind myself that one way to grow and learn is through honest dialogue. After all, we're all ignorant about something. It is educational for both of us, as we learn how the other lives and thinks. We walk away with at least one piece of clarity: that there is much in the world we do not understand.

As we take the last few steps to the famous Terracotta Army, she nods toward Roland, who is caressing Kymani. "You are lucky, he's a good dad."

"Yes, thank you," I mumble, acknowledging the accurate compliment but somewhat annoyed when dads are praised so freely for caring for their children the same way thankless moms do.

I shift my attention to the primary reason for our trip to Xi'an, the Terracotta Army. A collection of 8,000 life-size warriors sculpted in clay between 476–221 BC to help protect

Emperor Qin in the afterlife. They're considered one of the greatest archaeological discoveries of the twentieth century. In the event Qin could not live forever, he wanted to be prepared. He had his artisans build terracotta warriors, concubines, animals, carriages, food, tools, and all the accessories you can think of to be buried with him. He believed they would follow him into the afterlife, ensuring him complete protection and comfort.

The Terracotta Warriors are displayed in a sea of thousands, each one finely crafted and entirely individual. They are intimidating in their military formation and serious demeanors. The sheer number and magnitude of the project is awe-inspiring. The figures are individually modeled after a real person, with distinct facial characteristics, hairstyles, attire, and weaponry based on their position and rank.

✈

AS WE PACK THAT EVENING, readying to leave China the next day, I reflect on our time here. The racism and ignorance is difficult; though we try to not let those individuals affect our journey. We leave with overall fond memories, grateful to have seen some of the world's most incredible monuments. China has a fascinating culture with an interesting, deep and rich history. And the culinary scene was a delight. Our experiences here, both wonderful and unpleasant, were intense. We're ready for some relaxation in northern Vietnam.

VIETNAM

Alana and Roland enjoy cocktails at a resort in Ha Long Bay

Hanoi & Ha Long Bay

2 months old

February 6–14

———◆•◀———

"There is more to life than increasing its speed."

—Mahatma Gandhi

"I WOULD NEVER WANT TO DRIVE HERE." Roland's wide eyes gaze out the bus window onto the streets of Hanoi where a slew of motorbikes weave and dart in and out of traffic with zero regard for lanes, maximum passenger loads, or the appropriate weight-bearing restrictions of their vehicles.

"Isn't it intense?!" I agree, remembering how I felt three years ago when I witnessed it for the first time, in southern Vietnam with my siblings. "Beautiful though, once you get over the shock. A perfect example of organized chaos." The bikes flow together like schools of fish, weaving in and out as a giant entity not bound by lanes, lines, or rules.

We have only one evening in Hanoi. We walk through the lively local market, picking up essentials for Kymani. The bustling streets contain the constant low hum of scooters that buzz around like busy bees carrying people to and fro. We stop at one of the many quaint restaurants and sit on itsy-bitsy chairs on the sidewalk. We eat vermicelli and drink local beer as the world goes by.

The next morning we're sitting squished between our bags and the window in a run-down bus on the road to relaxation. We're headed for Ha Long Bay, with the explicit intent of leaving the busy city behind. We have no schedule, nothing to do, and nothing to see for an entire week. I will grow restless after a few days with nothing to do, but Roland needs to slow down, unwind, and recharge.

We arrive at our resort in one piece, largely thanks to our fellow travelers who helped us load and unload our luggage onto the first rickety bus, then an even shadier boat, and again onto one last iffy-looking bus.

By the time we arrive there's a camaraderie among us all. Travel is the rare situation in our adult lives when it's totally acceptable and encouraged to speak to strangers and even become friends for a minute, a week, or a lifetime.

We sigh in relief as we gaze upon the luxurious waterfront resort with meticulously cared for grounds. We usually don't opt for lavish accommodations, but on this island there are only two options: five-star or no-star. So here we are, living it up in a gorgeous resort for a week at the very reasonable rate of $150 CDN a night.

The path to the lobby is lush with tropical plants, bright flowers, and waving palm trees. We can hear the ocean expanding and contracting over the soft fine sand and the smell of the sea fills me with anticipation of fresh food, tropical drinks, and beach walks.

When we open the door to our room we pass the tasteful art on the neutrally painted walls, ignore the wood-accented ceiling beams that match the desk and headboard, glance briefly at the crimson and white comforters decorated with flowers and towel swans, and open the glass patio doors. Our bags must have landed somewhere inside because by the time we take in the view the only thing we're holding onto is each other.

We stand completely still. The calm water is a pale shade of blue-green reflecting water-color streaks of pink, orange, and yellow from the setting sun. The line between ocean and sky is almost indistinguishable but for the gigantic boulders that jut intermittently out of the water.

My eyes soften, my shoulders glide downward, and my breath slows.

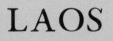

LAOS

Roland and Alana take a stroll with Kymani
at the MandaLao Elephant Conservation.

Luang Prabang
2 months, 1 week old
February 14–21

———◆•◆———

"It's opener there, in the wide open air. Out there
things can happen and frequently do . . . . And when
things start to happen, don't worry, don't stew. Just
go right along. You'll start happening too."

—Dr. Seuss

"DID YOU BRING A HAT FOR HIM?" A disdainful middle-
aged blond American asks, pointing to Kymani. "It's going to
be too hot for him."

Shit.

I'm digging through his diaper bag to make sure, but I
already know I didn't bring it. It's blazing hot and we're about
to go out into the sun to feed, bathe, and walk with the elephants at MandaLao Elephant Conservation. There is no way
he'll last half a day out in this heat, especially without a hat.

I pull out a thin white onesie from his bag and put the
neck hole over his head, letting the body of it drape over his
head and neck.

"This is the best I've got," I say to both the lady and Roland.
"Do you think it will work? I have his portable fan too."

The lady shrugs, absolving herself of the situation. Roland shrugs, optimistically.

"Let's try it and if he's not doing well then I'll come back," I say to Roland. Elephants are Roland's favorite animals, so I want to make sure he gets the full experience.

"The walk is in the jungle. It's covered with trees, so he'll have some shade," our guide reassures us.

I put the compulsory waterproof boots on and tighten them around the base of my knees, then strap Kymani in. I worry he's going to roast inside the dark carrier, so I prop him up so he's half in and half out. This way he gets a slight breeze to help cool him down.

Roland holds my hand as I step inside the slim canoe-shaped boat. It has small wooden slats for us to sit single file and a small outboard engine. I sit down quickly, feeling a bit unbalanced with Kymani. Roland and a few other travelers get in more gracefully. The small boat pushes away from the shallow shoreline, and we're across the river in less than thirty seconds. As I step onto land, two large Asian elephants flap their ears and pound their heavy feet into the dirt as they walk toward us.

We had not initially made plans to see elephants while in Asia because of the animal rights issues surrounding the industry. As tourists we do our best to use the power of our dollars responsibly, and animal "conservation" seemed a tricky one to get right. But in Vietnam we met a couple who had done their research and told us about this place where elephants once used for labor in the logging industry, which was now an illegal practice, had found a safe sanctuary to live out the rest of their lives.

On the bank of the river, Roland and I hold bunches of bananas behind our backs, slowly feeding the elephants one banana at a time. Mine likes the banana placed directly in her mouth, while Roland's likes to pick it out of his hand with her trunk. The elephants are patient with us, letting us stand beside them to take a few pictures so long as we continue to offer bananas as we do so. They don't seem interested in or bothered by Kymani at all. He has fallen asleep on my chest and is napping quietly.

We walk into the river with buckets in hand. Holding Kymani with one hand, I bend into a squat position to fill the bucket with my other. As instructed, I whip the bucket forward in a kettlebell swinging motion. The water splashes the side of the elephant, cooling her down. I repeat the motion over and over in the best one-sided water fight I've ever been in.

Despite my sunglasses, I squint from the brightness of the sun. We wait on the riverbank watching the other tourists glee-fully spray the elephants. The sun beats down on our faces, beads of sweat forming on my forehead. Kymani wakes from his nap. I take him out of the hot carrier to cradle him in my arms. I hold him and a portable fan with one hand and feed him a bottle with the other. I hope this keeps him cool and hydrated.

The group begins walking toward the forest, with the elephants leading the pack. The air becomes noticeably cooler once we are under the shade of the trees. Kymani continues to drink his bottle, a sign he isn't too hot. When he finishes I prop him back into the carrier, giving my arms a break. I adjust his makeshift hat and blow the fan on this back.

We enjoy a relaxing walk through the forest with the elephants. We stop on occasion to have some water or to give the elephants another small treat. I hate what these animals have been through for us to have this close interaction. I feel torn, and guilty for enjoying it so much.

After our walk, we're shuttled back to our hotel in Luang Prabang. At our quaint French villa we unload our stroller, baby bag, and backpack from the van, say thank you to our fellow travelers and guide, and wave as the van disappears down the street.

When we turn toward our villa, Roland and I simultaneously pause. A few meters in front of us are two young monks, hanging their bright orange garments on a clothesline. Their young, slender arms drape the fabric over the line, then smooth it out with long strokes. The bright fabric drying in the sun contrasts strikingly against the backdrop of the old white monastery buildings.

In Laos, it is tradition for boys and men to serve in Buddhist monasteries. Some become monks for a short week and others, for a lifetime; it's a rite of passage. What we are seeing is a window, a small glimpse into this spiritually pivotal time in their life, steeped in the traditions of their culture.

✈

WE ARE UP AT 4:30 A.M. TO WATCH the Tak Bat processions that take place every morning at sunrise. This ritual is a respected Buddhist practice during which the monks collect food from local almsgivers on their way to the temples. In somber silence, the monks walk in their sandals and bright orange garments, one in front of the other in the dim morning light. They stop and collect their rations from the locals and place them in the bowls they carry with them.

We decided to silently observe the proceedings from right outside our villa, instead of some of the more touristy routes. As observers, we are expected to keep our distance, be silent, not interrupt the monks in any way, and be discrete about taking pictures. We find a place to stand across the street from some local almsgivers, hoping to enjoy the ceremony from a respectful distance.

A group of ten monks comes toward us down the sidewalk. I watch closely, intending to be fully present in the moment. Roland has his camera out and is preparing to take a few pictures. The monks come and go quickly; the moment is beautiful and fleeting, like seeing a Monarch butterfly drift in front of you one moment and then disappearing the next.

Roland reviews the pictures and shakes his head, "The lighting's too low—I can't get a decent shot. Everything's blurry. I'm going to move in closer, try a different setting and get a better shot."

"Be careful," I warn.

Five more monks walk down the sidewalk across the street from us.

"We need to move to where there are more monks." He frowns and won't avert his attention from his camera.

"Roland, this is it," I say sharply. He's ruining the moment for a picture and killing my Zen vibe. "By the time we move somewhere else, it will be over. Don't worry about getting the perfect picture. Take this in. You're missing it."

Roland ignores me and moves onto the empty street to get a better angle. The monks turn their heads toward him, and I am embarrassed and frustrated.

After the monks have moved on, I start walking the fifty feet back to the villa. I'm so angry I don't say a word to Roland. I love that he captures so much of this trip with his camera, and I appreciate the lengths he goes to for it. But this morning, he took it too far.

Later that day we go to the Kuang Si Falls, a forty-minute drive outside Luang Prabang. It is the most ridiculous tourist trap I have ever seen. Young men do a couple pushups before wrapping their arms around their girlfriends, who adjust their bikinis and pout for a selfie. Tourists overwhelm the small, crowded waterfalls, taking away from whatever natural beauty is there.

I'm in a horrible mood and I'm not hiding my distaste for this place. Roland and I are still at odds with each other over this morning and the tension is palpable. All it takes is me pushing away his hand during a picture to throw us into a full-blown argument.

We accuse each other of ruining the moments. I huff at him for ruining a special moment this morning for the sake of some pictures and he tells me I'm ruining this time at the waterfalls with my negativity because it isn't meeting my standards. We're both right and we're both wrong.

Our fight has completely ruined the day. The hour-long drive back to our villa is filled with the thick silence of stubborn anger. Both of us look out our respective windows, not uttering a word to each other.

I hate fighting with him on any given typical day in Victoria. The stakes are far higher now, when traveling. I don't want to taint my memories of this place with some stupid argument. Inevitably, from time to time, we will disagree, but we need to be better at ensuring it doesn't escalate unnecessarily. It's not worth it.

Before the day is out, we both apologize to each other, for what we did, what we said, and for how we handled it.

Our last day in Luang Prabang is spent in good spirits. Luang Prabang is a UNESCO World Heritage Site, and we go on a guided tour. The busyness of the world and of my mind disappear when we step inside the still, noiseless space of the temple. A large golden statue of the Buddha occupies the center of the room, sitting tall with his eyes half open and his hands folded together in front of him. I close my eyes and give gratitude for my family, for our health, and for the generosity bestowed on me to be here in this moment.

MYANMAR

Hot air balloon ride over Began

Bagan

2 months, 2 weeks old
February 21–27

———•◦•———

"Travel is fatal to prejudice, bigotry, and narrow mindedness, and many of our people need it sorely on these accounts."

—MARK TWAIN

IN AN EPIC FAILURE OF LOGISTIC planning, we're running through the airport in Bangkok trying to get our luggage and ourselves on our next flight. We're in the middle of three back-to-back flights with three different airlines, flying from Luang Prabang, Laos, to Bagan, Myanmar. Geographically, Laos and Myanmar are neighbors sharing a border. I thought it would be a simple flight across, but nope: we have to fly down to Thailand then make our way back up to Myanmar. By the time I realized this, I had already booked our flights and accommodation, the cheapest I could find, with zero cancelation or adjustments policies.

As we charge through the airport I think back to how relaxed I was when booking this portion of our journey. How easy it had been to click a few buttons from the comfort of my couch after two glasses of syrah. Now I'm surrounded by the frantically busy airport and my hopes for making our next flight are dwindling.

The security line is packed.

"We're not gonna make it." I'm panting from the run through the terminal laden with baby and bags.

"Yes we are." His resolve surprises me, and I try to believe him.

A guard walks up to us, sees Kymani, and ushers us into a family security line behind only two other people.

"Kymani saves the day again."

Roland nods, distracted with the task of unloading liquids and electronics for the scanner.

"The next flight is better." This is my version of an apology for the frenzy I have put us through. "We have a three-hour wait at the next stop and it's a tiny airport, so we won't be rushed."

"Great." Roland nods, not showing a hint of anger or even annoyance, as if this has all been caused by some unavoidable and unpredictable element and not by his wife in a careless wine haze. I deserve an annoyed tone, some choice words, or the cold shoulder, but there's nothing. He is so much kinder than I would be.

✈

"THIS ANCIENT CITY IS ONE OF the most significant archaeological sites in Asia," explains our guide. "At the height of the Bagan empire's power, between the eleventh and thirteenth centuries, there were more than ten thousand Buddhist temples and pagodas. Over 2,200 of these monuments still remain, making Bagan the site of one of the densest concentrations of temples and pagodas in the world."

"Why are there so many temples and pagodas concentrated in one area?"

"Every emperor tried to out-do the emperor before him,

building bigger and better ones as gestures of worship. It became a status symbol."

I laugh at the idea that all this spiritual beauty is the result of a centuries-long pissing contest.

"Holy, is this real gold?" Roland asks, pointing at the dazzling Shwezigon Pagoda's wall.

"Yes." Our guide looks at our wide-eyed faces tilted toward the towering yellow shimmer. "Many ask about the extravagance of the temples among the visible poverty of Bagan. They ask why the money invested in this temple wasn't spent on something more practically useful to help the community. To the Buddhist people, it is more important to provide charity than to be comfortable in this life. These temples are built on the generosity of that belief."

I hope the sacredness of these temples and the practices of faith and charity involved in creating them provides the people with inner happiness and peace. I also hope that these temples continue to encourage tourism and contribute to their economy.

As we explore the temples, the gawkers and the pointers have found us again. A group of teenagers, on what appears to be a school trip, are the most obvious with their stares. A few of the boys start laughing and pointing in Roland's direction. Because we are in a place of worship, we keep our distance and ignore them, but I can tell from Roland's expression that he is getting fed up.

I feel his frustration and want to defuse the tension. "We're out in the middle of nowhere. They've probably never seen a Black person before,"

"I know, but they probably don't see many white people either. They don't point and laugh when they see you."

He's right. I didn't want to feel uncomfortable, and I was trying to make him feel better too. However, it's coming across like I'm making excuses for them, and trying to downplay their behavior. I don't know what else to say except the same old tired, useless apology. "I'm sorry babe."

We enter an unassumingly small temple, feeling worn out. Inside, a gigantic gold-painted Buddha fills the small space. The top of its head reaches the ceiling, and its shoulders touch both walls. We stand in silence, trying to understand what we are seeing.

"The man who built this wanted to show what it was like to live imprisoned," our guide explains.

A lump forms in my throat. The little room entraps the statue so that the figure, if it were alive, could never stand or lie down. The entranceway, although open, is far too small for the statue to ever get out. It's trapped in here, for eternity.

Feeling emotional and claustrophobic, I back out, pulling Kymani's stroller with me. A little kid, who appears to be about ten—*The same age as Josephine*, I think—comes running up to me from across the grounds.

Kymani gets a lot of positive attention everywhere we go in Southeast Asia. People stop us frequently, wanting to say hi and get a peek. They are kind, always smiling at him and telling us how cute he is. He is treated as an honored guest on every tour, in any restaurant, and at any show. Southeast Asia will prove to be, by far, the most baby-friendly region we visit on our year abroad.

I take off the white muslin blanket covering the stroller, anticipating the boy wants to see the baby. He stops a foot away from Kymani and I and points to Roland with one hand, then to me with the other hand, then brings his fingers together in unison.

"Yes," I say, nodding my head "we're together."

He points to Kymani, smiling and filled with curiosity about the situation.

"Yes, our baby," I confirm, continuing to nod.

The boy jumps with glee and runs back to a group of kids

who are waiting for the brave boy to report the news. He is shouting his findings as he barrels back to them. It's as if his discovery happens to be the most interesting thing he's ever seen in his life.

I wonder, now that he and his friends have had this exposure, what they will take away from the experience. Perhaps it will inspire them to imagine and seek out a greater array of lifestyles, ideas, and people than they've yet come across in their lives. Or maybe they are simply laughing at us—I'll never know.

✈

TODAY IS DEDICATED TO ROOM SERVICE, massages, and cocktails by the pool.

I've booked the longest massage possible, and I'm so excited to have my back muscles steam-rolled after months of carrying Kymani as we walk non-stop. I'm escorted into a room with a double mattress covered in crisp white sheets, lying on the pristine hardwood floor. A deep red pillow at the head of the bed matches the red and gold fabric hanging from the ceiling and encircling the room.

The lady hands me a neatly folded pile of gray fabric. "Put on please."

I unfold the clothes to find a plain tunic-style top and pants that are two feet too short and three feet too wide. *How am I supposed to wear this? Am I supposed to leave my bra on? Shit.*

I decide the bra needs to go and I quickly put on the clothes the best I can. The lady returns, scurrying back in with no warning, and comes quickly toward me.

"It's a bit big, I am not sure how—" before I can complete my sentence she is wrapping the waist of my pants together with a sash.

"Do you like hard or soft?" she asks.

"Hard, please," I respond. I've never understood the point of soft massages.

"Lay down," she offers with a smile.

How is she going to massage me with this shirt on? I lie on my front and close my eyes.

She sits straddling my legs and begins kneading my back with her palms. She presses hard, inching her way from my neck to my lower back then to each arm. She grabs my wrists and lifts me up into an aided yoga cobra pose, then lets my torso return to the mattress. Then she kneels on my butt and presses the weight of her body into my back. I let out a gasp of air, surprised at the intense pressure, and generally confused at the way this massage is unfolding.

She gets off me and picks up my feet, pointing them like a ballerina and lifting them toward the sky. She starts punching my leg with the side of her fist. Still holding my feet, she steps on my legs, shifting her weight from right to left. She puts her foot firmly on my tailbone, presses down hard and yanks my feet up in the air.

This is so bizarre that I'm afraid I'm going to laugh. My mind flashes back to when I was eleven years old, wrestling with my six-foot-three, thirteen-year-old brother, who holds my feet so I can't move and delivers rapid-fire kicks to my side in a torturous form of tickling.

I'm getting wrecked, and I don't know how to tap-out.

She turns me over, grabs my ankle, and starts pounding my inner thigh with her foot.

When she's done pounding, wrapping, and swinging me into positions I never knew I could achieve, I pull my sore body off the mattress, put on my bathing suit and cover, and thank the lady all in a minor state of shock.

Roland is lounging by the pool with Kymani. I whip off my cover and lie on the lounger beside him. He turns over to reveal his mom on video chat. "Hi Nadine!"

"Wow, you look sexy in that suit!"

I laugh. Bless her soul. "Oh dear, well, thank you."

I take the compliment instead of dwelling on the fact that I haven't felt sexy since I got pregnant a year ago. Right now it's weird to think of my body as anything but a vessel for Kymani's needs.

We point the camera at Kymani. "Kymani is a little rock star over here." His popularity does not surprise his proud granny.

She is attentive and interested in every story we tell her. She tells us the women in her mahjong group are always asking where we are and what we're up to. I beam at that, taking in the pride she has for what we're doing. She fills up my love batteries, giving me the energy to take on the world again.

We call my parents after. They spend the winters in Arizona and are currently enjoying the heat and relaxation of retired life.

I repeat our plans to come down to California for spring break, trying to convince them to meet us there. It's a six-hour drive from their place, but they express a willingness to make the journey.

"Josephine would be ecstatic to see you," I say, "and Kymani will have grown so much since you last saw him. I'll send you the details. We would love it if you came."

I'm excited at the possibility of meeting up with family and friends along the trip. It can get lonely on the road after a while. It's heartening to be with people who know you through and through, and though today it's been via video, we feel the effects of time spent with loved ones.

✈

I OPEN MY EYES IN THE DARK BEDROOM and search the nightstand frantically for my cell phone. Our 4 a.m. alarm is going off and I'm worried it will wake up Kymani. I turn off the alarm; Kymani, lying beside me, sleeps on. I slowly slide out from underneath the covers. Our guide is picking us up in forty-five minutes for a sunrise hot air balloon ride across Bagan.

For the first time on this trip, my stomach is reacting to something I ate or drank and is expressing its anger with an upsetting bout of the runs. It's been an unpleasant night of getting up every hour, either to feed Kymani or to run to the toilet or both.

Roland and I love to try new food and are fortunate to have iron guts that rarely ever give us stomach issues. However, because of Kymani, we've adopted a better-safe-than-sorry approach to cuisine so far; I worry if I get sick and dehydrated it will affect the milk I produce. So we've avoided street meat, gone only to restaurants with positive reviews, and if something appears even a little bit iffy, we don't touch it. We are careful where we buy our water, cautious of vendors re-filling bottles and snapping lids back on.

Our doctor provided us with a slew of medications before we left including antimalarials, which we have taken diligently, and some magic pills for diarrhea. On top of this, I've been taking advantage of the more relaxed drug restrictions in Asia (you can walk into any pharmacy and pick up medication without a prescription inexpensively) and grabbed a number of just-in-case meds such as amoxicillin, allergy medications for Roland, dimenhydrinate, infant Tylenol, and some cold and flu relief.

I took a magic diarrhea pill at 2 a.m., worried we would have to cancel our hot air balloon ride otherwise, and I'm feeling much better.

"I can't believe we're getting Kymani's first babysitter!"

Roland is obsessed with firsts of any kind, from Kymani's first smile to the first time we purchased a lawn chair together. I roll my eyes a little, making fun of him, though I secretly love this about Roland: his unabashed love for all things, big and small.

I'm a bit nervous, but the babysitter is offered by the resort, and this is a once-in-a-lifetime experience that would not be safe for Kymani to join.

A knock on the door reveals a short, sturdy lady in her early sixties. Her long black hair is tied in a long braid down her back.

I jump immediately into introductions as she places her bag on the chair and I realize she doesn't understand a word I'm saying to her. Her face is kind and patient and I laugh at myself to think how many anxious tourist mothers this lady has indulged before being left to do her work. She, undoubtedly, has raised ten children single-handedly. I take a deep breath and relax a little.

I point and show her the pre-made bottles, his diapers, and clothes. I try to tell her he's likely to sleep most of the time, but please feed him if he wakes up and it will put him back to sleep again. I remind myself we're only going to be gone for three hours, and, reassured that she knows exactly what she is doing, we thank her profusely before hurrying out the door to meet our ride.

Once I get over my nerves about leaving our infant with a stranger, the feeling is absolutely liberating. I never noticed it when Kymani was with us, but without him the constant strategizing to anticipate his every need is gone. I feel a weight lift.

Tucked into a large basket under a huge crimson red hot air balloon, Roland and I hug each other in the cool morning air. Dozens of hot air balloons are gliding slowly through the sky's layers of pale pinks, yellows, and blues. A light, cloudy haze blankets the lush grassy fields, thick bushes, and palm trees below. The ancient ruins of thousands of temples and pagodas dot the earth to the horizon.

My eyes prickle. It's the dawn of a new day and we are floating over the culmination of thousands of years of spirituality and tradition. I am overwhelmed by the beauty of it.

Like a beautiful dream, it's over too quickly. Local kids chase our balloon as it descends, laughing and waving, until we land softly on a sand dune.

CAMBODIA

Roland and Alana at Ta Prohm Temple

Siem Reap

2 months, 3 weeks old
February 27–March 2

"Stop worrying about the potholes in the road and
enjoy the journey."

—Barbara Hoffman

THE HEAT IS EXCRUCIATING. It must be thirty-five degrees
Celsius in the shade. Kymani's skin touching my skin burns.
I was here three years ago with some of my siblings, so while
Roland and our guide are taking a longer tour around the
Bayon Temple grounds I find a small, shady nook in my favor-
ite part of the temple to sit and nurse and enjoy the view.

A total of 216 massive stone faces, stretching over four
meters tall, their eyes closed, and their lips curved slightly
upward in serene smiles, preside benevolently over the stunning landscape.

Kymani falls asleep in my arms, so I stay nestled where I
am to ensure neither of us get heat stroke. The portable fan
blows on his little body, cooling him further. He is as tranquil
as the statues before me.

I could be at home watching daytime TV right now, but
instead I get to look at ancient ruins halfway around the world.

Being a mom to a newborn can be trying but enjoying these moments of travel while parenting makes it so much more tolerable. I find myself worrying less about the day-to-day stuff that fills my mind back home; I'm too preoccupied navigating our travels and enjoying each place we are in.

It helps that I've parented a newborn before, with Josephine. Although it was a decade ago, it's not completely foreign to me. We are fortunate Kymani is as healthy and relaxed as Josephine was. I'm not sure how much of his easygoing, adaptable personality is nature rather than nurture, but it has given us the opportunity to see and do much more than we expected. All this would be impossible with a baby of a different temperament.

Later our guide walks us through the museum, and we talk about Cambodia and what it has been through. A horrific civil war resulted in the torture, murder, and division of the nation's people during the Khmer Rouge regime (1967–1975). Cambodia is still recovering, working through the devastation, which killed two million people, one-quarter of the population at that time (1975–79). Half died by execution and half by starvation.

The extreme poverty is visible and heart-wrenching. The first time I was in Cambodia, I saw a boy no older than six on the sidewalk huffing keyboard cleaner. It shocked me. He was so small and way too young to be out there on his own, let alone high and abusing substances. I can still only imagine all the reasons he was trying to escape reality in that dark and dingy street.

Throughout our time here, as we walk in and out of temples, to a market or a restaurant, we see street kids, prostitutes, and beggars everywhere. It especially hurts to see a woman shaking, hitting, or kicking her baby to make it scream as we walk by, hoping for an empathetic dollar. At once I feel so grateful for Canada, for the luck of being born into the right set of circumstances and torn that I have never had to worry about basic necessities for my family while such poverty and hardship continues on.

✈

A VISIT TO SIEM REAP WOULD NOT BE complete without an early-morning sunrise walk to the famous Angkor Wat. The stillness of the hour makes the whole world feel slowed down. A hazy orange sun peaks over the ancient temple as it rises in the pale pastel sky. The soft morning light, stone structures, and palm trees reflect off the water in front of the expansive grounds. We sit quietly beside each other, with no desire to speak, taking in the sight before us.

We take advantage of the cool morning temperatures to tour the grounds, through the seemingly endless flow of columns, towers, and stairs, past sculpted murals depicting divine and earth-bound scenes in intricate detail.

We step outside to see a staggering number of people flowing toward us. As we move in the opposite direction we pass hundreds of Asian women carrying dainty parasols painted with flowers and birds to shade themselves from the sun. At first I think it's to counter the heat, but when I study their faces, I realize their purpose has a vainer motive. The women's skin is painted unnaturally pale, like that of a porcelain doll, all naturally warm undertones lost. To be as white as possible, they must keep the sunrays away. I understand more explicitly than ever in my life that, to them, to be white is to be beautiful. Although shifting now, this has historically been the message projected to all of us from magazines, billboards, and commercials: There is one skin color associated with power and beauty.

SINGAPORE

(From Left) Kymani, Roland, Alana, Melissa, Ciahna, and Andy

Singapore

2 Months, 2 weeks old

March 2-4

———————•·———————

"A journey is best measured in friends, rather than miles."

—TIM CAHILL

WE ARE RUSHED THROUGH THE PRISTINE corridors and rooms of Singapore's airport security and customs with speed and efficiency. In less than twenty minutes we have our luggage and are waiting in line to pay for two bottles of wine, gifts for our hosts. People walk by in expensive suits and designer dresses carrying luxury-brand bags. It no longer feels like we are in Southeast Asia.

Our friend Melissa greets us with open arms. "Welcome to Singapore! How are you? How was the flight?" She hugs Roland and I before introducing her four-year-old daughter, Ciahna, and saying hello to Kymani.

Melissa grew up in Victoria and we selfishly hope she and her family will move back one day. She and I both worked for the provincial government and used to meet for lunch or happy hour to strategize or vent about work. We became even closer when, in our early thirties, we separated from our ex-husbands around the same time. We leaned heavily on one another as we learned to cope with failed marriages and navigating single life for the first time in a long time.

Melissa quit her government job with the hope of getting back into international education, and soon found an excellent position in Singapore. Before we knew it, she was off. She met Andy, a fun and charming man from the UK with proud Jamaican roots, through her new work. They're now parents to two young daughters and have made Singapore home.

We are here to spend the weekend with them and are crashing in their youngest daughter Eloise's room. We are grateful for the free accommodation in this notoriously expensive city. But most of all, we appreciate being around friends.

Roland states is happiness to not be the only Black guy in the room.

We throw our bags and stroller into the back of Melissa's SUV. I put Kymani in one of the car seats, then squeeze myself between his and Ciahna's. It's past Kymani's bedtime. He is fussing, squawking, and crying, but he's so over-tired he won't take a bottle.

"Here, try Eloise's soother," Melissa, brushes it off on her shirt hands it back to me.

This is not going to work. He never takes a soother, but I don't want to be rude. I take it and give it another brush-off before popping it in his mouth. Kymani sucks and closes his eyes.

"It's actually working! He's never used one before. Awesome, thanks Melissa!"

I take my eyes off Kymani and look out the window. We weave through a maze of highways. Every car is fairly new, and everyone is diligently following the rules, obeying all signs, signals, and lines on the road.

"This is weird," I say to Melissa and Roland. "It's like being back in North America. Everything is so . . . orderly. Everyone is actually following traffic rules."

"Yeah, Singapore is not like the rest of Southeast Asia," Melissa laughs. "A lot of people come through Singapore halfway through their trip to take a break from the culture shock."

"It's weird to not see any scooters . . . and wow, some of these cars!" Roland points at an especially expensive vehicle as it passes.

"There are very strict rules here," explains Melissa. "The emission standards won't allow for old vehicles. Also, there is a lot of money, as you can see."

Melissa's condominium complex is a huge, indistinguishable white high-rise. The occupants include a large number of ex-pats from all over the world. They have developed friendships in this community, sharing not only communal space but also their experiences living in a foreign country.

When we open the door to their condo, Andy greets us warmly with hugs. We've met him a few times when they've come back to Victoria to visit, but our time together is never long enough.

Melissa gives us a quick tour. To the left of the entrance, she points out, is the live-in nanny's quarters. Apparently it's standard practice in Singapore; everyone with a kid has a live-in nanny. Therefore, most condominiums, regardless of size, come equipped with living space for them. I can't imagine living in such close proximity with a nanny, but I suppose you must get used to it.

Once the kids are tucked into bed, we sit on the veranda to enjoy a drink. The sun has set, but the air remains warm and heavy. A sea of city lights flows out from the balcony into the distant horizon.

"Cheers!" Melissa smiles, raising her glass.

We clink our glasses, sip generously, and take in the soul-filling moment of reuniting with old friends. We talk, laugh, and drink into the late hours of the night.

✈

THE FOLLOWING AFTERNOON, we are walking by the Supertree Grove at Gardens by the Bay. The gigantic man-made tree sculptures are an iconic landmark in Singapore that complement the city's stylish modern architecture. The lush vegetation that climbs the vertical structures is a tribute to the city's efforts toward environmental sustainability.

Melissa giggles and nods toward a group of three women staring at us. "I wonder what they are thinking, like we are from some far-off land where white women only marry Black men."

"Whoa," I say, realizing suddenly that the group of women are not the only ones, we are surrounded by people staring at us. "We've had a lot of this since we've been in Asia. At least here when you catch them, they look away."

"I know," Melissa agrees. "Andy has no interest in going to China for that exact reason."

I do a quick scan occasionally as we walk along the pristine sidewalks. We are certainly attracting some attention.

That evening, Roland, Kymani, and I go to the famous Marina Bay Sands Hotel rooftop to indulge in $25 Singapore Slings. We luck out, getting one of the few high-top tables available. The view is magnificent. The entire city shimmers with lights. The Supertree Grove lights up in a firework-like spectacle of glowing lights that explode then retract and change color. I could spend hours staring out at the flickering glow of the city, which puts me into the same hypnotic state as an evening campfire back home.

✈

ON OUR LAST DAY IN SINGAPORE we take a relaxing walk along a residential path that winds through a marina bay. Large waterfront houses line the shore and luxury vessels line the water. We play a game, guessing how much the yachts are worth and then how much it would take to run and maintain them. The city feels so pristine you could eat off the sidewalks. I bend down to touch the grass, half expecting it to be turf. It's not. It's lusciously thick, impossibly green, perfectly manicured grass. I see the allure of Singapore. It's clean and safe with a ton of opportunities and a large community of ex-pats. With the promise of high salaries, a live-in nanny, close friends, and a great lifestyle, I can see why Melissa and Andy choose to live here. Still, as we part ways, I'm hopeful that we'll lure them home one day.

THAILAND

Roland and Kymani at Wat Pho temple

Bangkok

2 months, 3 weeks old

March 4-9

———◆•◆———

"No one is born hating another person because of the color of his skin, or his background, or his religion. People must learn to hate, and if they can learn to hate, they can be taught to love, for love comes more naturally to the human heart than its opposite."

—NELSON MANDELA

BANGKOK IS CHAOTIC—THE STREETS are wildly busy, packed with honking vehicles and full of life. *You will either love it or hate it*, states our travel book. *I love it*, I decide, as I watch the city through the window of our cab, caught in the current of a rushing stream of cars, tuk-tuks, and motorbikes. The streets are a patchwork of ancient spiritual relics, run-down buildings, and modern skyscrapers that rival Singapore's: an obscure mix of traditional and modern.

The sidewalk is alive with people walking, ordering street food, and sitting in bright red plastic chairs eating and sipping Singha and Chang lagers. A block further down, two young men unload packages of flowers half the size of themselves from a white delivery truck to be sold. As we pass the glass doors of the market, I get a quick glimpse of the massive cascading bunches of colorful flora filling its corridors.

At Chakrabongse Villas I open the cab door and am hit with thick, humid air heavy with the scent of tropical flowers. The place is such an unexpected oasis in this big, dirty city that I stop with my hand still on the cab door, closing my eyes and taking a deep, meditative breath. As I breathe out, my eyes flicker open again, eager to take in the lush, serene gardens. I am glad for this refuge among the high-energy buzz of the city.

Early the following morning we are efficiently escorted by a local expert through some of the well-known markets. We have come before the crowds get too thick, pushing Kymani's compact stroller through the narrow alleys, maneuvering around the amassing crowds.

Examining the stalls, I'm surprised at how little I recognize. Large steel bowls of different colored liquids are identified as curries. Beside it, on a small card table with a plastic tablecloth, are large green plastic bowls of nuts—or legumes? They're too shiny to be nuts. I turn to ask our guide what it is but she's busy showing Roland a juice stand. Across the narrow pathway is a table with fruit cut and carved next to bunches of what look like weeds but probably are not.

"This is fried pork," the guide informs, drawing my attention back to her. She is pointing at a glass cabinet filled with hanging red meat.

"Each market is famous for different things," our guide explains. "What are you interested in buying?"

This is our last stop in Asia. We go home to Canada in a couple of days to see family for a week before taking Josephine to Disneyland for spring break, so I'm excited to pick up a few things without fear of overloading our suitcases.

"I'd like to find a couple gifts for my daughter," I say. "She's ten and she loves cats."

Our guide nods and walks us out of the open food market

and through an alley. We turn a corner and, without warning, find ourselves in a densely packed street full of vendors. Plastic tarps and tent shades are roped together like a quilted roof, offering relief from the heat of the sun. We walk from booth to booth of seemingly random selection of items. Hair ties and brushes, earrings, smartphone covers, fans, lamps, clothes, shoes, toys, linens, and bags. I choose some jewelry, a purse, a couple of unicorn cat squishies that smell like strawberries, and a pair of blue ballet flats with cat faces on the toes.

We're reaching midday and despite the shade of the covered markets, the temperatures are becoming unbearable. Kymani, who is usually so calm and relaxed, is squirming uncomfortably in his stroller. We take off his shorts, leaving him in only a thin short-sleeved white onesie, and attach the portable fan to his stroller using a holder meant for attaching smartphones to bicycles. His eyes shut tight, and his mouth opens, expressing his discomfort. He clenches his fists and shifts back and forth in his stroller.

"Maybe I should try to feed him," I say to Roland and the guide. "Is there anywhere cool we can go?"

Our guide rushes us across the street and into a shopping mall. A gust of air conditioning hits us upon entry. Kymani is typically a great eater, sucking happily for nourishment and comfort, but despite not having eaten in two hours, he only takes a couple of sips before stopping, moving his head away, and crying again. He fusses and squirms as I change him into a fresh diaper and new outfit. He remains the same after twenty minutes of trying different tactics and giving his little body time to cool off.

"It's not the heat, something else is wrong," I say definitively. "I'm sorry but I think we're going to have to go back to the hotel. Maybe he picked something up on the plane."

"No problem," the tour guide replies empathetically. "Let's grab a taxi, they're better than the tuk-tuks because they have air conditioning. We will get you home."

A few minutes later we are in a cool cab heading back to the hotel. We thank our guide for her flexibility and for getting us home efficiently. She refuses to take the tip we are trying to offer, saying it wouldn't be fair given that we didn't get to finish the tour. It's our first day here and we can already see why travelers always mention the kindness of the Thai people.

I give Kymani a dose of infant Tylenol to lower his fever and make him more comfortable. I sigh as I think back to a conversation we had with Roland's pediatric friend before we left. He had expressed concern about us traveling to Asia with such a young infant. He warned us about how delicate babies can be, and how critical it can be to get urgent care if they get sick.

Upon his advice, we diligently made lists of all the emergency numbers to call and the best medical facilities in every city we planned to visit. We made sure our travels were in low-risk malaria zones and regardless, to diligently use every recommended malaria preventive including mosquito nets for his stroller and bed. We also keep up Kymani's immunization schedule wherever we are.

"If anything serious happens," Adam, the pediatrician, told us, "go to Bangkok. They have some of the best medical services in Southeast Asia." I'm glad we happen to be here already.

We spend the rest of that day and the following watching Kymani's temperature, ensuring he's getting enough liquids and sleeping comfortably in the cool, dark hotel room. By the end of the second day he's smiling, eating, and interacting playfully again.

When Kymani is well enough to venture out, we walk to the Wat Pho and Wat Phra Kaew temples and the Grand Palace, which are conveniently across the street. Honestly, we're both a bit templed out, but we need to stretch our legs and get outside. Plus it's raining, which keeps the heat at bay, ensuring Kymani is comfortable.

"Oh wow!" I exclaim as we enter the temple grounds. My mood shifts quickly from impartial to excited as I take in the brightly-colored and intricately decorated structures that surround us. The temples are stacked in a pyramid-like formation, with the top stretching thin and tall to a spike. The outer walls are ornate, covered in flowers and vines that swirl over small mosaic tiles of vibrant blue, red, green, and gold. Much to our surprise it's entirely different from all the other temples we've visited.

"I'm glad we didn't miss this!" Roland smiles.

"I feel like we are in a different world!"

The stroller-friendly grounds make it easy for us to meander. We're in no rush to go or be anywhere but here, physically, and mentally. The grounds relax me. Like stepping into a favorite yoga class, I leave all my stress at the door and take in the tranquility.

✈

KYMANI HAS MADE A FULL RECOVERY by the last of our five days in Bangkok. For our final outing in Asia, we're going on a historic day trip to see the Death Railway in Kanchanaburi. The railway earned its name during World War II when over 100,000 prisoners of war died over the course of its sixteen-month construction.

Before we reach the railway, we stop at the Kanchanaburi War Cemetery. The air is thick with the damp heat, but also, it feels, with the somberness of the site. Thousands of prisoners of war are buried here, victims of Japanese imprisonment put to work building the Burma Railway.

Coming to a monument like this is soul wrenching but provides us with a deeply affecting opportunity to learn from our past. It's the perfect setting to open your heart and reflect on how humanity must always strive to treat each other better.

This, in part, is the reason I am standing here with my mouth open in shock.

A group of young adults are boisterously laughing and pointing at Roland. They speak to each other quickly, then erupt into giggles. They cover their mouths, unable to contain their amusement, pointing at Roland and then doubling over, their bodies folding over at the uncontrollable hilarity of seeing a Black person.

Roland and I have been together for four years. In that time, I'd only ever witnessed two acts of racism toward him. Once it was a homeless guy, staggering across the street in a drunken stupor. He shouted a barely comprehendible slur. Due to the likelihood of mental illness and definite substance abuse involved, I didn't put much weight in it. The second instance was around a late-night campfire, when someone's drunk parent joked that Roland was so dark the only way she could see him coming was by his white smile. Again, I dismissed it because she was old and ignorant but not hateful, and because when I checked in with Roland, he shrugged it off.

Of course, over our four years together till that point, there had been other incidences. Acts of racism—whether covert or overt, micro-aggressions, or full-on hostility—are a constant reality for Roland. I didn't see it; Roland wasn't pointing it out to me, and we didn't talk about it.

I have seen movies, read books, and watch the news. I know racism exists in the world, but I have been naive to the realities of it. I assumed most people think like I do. I thought racism toward Black people was an issue largely concentrated in the United States, specifically in the south. Many of the race-based stories I consume are set in a different time. As I understood it, we had evolved into a more progressive state. When I heard or read about a recent instance of racial preju-dice, I thought it was a horrible, isolated incident.

My personal ignorance has worn thinner and thinner over

these past six weeks in Asia. Standing here, I can no longer pretend to myself that widespread racism doesn't exist. It has been so prolific, so constant. Watching these young adults openly mock my husband is the final bucket of cold water to my face, waking me the fuck up.

Roland looks me in the eyes, "I need to go speak with them."

My kind, empathetic, loving, and tolerant husband has reached his breaking point. After countless stares, requests for pictures, inappropriate comments, and an endless stream of pointing and laughing, he's about to lose it on these tourists, and my naive, white bubble is bursting. I am shocked, scared, and vacillating between sorrow and fury.

I try speaking, but nothing comes out. He approaches the group as I watch them, still in disbelief. My emotions swirl—anger, fear, sadness—as my attention shifts between Roland, Kymani, and the group.

My brain finally catches up with me. *Alana, start walking. Go stand beside him.* My body pulses with adrenaline as I take shaky strides to catch up with him.

I expect Roland to be in a full-on shouting match or worse, and I'm worried that things could escalate. Roland has been infinitely patient with the hundreds of people hounding him these past six weeks. After being so tolerant and restrained, I'm worried that his anger cannot possibly come out in any other form than a blistering, fiery rage.

When I reach Roland, I search his face for signs of his emotional state, but his eyes are making contact with every member of the group, which have not stopped their shocking behavior.

"Do any of you speak English?" His deep tone penetrates the high pitch of the group's laughter.

One of the young men who appears to be the ringleader steps forward. He is laughing so hard he has to catch his breath. Between spurts of giggles, he manages to utter, "I speak English."

"What are you doing, what's going on here?"

Silence.

Then the group erupts in laughter again, bordering on a frenzy.

Roland's stance squares. "How *dare* you and your friends point and laugh at me because my skin color is darker than yours."

Three of the seven stop laughing and look at Roland intently.

"How would you feel, if you walked into a room and a group of people pointed and laughed at you because of the color of your skin?" His tone is serious and sharp with intent, but not angry or hostile. "If you came to Canada, where I'm from, and people laughed at you for your physical characteristics, how would you feel?"

There is a long pause. The entire group, except for one young woman, has stopped laughing. She laughs so hard she collapses to the ground rolling around on the ground holding her stomach. I wonder if she's intoxicated. She pulls herself off the ground and hovers in a squatting position, sitting on the back of her heels. I think the madness is finally going to stop but she points at Roland and clasps her mouth with her other hand and begins her shrieking laugh again.

Roland turns away from her and continues to address the rest of them.

"You don't point and laugh at any of the white people here. I hate to break it to you, but you and your friends aren't white either. You should know the shade of someone's skin isn't a value scale. Do you realize that when you treat a person like this you're reinforcing that the further away someone's skin color is from white, the less valued they are? That includes you! It's not okay. It's not *right*." Roland shakes his head and frowns, and my heart hurts. "You have no right . . . . This kind of ignorance . . . it's deeply hurtful. And it damages our entire society."

The tense empty space between Roland and the group is filled with the heavy weight of silence. Even the woman on the ground has brushed herself off and is standing with a serious expression on her face. The ringleader stares down at his shuf-fling feet. Finally he peels his eyes off the ground, making eye contact with Roland.

"I am sorry."

Roland takes a deep breath. "Thank you."

There is more silence, though the tension has lessened. "The next time you see a Black person, do not point, and laugh at them, for any reason. We need more love in this world, not hate."

The young man nods and turns slowly to his friends. There is an awkward parting as the group moves away.

Roland turns to me. "I couldn't let that one go." He lets out a huff of exhaustion, his muscles still tense from the adrenaline.

I open my mouth to say something, but nothing comes out. I am a bundle of emotions.

"I'm sorry, babe," I finally manage. That same old terrible refrain. "I'm so sorry that you had to go through this, and I wish this world were different." It is a small condolence, and he deserves more. My heart breaks. I give him a long hug, hoping desperately that I'm transmitting all I'm feeling, what I am failing to convey in words, from my body into his. "I love you."

"I'm so tired of it, the ignorance is unbelievable," he shakes his head again in disappointment. "That they think it's okay to point and laugh—and for the color of my skin. They don't know anything about me. It's just pigment." He sighs at the magnitude of the issue. "Who knows how much they understood, but I had to say something. I hope the next time they see a person of color they treat them like a human being."

I hold him for a long while and tell him again that I love him. I hate that I can't think of more to say. Partially I am in shock, but I'm also at a loss for what to say because I'm scared to say some wrong, ignorant, white thing that will do more harm than good. All I want to do is show my love and try to make it better, but I have no idea how. It's a slap in the face. It's a hard realization: that I do not understand what my husband has gone through in his life, and what he is going through right now.

As we get back on the tour bus, we spot another biracial couple. Roland nods, "Hey man, where you from?"

The couple are from New York, the Bronx. We stick together for the rest of the tour. Having each other gives us some comfort. Talking with them is a pleasant distraction from the incident that has burned a little hole in our hearts.

✈

ALTHOUGH IT HAS BEEN AN incredible trip so far, it's been hard too. Roland, however, refuses to let it ruin his experience. He says his parents raised him to be tough and to not let ignorance plant a seed in him and allow it to grow.

On our long flight back to Canada, I turn to Roland, "What was it like growing up in Canada? Did you experience things like what I saw on the trip?"

Roland was born in Vancouver, spent his grade school years in Winnipeg, and lived for a several years in Montréal and then Toronto before moving to Victoria, BC.

"When I was younger, sometimes I was teased about the size of my nose and lips. Kids wrote racial slurs in my yearbook. Occasionally an ignorant comment would come my way." He describes being followed by security guards in various stores.

I listen, with sympathy and a new understanding. "I feel so naive. I thought as a society we were so much further ahead. I feel completely unprepared to provide any advice and guidance for Kymani."

"Well, I will talk with him about a lot of this."

"I know, but I should too. I need to be more aware so I can be a better parent and partner—and person."

Back home in Canada we pride ourselves on being multicultural and accepting. Although, in recent past we have become more aware—in 2018 we still liked to think acts of racism did not happen to the same extent as the rest of the world. Over these first six weeks of our trip, we've witnessed blatant ignorance and racism, but these acts are not limited to Asia. As I write this book in the wake of our adventure, and in the midst of a global pandemic and the Black Lives Matter movement, I am more keenly aware of this than ever.

A few months after we returned from our year abroad, we went to Roland's sister's place for Easter dinner. We had a joyful night, still basking in our return and thrilled to spend time with family we had missed so dearly when we were traveling.

We arrived home late. Nearby, a group of young adults laughed and joked drunkenly. This happens on occasion as we live beside a bus stop on one of the major streets that go downtown and run between to the local college and the university. We didn't think much of it, though I remember double-checking the front door was locked before going to bed.

The following morning, Roland woke up early with Kymani. Holding him in his arms, he walked down the short driveway to his car parked on the street. He had left some Easter treats and cards from his sister in the trunk. The early-morning sun reflected off the hood of his car, exposing the shine where the light layer of dust had been wiped off by someone's finger. As he got closer, he stopped in his tracks. Scrawled across the hood of his car in big letters was the N-word.

Angry and distraught, he clasped onto Kymani tighter and whipped his head around, but the empty street offered no clues. He kept moving. He opened the driver side door, sat down, and, careful to protect Kymani's head, bent to pull the leaver that opens his trunk when something caught his eye in the rearview mirror: There it was, written again in large block letters across the back window.

The feeling of anger and pain sunk in as Roland assessed the ignorant racist act. This experience was more intense and heartbreaking than previous racist acts directed at him, because this time the moment was shared with his young, vulnerable, beautiful Black son. Through tears, Roland looked down at his son and said, "I'm so sorry, but I will try my hardest make a difference, I promise you."

Instead of wiping the hood of his car clean and continuing with his day, he pulled out his phone and filmed the racial slur written on his car.

As Roland tells me what happened, the blood drains from my head rushing to my distressed heart. My mouth gapes open and my eyes dart back and forth searching my brain for something that will help me digest his words. Before I lose my grip, I put my coffee mug on our black granite kitchen island.

My chest constricts and my stomach turns as he tells me he is calling the police to report the hate crime. He also shares it with his family and friends on social media, to help build awareness of how bad and common racism truly is. This was his way of taking back and owning the power of the racist act to create a much greater impact.

My mind races to catch up with my agonizing physical response. *My husband and my son will never be free from racism*, I think, my eyes tingling with the tears filling my vision before rushing down my cheek. The discrimination and hate my husband and boy are subjected to is not only a condition of the outside world, but of our hometown. The hometown I loved for being so progressive and liberal.

I close my eyes and take a deep breath. What can I do, where can we go to ensure their safety, to make sure nothing like this will ever happen to them again? *Fuck, there's nothing I can do*, I think as I clasp my shaking hands together to ground myself. No matter where they go, no matter what they do and no matter how undeserved, they must live in a world that, Roland says, makes him feel unsafe and unwanted.

CANADA

Josephine holding up a Canadian flag

Victoria

3 months old

March 10–16

———◆•◆———

"Two of the greatest gifts we can give our children are roots and wings."

—Hodding Carter

JOSEPHINE APPROACHES ME WITH A quivering smile, her arms outstretched to give a warm welcome home. As she takes a few steps closer her smile turns into a pained expression and tears come. I take her in my arms, holding her close. Her slim shoulders shake as she embraces me, letting out all her emotions.

"I missed you," she utters.

"Oh baby, I missed you too." I squeeze her tighter, then place my hand on the back of her head and let it run down her long, sun-streaked hair. "It's so good to see you."

Tears streak her face as she flickers her eyes up at me. I kiss the top of her head and hold her for a long time in the foyer of Nadine and Ed's place. It's been six weeks, by far the longest we have ever been apart in her ten years of life. Given the scarcity of her messages and the lack of emotion or real focus on our video chats, I thought she had barely noticed we were gone. Seeing each other in person again, I realize the truth of the situation.

I feel the pangs of mom guilt for leaving. I wish we could take her with us for the entire year, but that wouldn't be fair to her or her dad. "Why did you leave? Why are you doing this trip? It's too long."

I continue holding her as she works through her emotions. "Babe, why don't you and I go for a walk alone, so we have some time to chat, okay?" She perks up at the idea of getting me to herself and nods her head quickly in agreement. She turns her attention to Roland and gives him a huge hug. He holds her tight, puts his hand on the back of her head protectively.

It's a beautiful sunny March day in Victoria, and I'm very happy to be back in a temperate climate. As we walk along the path, I close my eyes and breathe deeply. The air smells like home; fresh and crisp with the distinct aroma of the ocean and evergreen trees. Josephine is especially quiet. I need to break the ice.

"Baby, I know we were gone a long time, and it was tough. I wish I could be with you all the time, but we talked about this. We had to find a fair way to split up the time with your dad. We now have three weeks together to explore California."

"I know. But why did you even have to do this trip to begin with?" She counters, getting straight to the point.

I remind myself that it's a fair question, even if we've gone through it before. "This is an amazing experience for all of us, a once-in-a-lifetime opportunity to see so many beautiful places. But sometimes it will be hard. We'll miss each other when we're apart. I know it's difficult, and it can be sad and lonely." I reach for her hand. Hoping to rouse her excitement, I smile brightly and lift my voice a couple octaves. "But I promise, once we're exploring Europe for six months, you'll know it was worth it!"

She flashes a disbelieving glance my way but remains quiet. Her emotions are taking precedent. No matter what happiness could come later, in this moment, she is sad and missing her mom.

I want to tell her all the ways this trip will benefit her. How the journey will open her mind to a wide variety of cultures and ways of life. I know she will be shaped by what she sees, and it will help her to be a kind, educated, compassionate, and independent woman. I want to do this with her, to create memories and bond, while she still likes me, before she is a teenager. And I want her to know that there's a great big world out there so that whatever drama comes into her teenage world doesn't seem so colossal. I want to build her wings long and strong so she knows she can fly anywhere, that the world is hers. Instead, I decide spending some one-on-one time together is probably going to have a better immediate effect. She needs to *feel* loved, not be convinced through discussion.

"Why don't we go play at the park for a bit?" I ask. "We can continue this conversation whenever you like. Let's take advantage of this beautiful day and the time we have together."

Josephine cheers up a little and agrees with a smile and a nod.

Walking to the park, I think about how this next leg of the trip is going to be tough on both of us. We have three weeks together in California but then must endure three months apart after that. On top of this, she has to contend with the fact that there's a baby who needs a lot of my attention. Traveling can be stressful without these intense dynamics at play. Everyone will have a lot of adjusting to do.

UNITED STATES

Josephine in Disneyland

California

3 months, 1 week old

March 16–April 4

———◆•◆———

"In Los Angeles, everyone is a star."

—Denzel Washington

"WOULD YOU LIKE FREE TICKETS FOR the premiere of IMAX's *Pandas*? It starts in fifteen minutes!" The stout lady's dark brown hair is pulled back into a ponytail, the strays clasped out of her face with black metal barrettes. She speaks nervously, grasping the stack of tickets in her hand.

I study her face to decide whether I trust her. She certainly does not come across as a typical charismatic hustler.

I glance at the TCL Chinese Theatre, the crowds streaming through the front door. I look back at Josephine, Roland, and his friend Darren, who is from Toronto but lives in LA as a comedian/actor/writer/everything cool. They're all frozen, silent, as if they too are thinking *What's the catch, lady?*

"I'm not sure," I utter after an uncomfortable silence from all of us. "I don't know if the baby can last through the show." Always blame it on the baby; it's the best excuse.

"Oh," she waves off my concern, "it's only forty-five minutes. It's really short." More silence. "It's free," she urges.

I let go of every instinct to run in the other direction. It could be an amazing experience if it's real. "Sure, great, we'll go. Can we all sit together?"

"Yes, no problem, if you don't mind sitting up front," she responds riffling through her tickets trying to find five together.

"No problem." I'm still waiting for the part where she wants my credit card *just in case*.

She hands us the tickets and points to a man standing beside her. "He will escort you in."

My entire body clenches under the shadow of the thick-muscled man towering in front of us. I am now convinced we're about to be shown to a back alley and robbed. Still, I reluctantly follow him, keeping Kymani's empty stroller between us and feigning confidence to my family and friend. He escorts us through a series of entrances, through a quick security check, and then through the front door. He stops. I jump. He turns to us. I lean back two inches to see his expression. He looks me dead in the eyes.

"There's free drinks and popcorn at the concession stand if you like ma'am." He points to an array of popcorn bags and drinks lined up on the counter. "Enjoy the show."

"Thank you," I say after he's taken a few stepped away. I turn around to face the group. "Wow, I think this is actually legit."

"This is amazing. It's like we're celebrities!" Josephine exclaims. "Mom, can I go get some popcorn?"

"Of course, baby, go for it."

"I'm so glad you get to see the inside of this theatre, it's gorgeous," Darren remarks enthusiastically. "It's where most of the premieres are. The big ones anyway."

"Wow," I say, the luck of our situation sinking in. "This is fantastic."

We are ushered to our seats in the front row. We are trying to be LA-cool but are failing terribly as we crane our necks and stare at the large round centerpiece in the ceiling: the layers of jutted spikes among swirling contours over Aztec-like carvings look like something from another world. I caress the soft red seat with my hand and wonder what celebrities have sat in this very seat.

The film's director walks to the front of the stage, standing a mere fifteen feet from us. He beams with pride as he introduces the documentary, describing briefly how the show came to be and some of the challenges they had to overcome to complete it. With heart, he thanks the many people who contributed to the making of the film, including Kristen Bell, who narrated it.

As the theatre lights dim, I turn to Roland, "This is so cool." Roland's got a grin the size of Texas and a sparkle in his eye; he's also in total awe.

I relax into my seat, resting my head on the back of the chair so I can comfortably take in the enormous screen in front of me. I hold Kymani in my arms and take advantage of the dark room to feed him, hopefully to sleep.

The documentary is fantastic. How could it not be, really? Pandas are the cutest creatures on the planet. Watching them roll around and play with each other for forty-five minutes keeps us happily entertained. Plus, when Kymani didn't sleep through it he was hypnotized by the large screen.

As we sit down to eat supper, we are delighted by the diversity around us. Nobody notices or seems to care what color we are, and nobody is wondering what we're doing together. This is the United States. I know very well this is not a racially harmonious utopia, but still, nobody is staring, pointing, or laughing, and we are surrounded by people of many different backgrounds. I am so grateful to blend in for the first time in a long time. It's also a nice break culture-wise. There are no major cultural differences (aside from the staggering number of dog-carrying, cosmetically-enhanced prima donnas), no language barriers, easy transportation options, and food we are familiar with.

Josephine grins ear to ear when Darren agrees we can go to the Ripley's Believe it or Not Museum after dinner. It was hard to be away from her for six weeks, and even harder to see her so sad when we returned. I'm so happy she is being dazzled and thrilled at every turn here, from the premiere, to Hollywood Boulevard, to Venice Beach and Universal Studios. It reassures me to know she is seeing firsthand the magic of travel.

✈

MY PARENTS DRIVE IN FROM THEIR winter home in Arizona to spend a couple days with us in Anaheim. At dinner, Kymani is passed between Grandma and Grandpa's laps. Josephine is snuggled in between them in the booth, telling them all about her adventures so far. It's heartwarming watching my parents interact with our children. There is a special bond that radiates between them: the relationship has no complicating factors, it's simple and all love.

The following day, the six of us drive to Huntington Beach. It isn't warm enough to sunbathe or swim comfortably in the ocean, so we rent a tandem bike and take turns riding up and down the boulevard. Between rides we huddle together on the beach, the cool wind blowing over us as we soften our gaze onto the water. We talk for hours, catching up on each other's lives. It's a memorable day, not because it is particularly nice out, or because we do anything amazing. What makes it memorable is the feeling of having everyone together. I love watching my dad race up the boulevard with Josephine who is giggling uncontrollably. My heart melts when my mom holds Kymani on her lap and we watch him squish sand between his fingers and toes.

More family pours in after my parents leave. Roland's sister Tricia, her husband Brian, and their two boys Jamal and Jalen move into a hotel room down the hall from us. Roland

(From left) Jalen, Jamal, Brian, Tricia Kymani,
Alana, Josephine, and Roland in Disneyland

and I are pumped to be together, and Josephine is over the moon to have her cousins to play with. We spend the next six days in a kid-oriented happy haze. They spend most of their time in the pool, entertaining themselves for hours with made up games, splashing about. At Disneyland we divide and come back together, taking various kids to different rides based on their interests. We gather at night to watch the iconic fireworks and enjoy laughter-filled dinners together.

We are missing Ed and Nadine and wish they were here. It's too big of a trip for them, especially given Ed's declining condition. Tricia does a fantastic job of sending them lots of pictures and getting them on a few calls throughout the trip. This helps everyone feel together, the best we can.

We leave California feeling happy and delighted. We are grateful for getting some sunshine, enjoying a culture closer to the one we are used to, being thoroughly entertained by rides, and shows, and relishing special moments with family.

EGYPT

Roland and Alana at the Pyramids.
Photo credit: Mohamed, our beloved tour guide

Cairo

4 months old

April 10–16

———◆•◆———

"It's better to see something once than to hear about it a thousand times."

—Asian Proverb

AS A CHILD, ANCIENT EGYPTIAN culture facinated me. The mummies, pyramids, cat worship, kings, pharaohs, hidden treasure, and booby-trapped tombs were so intriguing it seemed impossible that they belonged to the real world. I checked out every book on the subject from the library and immersed myself in their world.

As we walk out the door to meet Mohamed, our guide to Cairo and Alexandria for the week, I look over at Roland in disbelief. I am covered from head-to-toe in respect of local customs. Roland wears shorts and a t-shirt, which will be considerably more comfortable in this heat. *This is bullshit.* I sigh and roll my eyes at the double standard. On the plus side, my pale pink and white stripped jumper is way cuter. A small victory.

Mohamed greets us with a charmed smile and generous handshakes. He offers to help us get our bags and stroller on the elevator and into the minivan. I instantly trust and like him.

"Is there an ATM close by?" I ask Mohamed. "I need to take out some cash."

"Yes, there's one-half a block up the street," he responds. "I'll take you there."

"That's okay, thanks. I'll run over and be back in a minute," I offer, turning to go.

"I should come with you. Egypt is perfectly safe, but you must be careful. Either Roland or I should accompany you."

I pause for a moment, digesting this information. I'm torn between my desire to respect the culture and my desire to reject the limitation to my own free movement. Mohamed walks toward the bank, I follow silently, opting not to make a big deal of it.

Outside Cairo, we drive, searching the horizon for the iconic landmark. The desert stretches out in waves of golden sand curling in every direction.

"There it is!" I exclaim.

My heart beats at an excited pace and a few plump tears escape my eyes. I can't believe I'm really here!

The pyramid is smaller than I expected, and oddly not as triangular—the top flattens out ever so slightly. This doesn't curb my excitement; in the past three months of travel I've learned that things are rarely exactly as I pictured.

"There's nobody here," I say, shocked. "We have the pyramid to ourselves. This is unbelievable!"

"These are the lesser-known pyramids," says Mohamed in response to my excitement. I resolve to update my education by downloading some documentaries in the evenings. "This is the second pyramid ever built. The first is over there," Mohamed points at the desert in another direction. "We will drive by that one after, it was a failed first attempt, and is shaped a bit funny. This Red Pyramid is a vast improvement. It is the third largest Egyptian pyramid, after the ones at Giza, but it's excellent to visit because there are fewer tourists."

Roland, Mohamed, and I step out of the van to take some pictures. Kymani remains asleep in the air-conditioned van along with the Simon, our driver who doesn't speak English, but Mohamed assures me he is happy to watch the baby.

My gaze works its way up to the peak of the pyramid, which stands out surreally against the pale blue sky.

Mohamed turns to us. "Would you like to go inside?"

"You can do that?" Roland asks. "Yes, of course we would!"

I love Roland's enthusiasm, but I'm assessing the stairs and wondering how long Kymani will sleep for. "What about Kymani?" I ask him.

Mohamed gestures to the van, "Don't worry, Simon will take care of him," and ushers us toward the pyramid. "He has three kids; little Kymani will be fine."

"Okay, but let's be quick."

Our legs are shaking from the climb up the steep stairs, which go halfway up the pyramid. When it was first built, Mohamed informs us, there would have been several fake entranceways. Theories suggest this was to trick thieving tomb raiders. We make our way inside the confined passage, which runs a sharp vertical sixty meters back down. I turn around to descend the ladder-like structure, carefully feeling for the small wooden planks to support the balls of my feet as I inch my way down. In the belly of the pyramid, a strong sharp stink I associate with neglected cat litter stings my nose.

We explore the inner chambers, climbing into and around the dark, musty rooms. I think about the early nineteenth century explorers and imagine the treasures that would have been discovered here. The harsh smell never subsides, and even with a scarf held over my mouth, the pungent sting is becoming unbearable. We backtrack, weaving our way through the ancient tombs, and climb the ladder, motivated to reach the dry desert air.

When I open the van door, Kymani's eyes flicker awake. Perfect timing.

The tiny Imhotep Museum is also void of tourists. We wander through the silent rooms, reading the labels of the relics on display. My eyes grow wide, and I gasp, pushing the stroller in a brisk walk toward a coffin shaped case at the far end of the room.

The mummy's gray, clay-like head lies peacefully with its eyes closed. He is wrapped in a cocoon of cloth from his neck to his ankles. "You can see his toenails!" I exclaim, bewildered that someone from thousands of years ago can remain so well-preserved.

By the time we finish at the museum, the dry heat of midday is upon us. I'm still tired from our overnight flight and ready to head home. However, Mohamed insists we go inside this pile of rocks first. With extended arms he walks toward me. "Come, I'll help you carry the stroller." *Ugh*, he squashed the one excuse I had to wait in the cool van instead.

But my eyes light up when I read the sign above the entrance. "This is a tomb!?"

Mohamed beams at me, like a proud parent watching a toddler discover a world all-too familiar to him. He leads us inside the short mud house–like structure. There are multiple rooms with walls covered from floor to ceiling in hieroglyphics. Their sheer number floods our vision. They are exquisite, but also so much more than decoration—stories of everyday life: of fishing and making baskets, of important battles and tributes to the pharaohs and gods. There are no guardrails, no glass protection, and no formal security. I can't believe these monuments are still intact given the lack of visible effort to ensure their lasting survival.

Before we go home that afternoon, Mohamed takes us out for tea at a small café on the perimeter of Tahrir Square where the most recent 2013 protests took place. Here, thousands of people demonstrated against Mohamed Morsi, who protesters considered a corrupt president after giving himself unlimited power. The protests turned violent, and tourism declined substantially in its wake. We talk about politics and where Egypt is headed. Mohamed is passionate about his country, yet honest about its challenges and where he hopes it will improve.

Outside of dinner, we don't go out at night. Kymani goes to bed early, but also we are under the impression Egypt is better experienced in the light of day when Mohamed is with us.

✈

THE SPHINX AND THE GREAT PYRAMID of Giza are famous for good reason. Despite the eyesore of unfinished buildings leading up to it, the garbage that line the streets and the banks of the river all around, the relentlessness of the hustlers when you arrive, and the coachloads of gawking tourists, it's still amazing.

Roland is crouched down on one knee, angling his camera lens vertically. "These pyramids are enormous!"

I frame the pyramids with my hands. "Can you imagine them being any more magnificent than they are today? Picture them with a glimmering white limestone exterior, like pearls in the desert."

Meanwhile, Mohamed lifts Kymani up in the air and tickles him with his beard. Kymani clenches his body, his little fingers wrapped into fists as he bursts into giggles. Mohamed intuitively knows when I'm getting tired of carrying him and offers to take him in an it-would-be-rude-if-you-refused kind of way. Kymani is four months old, and Mohamed is thrilled to declare him the youngest tourist he has ever had the pleasure of working with. Without a doubt, a major part of the charm of this country for us has been the generous hospitality Mohamed has shown us.

Mohamed insists on keeping Kymani while we mount some camels and take the rite-of-passage ride with the pyramids in the background. I throw my leg over the colorfully tacked saddle, adorned with large tassels and bright geometric patterned blankets. The guide tells me to hold on tight and I grasp onto the horn of the saddle for dear life as the camel works its way jerkily up to standing position. Once up, I ease my grip and unclench my jaw. Beside me, Roland's eyes are wide with a mix of fear and excitement, his facial expressions moving quickly between smiles and *whoa*s.

It takes only a few steps, atop these unfamiliar animals, under the Egyptian sun, to forget you're on a heavily orchestrated (read: kind of cheesy) tourist venture. I ignore that part and let myself be swept away in the fantasy of being on a glamorous expedition across the sand dunes, gazing at the ancient wonders from afar.

✈

THE FOLLOWING DAY, MOHAMED takes us to the Egyptian Antiquities Museum. We've been inside for a brief ten minutes when a short woman, covered in a black niqāb, walks briskly up to me. A sense of panic rises from my stomach to my throat. *Oh no.* I replay the last few minutes, worried I did something wrong. She fixes her gaze on me with her almond shaped, gold-speckled brown eyes, dramatically encircled with kohl.

"Can I take a picture?" she asks.

I move a little and glance behind me. Take a picture of what? *Am I standing in front of something?* I jump at the unexpected hand she wraps around my shoulder. Her rhinestone-encrusted smartphone is angled high in front of us, ready for a selfie.

"Oh, sure!" I say, still a little confused. I tilt my head toward hers and smile, acting as if we are close friends.

"Thank you!" She disappears into the crowd.

"What was that about?" I ask Mohamed.

"She's probably from a small village," he theorizes. "This is likely a big trip for her to come into the city, and she is not used to seeing westerners. She wants a picture to remember and show her family and friends."

"Oh," I say, relieved it's not because of my exposing attire. I'm glad I decided to be conservative with my wardrobe choices, but even still, I'm showing more than the local women.

I could spend days in this museum, which is packed with extraordinary treasures. Again, I note the lack of technology and security; these priceless relics are out in the open with nothing to protect them or keep tourists from pawing at them.

We pay a little extra to walk through the mummy room. Here, there *is* security, at the entrance, inside, and at the exit. The rooms are temperature- and air quality-controlled, and the mummies are fully protected in enclosed caskets.

It is astonishing to walk among the dead pharaohs and nobility. We examine their faces and bodies, pointing out the preserved teeth visible through thin-lipped mouths and tufts of exposed hair. I stand staring in awe at Ramses II, the powerhouse of ancient Egypt. People adored him, and generations of subsequent rulers idolized him. His legacy includes some of the most famous sites in Egypt, including the Karnak Temple Complex in Luxor and the Abu Simbel temples, forty kilometers north of the Sudanese border.

✈

EGYPT HAS A DEEP AND SIGNIFICANT connection to its religious past. Mohamed assumes we are Christian because we are westerners. We figure there's no real point trying to explain that although we are spiritual, we don't subscribe to any religion.

Mohamed explains, "Religion has been used as a way to divide the people of Egypt. It is my hope that in the future, we can work together without conflict."

Coptic Cairo is home to many historically significant Muslim mosques, Jewish synagogues, and Christian churches. "You see," says Mohamed, "they used to practice their religions side by side in a mosaic, guided by principles of mutual respect. However, it did not last. There began persecutions and horrible violence to gain or maintain control of the populations through their beliefs," he explains in a plot that is far too common the world over.

Mohamed shows us a map, illustrating the understood journey Mary, Joseph, and baby Jesus took after the Messiah's birth in Bethlehem. He guides us up the quiet cobblestone street to the church, which is believed to have housed the holy family for some time before they continued.

Saints Sergius and Bacchus Church is a sand-colored structure with an oval, stadium-like center, a rectangular tower, and a flat square entryway. Inside are multi-story vaulted ceilings with exposed beams stretching across the domed roof. Tall, slim white stone columns hold up arcs of finely painted green and gold that curve down on either side of the worn wooden pews.

I want to linger in the spiritual sanctuary but Mohamed ushers us along to the real reason we are here. A brick entrance, coated in white paint, leads us downstairs to the basement where a series of low, cramped rooms are staged, displaying a few rudimentary pieces of furniture and some candles to recreate the space that Mary, Joseph, and Jesus are believed to have resided in. Staring down at my feet, I wonder how it is that I'm standing in the same place as they once did.

Cairo continually surprises me with its depth and complexity.

In the late afternoon, we stroll down the pedestrian-only El Moez Street. It is lined with well-kept, medieval-style buildings containing antique stores and vendors. The sidewalks along this kilometer-long stretch are believed to be the oldest in Cairo.

As we walk, Mohamed points to three teenage girls preoccupied with their cellphones. "You see, things are changing here. Many of the young Muslim women are choosing not to cover their heads." This is one of many unprovoked efforts he has made this week to break myths and stereotypes about the Muslim religion and culture to us. "They care a lot about fashion."

"I suppose they would have to modify to maintain modest coverage," I say.

"Well, they need to cover up like that to prevent fights."

"How so?"

"If they are not covered, the men stare and flirt with them— maybe make a pass. This causes their husbands to get upset, you see, causing fights. And if the men don't engage—well, then the women get pissed off! So, this is better."

I keep silent but the disappointment blazes inside of me. Misogynistic untruths like this are what lead people to blame sexual assaults on the "slutty and revealing" clothing worn by the victim, rather than the person responsible.

I remind myself that Mohamed was raised in a very different culture. I am fortunate to come from a place where I can stand on the shoulders of the feminists who came before me, and where change in the name of gender equality continues to be a primary social concern.

I was raised to use my voice when faced with sexist comments, but here I am wary to say anything, even to this kind man I've grown to trust. If I did, would he dismiss me as another crazy, emotional woman?

I look to Roland for backup. I am frustrated by his silence. Coming from him, a few choice words could be powerful, as they would not appear defensive. Then it dawns on me. All those times I was silent in Asia. I could have said something. It maybe would have been different coming from me.

We need to stand up for each other, be each other's allies.

I would be remiss if I concluded our time with Mohamed on a sour note. He remains the best tour guide we have ever had—kind, warm, and generous with his time and knowledge. He received us like family. Most guides won't share their perspectives on their country or discuss politics, but he was honest about his views, which made the experience enriching. He treated Kymani like a prince and was helpful in many ways. Certainly, his outlook on this issue disappointed me, however, we all have things to learn.

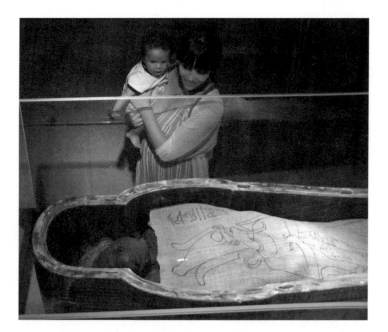

Alana and Kymani with an ancient Egyptian mummy

Luxor

4 months, 1 week old
April 16–21

———————◆•◆———————

"I am not free while any woman is unfree, even when
her shackles are very different from my own."
—AUDRE LORDE

MY INNER FEMINIST JUMPS FOR JOY as our new tour guide
walks toward us with confidence, a dark blue hijab over her
hair and fluttering behind in the desert sun.

Nahma introduces herself to me with a soft, gentle voice
and a firm handshake, then turns to Roland, clasps her hands
together and bows. "I'm sorry, in our culture we do not touch
other men."

Roland retracts his hand with a smile and bows back.

Nahma wastes no time and dives straight into our itinerary
for the next few days in Luxor, which is an hour flight south
of Cairo. Already we have noticed this less populous city—1.3
million versus Cairo's 20.5 million—is far more attractive. We
drive along a tidy promenade that hugs the Nile and I admire
the manicured greenery than stands out among the golden sand.

Our first destination, the Karnak Temple Complex, is
intimidating. Its grandiose columns, walls, and statues are built

at a scale meant for the Gods rather than us mere mortals. Our heads are cranked skyward as we make our way through the vast compound, admiring the statues of pharos and gods that stretch toward the heavens. Hieroglyphics cover every surface.

I've been dedicating time, after Kymani goes to bed, to documentaries about ancient Egypt. In fact, this has become my number-one piece of advice after a year of traveling: read books and watch movies about the places you are going. Doing this heightened my sense of connection to the places we visited, by forging a relationship to the locations, historical figures, and culture. It also increased my ability to retain further information, and ask intelligent questions of our knowledgeable guides, which in turn felt like a gesture of respect.

"It's rare that women and animals are depicted as symbols of praise and worship in ancient worlds, it is one of the many things I admire about ancient Egypt." I say to Nahma.

Nahma smiles and nods in agreement, pointing out the various gods adorning the temple. "Here is Horus, the God of vengeance, and there is Ra, the God of the sun. You will find many of Hathor, the Goddess of motherhood."

When Nahma isn't pointing out culturally significant features, she tells me about her life in Egypt. She has previously been engaged twice but has since sworn off men and prefers to live independently and take care of her mother. She says there are not many women tour guides and that most of her friends, after having children, stay home instead of working. "Things are changing though. More women I know are leaving bad marriages, getting an education, and some are even refusing to get married at all, like me, because they don't agree with the expectations put on them as a wife or mother."

She asks me about life in Canada, and I explain that education rates for women surpassed that of men in the last census for the first time in Canadian history. I tell her all my friends who have children return to work.

She turns and nods at Roland, who is carrying Kymani a couple meters behind us. "Your husband is a dedicated father."

"Yeah, he is. Parenting responsibilities are now shared more than previous generations, but I am especially lucky. He would gladly care for him all the time."

She stares ahead in a wistful, even longing way. "It sounds nice."

"Well, we have a long way to go. Women aren't equally represented in executive positions, and they're not paid the same as men. Not all is fair in love and work," I smile, realizing too late that my play on words may be lost on her. "Roland and I are both divorced, actually. It's pretty common."

This surprises her most. She rapid fires numerous questions, and so I explain our family dynamics, and that I have a daughter from my previous marriage, who will be joining us in a few months. I tell her the reason we decided to end things was in pursuit of a happier existence, not because of abuse or anything deeply serious.

She listens attentively then pauses, squinting her dark brown eyes. "It's very different from what my friends and I experience."

The entranceway to Luxor Temple boasts a soaring obelisk and a towering open doorway book ended by two colossal statues of seated Gods. I can't imagine how they ever carved and erected these massive forms—what a feat it must have been for the time. The midday heat is starting to come upon us now, and I'm worried about how long Kymani will last in his carrier, which acts like a little oven.

Tour guides like to build things up, keeping the most impressive things for last. I turn to Nahma and Roland. "I'm not sure how long we'll be able to stay in this heat. Nahma, can you please take us to the significant parts first?"

As predicted, about ten minutes into our walk, Kymani fusses.

"I need to feed him. I'm going to find some shade off to the side and I'll come find you when we're done."

In Cairo, Mohamed encouraged me to nurse wherever, even in a mosque. Nobody stared or made me feel uncomfortable about it. However, Nahma's eyes dart back and forth with worry.

"I'm fine," I reassure her, "I'll be over here." I don't have much of a choice in the matter; I can't tell him to wait thirty minutes while we finish the tour. When he's hungry, he's hungry.

I find a rare piece of shade along the shoulder of the main walking path and turn my back to the oncoming tourists. A breathable white baby blanket covers us so I can peel the layers off underneath. I expected Nahma to continue the tour with Roland, but she is standing, creating a barrier, between the oncoming tourists and me.

The blanket stays intact, but my shawl slips off my shoulder, exposing a small corner of skin. My arms are preoccupied holding Kymani, so I leave it. Nahma's hand lightly grips the fabric with her thumb and forefinger and delicately glides it back over my shoulder. Despite her gentle touch, I feel the embarrassment radiating from her. She is trying to help, but I'm annoyed. Though I'm covered and nursing my baby, something every mother does all around the world, she is struggling to bear witness.

After Kymani is satisfied, we finish our tour and Nahma escorts me to the air-conditioned car. Nahma leaves me to retrieve Roland, who is lingering, taking some final pictures. When she reaches the gate, the men won't let her pass. She waves her tour guide identification at them, cussing them something fierce. I roll down my window to help, but she is shouting in Arabic. I have no clue what's going on.

Nahma comes stomping back to the car, sand flying beneath her steps. Her head is shaking back and forth rapidly in disbelief. "Those are bad men. I told them, my client is still inside, but they won't let me pass." She is vibrating with anger. She purses her lips tightly, takes in a deep breath, clamps her fists on her hips, and squints back at the security guards.

"Don't worry, Nahma," I say. "We can stay in the car and wait. Kymani will feel better in here. Roland sometimes gets caught up with the picture taking, but he won't be long."

Nahma huffs in exasperation. "This isn't right. If I were a man, they would never do this." She doesn't wait for me to reply and marches back to the gate to give them another earful.

I smile ear to ear at her determination. Maybe this is why she had been so nervous about me nursing when Mohamed wasn't; she doesn't have as much clout to defend me, should she be called upon to do so.

The men at the gate don't acknowledge the woman in front of them spitting frustrated words. They remain stone-faced, ignoring her as if she is nothing but a pesky housefly.

Roland, now within earshot, hurries over to the gate before things escalate any further.

Back in the car, Nahma is shaking and flustered. She goes back and forth between ranting and apologizing to us as we drive back to our hotel. We reassure her she has nothing to apologize for and we're glad she stood up for herself. I tell her we will stick together to avoid any further issues and flash a look at Roland that tells him he needs to stay closer to us in the future.

The rest of the afternoon is spent in luxury. We take Kymani to the outdoor hotel pool surrounded by short, manicured grass and tall palm trees. Our feet are relieved to the touch of the cool tiled floor. Laying in lounge chairs, shaded by a large umbrella, a man in a crisp white shirt, deeply-pleated pristine white pants, and polished black shoes appears out of nowhere to offer us beach towels and take our cocktail orders. This is absolute bliss.

✈

THE FOLLOWING MORNING, WE ARE up at five to take advantage of the temperate morning climate and arrive at the

Valley of the Kings before the other tourists. We've learned through trial and error that attempting anything past noon in this heat is a non-starter for Kymani. This child is going to make a morning person out of me, whether I like it or not. Good thing he's so darn cute.

Across the river from Luxor, the Valley of the Kings and the Valley of the Queens are gems veiled by the vast desert hills: hidden mazes of tombs built to house, in secret, the remains of pharaohs and other members of high society. The complex passageways were created to prevent thieves from finding the tombs and taking the treasures meant to accompany the dead to the afterlife.

We pull up into an unremarkable spot in the desert with nothing but endless rolling sand. The cave-like crevices are dug into the side of the hills, with small signs beside them. These are the entrances to the tombs.

My jaw drops as we enter the tomb of Ramses IV. The walls, from the floor to the ceiling, are covered in column after column of hieroglyphics: symbols and pictures recounting the stories of Ramses's mortal life, his passage to the afterlife, and the afterlife itself. Also written on the walls are spells from *The Book of the Dead*, prayers, and instructions to ensure the smooth transition from here to the other side. Each column of text is the width of my hand, written in bright blue, red, or gold paint, faded but still visible. My eyes follow the columns up until they land on the ceiling, which depicts a perfect clear night sky filled with stars. In the center are images of animals and Egyptians worshipping.

The deeper I walk into the tomb, the more preserved the colors are on the walls and ceiling. I reach the end of the corridor and find the chambers, which are equally remarkable in their embellishments.

We continue to work our way through a few other tombs, including that of Tutankhamun, or King Tut, whose coffin is still inside. The discovery of his tomb in 1922 brought about a renewed western interest to ancient Egypt. His tomb is smaller and less elaborate, as its artists and engineers did not have time to complete it due to his unexpected and untimely death. Although not as impressive, it's famous because of the treasures discovered there, including his infamous golden mask, which is now on display at the Egyptian Museum in Cairo. Such findings are rare, as most tombs were looted a long time ago, leaving nothing but the paintings on the walls.

We arrive at the Valley of the Queens at 11 a.m. The heat is relentless. We make it through my favorite, queen Nefertari's, tomb before Kymani breaks down.

We run from the tomb's entrance to a small shelter with a roof and some benches, where a number of local men are hanging out, also escaping the heat. I need to feed Kymani.

I drape the white baby blanket over my shoulders, arms, and Kymani, but the lack of airflow has him squirming in discomfort. Nahma pulls my shawl up, then pulls down the corners of the blanket to cover us while standing protectively over me. I point our portable fan on Kymani's core, but it blows my cover up, threatening to expose us. I pass the fan to Roland, so I can use both of my hands to help Kymani latch. He is flushed and screaming in frustration.

I pull Kymani out from under the cover and hand him to Roland. Roland blasts the fan as hard as it will go and he begins to calm down, but he's red and damp with sweat. With a quick nod, Roland and I mutually decide to call it a day.

I've tried to temper my expectations, but for a moment, I am disappointed we are unable to explore the rest of the tombs. Kymani constantly blows me away with his tolerance for our adventures, and I remind myself, I have no right to complain. Instead, I focus on the astonishing things we were able to do today. I still can't believe we're here.

Abu Simbel Temple

Abu Simbel

4 months, 2 weeks old
April 21–25

"Travel makes one modest. You see what a tiny place
you occupy in the world."

—GUSTAVE FLAUBERT

THE VEHICLE SHAKES AS IT makes its way over the cracked
desert highway. It will take us three hours to drive to Abu
Simbel. Two vans in front of us and one behind us all carry
tourists. We slowdown in unison as we pull up to a checkpoint.

Two guards, with expressions too serious for their smooth
youthful faces, walk toward us. Their stiff, dark cargo pants
are tucked into black laced-up boots. They each hold a
semi-automatic weapon against their puffed-up chests, which
are protected by bullet-proof vests.

The driver hands one of the guards a stack of our passports.
He peers into the van; his gaze sweeps past me and halts on
Roland. He rifles through the passports' covers, all Canadian.
Frowning, he opens each one, flipping to the page displaying our pictures until he finds Roland's, pauses, and rubs his
manicured thumb over the portrait and hologram. Repeatedly,
he examines the passport and glares at Roland through the
window. In a sharp tone, he questions the driver in Arabic.

The driver turns to Roland. "Tell him your name and date of birth."

My heart pounds. The engine is shut off, inviting the Egyptian sun to infiltrate the air-conditioned vehicle. Beads of sweat form on Roland's forehead. I wipe my sweaty hands on my pants.

Roland dictates the correct information to the guard in his Canadian accent.

The other guard walks around the van, sweeping the underside with a mirror for anything hidden underneath.

Without a word or change in his stern glare, the guard hands the passports back to the driver.

I release the breath I hadn't realized I was holding.

After five more minutes, they let us continue down the highway. Our convoy of vans fly down the black strip amid the ocean of sand to the southern tip of Egypt, toward the border it shares with Sudan.

✈

THE ABU SIMBEL TEMPLES ARE TUCKED into the back of a mountain ridge on the banks of the Nile. Being of similar height to the faces of Mount Rushmore, the gigantic statues on the temples' exterior tower over us. Standing at their base, I crane my neck to take in the icons that guard the entrance. I place my hand on my forehead like the beak of a hat to cover my eyes from the bright sun as I examine the sphinxlike shape of a head. These imposing figures were created to remind those traveling north on the Nile, toward the heart of Egypt, that they were entering the territory of the powerful Pharaoh Ramses II and his wife Nefertari.

The monuments, built in honor of one of the most influential kings of ancient Egypt, include statues of his favorite children and depict stories of his conquests and major achievements. Inside, a number of chambers with carved art occupy the walls that tell of tributes to the gods, of battles, and of everyday life.

I spend long pensive moments gazing at it all, hoping that if I do so long enough, the images will sear themselves into my memory and stay forever.

Kymani and Roland lounging in the sun

Sharm El Sheik

4 months, 2 weeks old
April 25–May 1

———————◆•◆———————

"I myself have never been able to find out precisely what feminism is: I only know that people call me a feminist whenever I express sentiments that differentiate me from a doormat."

—REBECCA WEST

AFTER THREE WEEKS OF EXPLORING the riches of ancient Egypt, we take a week to relax in an area known for its resorts. When we arrive, Roland's bag isn't at the baggage claim, despite our direct flight.

Roland asks a security officer where to inquire about the missing luggage. He frowns, and without making eye contact says, "Wait here, I'll be back."

Within minutes, the small airport empties of everyone who was on our flight. We sit and wait in the empty space, until the security guard comes back to tell Roland his bags went through another security area, and he has to come retrieve it.

By now, I have been on enough planes with Roland to be aware, and defensive, of the way security treat him. We've been traveling long enough to be weary of scams, even in seemingly legitimate situations like dealing with airport security. We are not in North America anymore, and the standards we take for granted don't exist uniformly across the globe.

"Why are his bags over there?" I ask.

The security guard ignores me and repeats to Roland, "If you want your bags you need to follow me."

I grab my partner's hand. "He is not going with you by himself, so you can either bring his bags here or we are all going with him. We stay together."

The guard doesn't appear to have heard me, so Roland repeats my statement.

"Wait here."

What kind of racist bullshit is this? And he won't listen to me, but he'll hear Roland. What kind of sexist bullshit is that?

"What the hell is going on?" I ask Roland when the security guard is out of earshot.

"I don't know, babe," he says shaking his head, disheartened by the constant airport struggles.

The security guard returns. "Come."

"Is there a reason for the security concern?" I prod again.

Ignoring my question, the guard points to a conveyor belt. "Retrieve your bags and go through those x-rays."

I am not used to being ignored or treated with such blatant disrespect. I walk up to the fat security guard slumped in his chair in front of the x-ray machine.

"Excuse me, can you please tell me why we are the only ones from the entire plane to be escorted through this security and forced to have all our bags x-rayed?"

He turns to his friend and giggles something in Arabic. I want to jump over the counter and slap him.

Roland waves a pointed finger to the two men "It's not funny. Why is it that I'm the only Black person on the plane, and I'm the only one who has to go through the extra security? This is not random."

With no reply, Roland heaves our gear onto the machine.

After they let our bags through, I take my phone out and snap pictures of the security guards, uttering threats that I will report them. They now acknowledge my existence, and miraculously speak English. "No! No, no pictures!" I am so angry I keep snapping as I make my way out the airport doors.

I place my cell phone in my pocket, worried my shaking hands will drop it on the cement, and observe our surroundings. The only moving thing is the heat waves pulsing over the scorching pavement. There are no travelers, no taxis, no guards, nothing. We can't go back inside, so we start walking, hoping we'll come across a taxi stand. Finally, we find a group of men sitting under a tree. One jumps up and asks us if we need a ride.

Of course, this is not a licensed cab. I scan the desperately vacant landscape offering us zero alternatives. We have to negotiate a price before we leave, but we have no clue how far our resort is. We are too hot and tired, so we let the driver rip us off, charging us double what it should.

I begin relaxing a little once in the foyer of our resort. We are within the compound and can seclude ourselves from all the hassle and hustle for a week.

However, as it turns out, it's not much better inside. The staff don't acknowledge me when I speak to them. Instead, they respond through Roland. The waiters brag and joke about how many wives they have. There is nothing to do here but sit and be treated like a second-class citizen.

✈

WE KNEW SOME PLACES ON THIS TRIP would be amazing and others disappointing. Sharm El Sheik was upsetting, but the challenges we faced are gifts of knowledge, and opportunities to find deeper empathy and understanding. I'm grateful, in hindsight, for the stark reminder of what women face around the world.

Egypt will be remembered as a magical place. The enormous pyramids built in the midst of vast sand, temples with columns of carvings as high as giant sequoia trees and tombs adorned with intricate artistry. Regardless of the challenges, as I write this book, tears come to my eyes at the memory of standing, by the ancient relics I'd dreamed of seeing since I was a kid.

ENGLAND

*Roland, Kymani (who's bursting with excitement),
and Alana at the London Eye*

London

4 months, 3 weeks old

May 1–13

———•◦•———

"In London, everyone is different, and that means anyone can fit in."

—PADDINGTON BEAR (MICHAEL BOND)

"I FEEL FREE AGAIN! I LOVE THIS CITY!" I exclaim as we leave our Covent Garden Airbnb, on a mission to find coffee and a bite for breakfast. We've barely been here a day and I already feel like a weight has been lifted off my shoulders.

Everyone speaks English, people treat me like a human being, I know what I'm eating and how to order it. I'm walking down the street without an escort; I am safe, and I am completely ordinary. It's a relief to not be stared at and hassled at every storefront to "come inside, looking doesn't cost anything." Plus, on every corner there's either a pub or a coffee shop. These are my kind of people. It's the big and the small things that make me happy and feel at home.

We are in London to join in the festivities surrounding our friends Emma and Damian's wedding. We've arrived a few days early, giving us enough time to hit some of the major tourist attractions. Today we have a relaxed schedule of coffee, a museum, then beer.

The British Museum is a short few blocks away, so we enjoy the leisurely stroll while sipping on desperately missed Americanos. Instantly, we notice how diverse London is. Outside of California, we have been the minorities in the countries we've visited over the past two months; it's a nice change to suddenly blend in. It gives me perspective and empathy for people of color in my very-white hometown in Canada.

"I love the diversity here," Roland says, reading my mind yet again. We've been spending far too much time together . . . it's getting weird. "There are a lot of Black professionals."

I sigh with more relief than I expect. "It's wonderful, isn't it? I've never felt so demeaned as I did in Egypt, like my voice didn't count for anything. I often, especially at the end, felt so unimportant and unequal. I loved everything we saw, but there was a lot of sexism. A month was too long under those circumstances." I pause and think of Nahma and how she described her and her friends' lives there.

"It's nice to not feel on display here. There were countless moments in Asia and Egypt where people would be watching me and I would think 'I hope I'm representing women well, or biracial couples well, and I really hope I'm representing Canada well. As if their judgments of an entire segment of the population or an entire country could be based on that one interaction with me is kind of a lot of pressure."

Roland nods, laughing long enough to tell me this is not new to him. Of course it's not.

"I guess over the past few months I've been getting a glimpse into your everyday, hey?"

"Well," Roland pauses and thinks about it. "It's been an intense crash course for you. You've lived in a world where anything you do only reflects back on you as an individual. If you succeed or fail at school or work, the congratulations or judgment will only ever be for Alana. Whereas if I fail, I worry I've made it harder for the next Black person that comes along.

If I mess up, I may have reinforced a stereotype. If I succeed, I might have changed people's perception about what Black people are capable of, thereby contributing to making it easier for the entire race."

Here I am complaining about a couple months of people noticing me at restaurants and museums. "That is an unfair amount of pressure."

"Growing up, every time there was a major news event about a murder or a crime committed, my family would gather nervously in front of the TV. We would pray the perpetrator wasn't Black. Because if it were, it would make things that much harder for us."

I close my eyes and shake my head. "That must be exhausting." I take his hand and squeeze it. "These next two weeks will be good for us—back in a country we're more familiar with and lots of time with friends coming up."

I can see the excitement in Roland's eyes at the prospect of interacting with friends again. We're both social extroverts; we really do need this. We joke, but we are kind of running out of things to say to each other.

Inside the British Museum there are treasures from around the world. There's a lot of controversy surrounding this, as they were taken from other countries that invariably—and fairly—feel their monuments should be returned to them. The Rosetta Stone, discovered in Egypt in 1799, is one such artifact. This stone has three decrees in different languages including ancient Greek and ancient Egyptian hieroglyphics, that together provided humanity the key to deciphering hieroglyphics. This revealed the mysteries of ancient Egypt to the world, as it enabled us to translate and understand hieroglyphics.

"We didn't even need to go to Egypt," I joke. "It's all right here!"

"No kidding," says Roland as we stroll among the mummies.

"Well, it's not really the same anyway," I qualify. "It's like the difference between watching a movie about a puppy and having one in front of you to play with. I hope these artifacts inspire people to actually go to Egypt one day."

After a few hours of roaming around the museum we venture off to find a pub for a cold pint and greasy grub. We find one close to the Airbnb and ask the hostess if it's okay that we come in with Kymani. The woman frowns begrudgingly in Kymani's direction then mutters, "As long as you're out by 7 p.m."

I'm a bit shocked by the anti-kid hospitality but shrug it off to enjoy a pint . . . or two.

We enjoy the next four days doing ridiculously touristy things like getting on the classic red double-decker tour bus, which takes us to Westminster Abbey and Buckingham Palace. We walk along the water to see the Tower of London and the London Eye. We also visit the National Gallery, which is free to enter. I love the London policy whereby the galleries and museums are free for everyone, which they do for social inclusion and participation. They believe everyone should have access to these cultural centers—that cost should not be a restriction to appreciating history and the arts. Bravo, London!

✈

THE BUS DRIVER FOR STONEHENGE insists we cannot bring the stroller onto the bus. We show him how it collapses and how the wheels tuck into the base, turning it into a car seat. A twelve-hour tour without his seat to sleep in will be an impossible venture. The driver reluctantly lets us bring it on.

As we step up inside we see the only vacant seats are in the very back row. We ask if it's possible to open the back door of the bus to help us get him in, but the driver says no. Everyone on the bus stares at us. Nobody offers to help, and nobody offers to switch seats with us. Roland hoists Kymani, in his car seat, over his head to get down the narrow aisle.

"This isn't the most baby-loving place we've visited, is it?" I say to Roland as we speed along the highway toward Stonehenge. "I guess we've been spoiled with people fawning over Kymani till now. Here, most people act like he is an inconvenience."

Kymani, happy to prove everyone on the bus wrong, falls asleep in his converted car seat. "I can't believe this is the only tour company that would allow us to take him. It's a bit of a different culture in that sense, eh?" I ask with typical Canadian flare.

"I guess so. I don't see any children out with their parents at the pub or even in restaurants."

"I understand not every baby or kid would behave on an all-day bus tour. But as parents, can't we make that informed decision based on what we know about our kids and ourselves? The same goes for the restaurants and pubs. There's this perception that the presence of a child will ruin everyone's experience, instead of adding to it."

"Well, I'm glad we found this tour. It'll be a great day. Plus, it's awesome that Kymani gets to celebrate his five-month birthday at Stonehenge."

"He has the best birthday-month-baby shots of any kid on the planet!" I laugh. "Oh, and there it is!"

Stonehenge is fascinating, partially in that it's ancient—dating to 3001 BC—and still around for us to visit, but more so because of the mystery of it. It's interesting to listen to the theories of why Stonehenge exists, and even more interesting that we humans really have no idea. It's hard to imagine what would have been so important five thousand years ago to build such a monumental structure. Current theories suggest it was a place of spiritual significance, or a healing center. It amazes me how so many stunning structures, paintings, sculptures, and monuments exist around the world all dedicated to the spiritual realm.

At five months Kymani can barely sit up on his own. He holds on for about five seconds before he tumbles back into a horizontal position. We spend ten minutes setting up his little FIVE MONTHS OLD sign and positioning him close to the guardrail, with Stonehenge visible behind him. Several times I sit him up, then run out of the shot.

Roland clicks quickly before I have to rush back and stop him from tumbling onto the grass. All the while, we are singing "Baby Shark," and clasping our hands together in imitation of a shark to get him to smile. After a dozen attempts, Roland gets a great shot of Kymani sitting up next to his sign with the monument perfectly visible in the background and a big smile on his cute pudgy face. Success!

EMMA'S SISTERS ARE THROWING A ladies get-together to celebrate the bride. It's a clear, warm day, and in the heat of the sun, as we play a game of mini golf, a few beers go down quickly. Soon we are tipsy and laughing garrulously at our inability to play this game, even with our increasingly lax rules. We stagger through the last few holes and clink our plastic cups together before downing the rest of our beer. Everyone is in great spirits and ready to continue the celebration with some food, games, and a hot tub at Emma's sister's place.

We nibble on some snacks back at the house as the champagne bottles start popping. The host sets up a game of "champagne-pong," which we all agree is a much more amusing version of ping-pong.

By 10:30 p.m., I am holding my hair back, hovering over the kitchen sink, and throwing up. Emma's sister, a confident woman with an I've-always-got-it-together demeanor puts me in a cab. I make it back to the Airbnb but cannot for the life of me get the stupid key into the lock. Finally, the door opens.

"Damian! Baby!" is how I greet Emma's fiancé and Roland, throwing my hands in the air, swaying to and fro like an inflatable dancing man at a used car lot. I mumble some sort of "Nice to see you. I'm tired. Good night!" I give them both a hug and head straight to bed.

✈

THE NEXT MORNING, I WAKE UP soaking wet. *Oh my God, what is that?* My head is pounding, and my hands are shaking. My guts turn as I muster the strength to lift my body off the bed and survey the bed and my clothes. The wetness is limited to the top half of my body: one of my boobs is engorged and aching; the other is normal.

Holy shit.

I forgot to pump-and-dump before I went to bed. Kymani is doing a combination of nursing and formula and I went for so long without nursing (or pumping) yesterday that my breasts swelled and must have self-expressed while I slept.

The smell of stale, rotting milk wafting from me turns my stomach even harder. I walk into the living room looking like a rat that's barely pulled itself out of the sewer water. Roland is sitting with Kymani on the couch, reading him a book.

"I'm sorry babe. I can't do it," I say, barely able to form a proper sentence. "I just need some water, and a shower. I need to go back to bed."

Roland gives me an empathetic smile, granting me a parenting pass.

✈

EMMA AND DAMIAN'S WEDDING ceremony was an intimate affair back in Canada, so today is all about the celebration. We start with a classy afternoon tea. The three of us are dressed in our formal garden attire and are looking rather smashing. Kymani is especially adorable in his beige linen pants, blue striped suspenders, and matching fedora. Roland is as stylish as always, in his gray dress pants, button-up shirt, and white hat. I'm in a flowing dark blue dress dotted with large pink flowers, my long hair bouncing in fat, loose curls and decorated with a stylish blue fascinator.

Tea is served in delicate china cups rimmed with pastel pink and blue flowers. Emma's sister takes Kymani from me with a quick, confident swoop. The swinging motion puts a big smile on Kymani's face. He leans in to grab at her hat, but she expertly diverts his attention by taking his hand in hers and kissing it loudly.

I take advantage of the moment I have two hands free to grab a scone. There are small containers of jam and cream, presumably meant to accompany the pastry. I pause, feeling the sudden silence of the five guests around me.

"What? What have I done?" My face flushes with embarrassment.

I scan their faces, hopeful for a clue. A tall brunette with kind deep brown eyes looks at me with curiosity. "We want to know which one you choose first, the jam or the cream."

"Oh," I say, "do you recommend a certain way?"

The friends laugh in unison. "Well, it's a bit of a debate . . ."

"Not really," chimes in a tall blond gent in a sharp blue jacket and white button-down shirt with an extra button undone. "It's clearly jam before cream." He raises his eyebrows and gives the brunette a playful smirk.

The group erupts into heated controversy. They passionately defend their perspectives, debating in their fine clothes and smart accents. I could listen and watch them for hours, giggling to myself about how very English it all is.

The evening progresses into a small local pub down the street. All things proper are left at the door as pints are paired with greasy finger food. The room quickly gets loud and ani-mated. Kymani is giving it a good shot, trying to nap through it, but loud, high-pitched tipsy lady squeals and clapping wake him up. It's an early 8 p.m., but the boss baby has spoken, and it's time to go. I say my goodbyes and walk home in the pouring rain. It's Roland's turn to have a few too many drinks tonight.

We leave London feeling grateful for how well it has treated us. It's one of our favorite cities in the world, and we hope to be back soon.

PORTUGAL

Overlooking Porto
Photo credit: Ravi Mohabir

Porto

5 months old

May 13–20

———————◆•◆———————

"Life was meant for good friends and great adventures."

—UNKNOWN

WE ENTER A VERY SMALL BAR WITH our compact stroller, navigating through the narrow spaces between tables, chairs, and the bar. *Where could they possibly be? This place is tiny.*

"Your group is outside, around the back," says the bartender, pointing to a door at the back of the restaurant.

"Perfect, thanks!" says Roland, leading the way.

"Ah!" exclaim Melissa and Ravi when they see us.

"You made it!" Melissa calls, getting out from under the picnic bench to come give us a hug.

"So glad you could be here," Ravi says, giving Roland a hug.

"We wouldn't miss it for the world, man," Roland replies.

We order drinks and settle into our seats, excited to meet and get to know the ten other friends and family members gathered around the table, some of whom I recognize, having met at various parties and gatherings throughout our friendship with Melissa and Ravi.

The couple worked with Roland on a large government IT project a few years before I came into the picture. By the time I was introduced to them, they had become Roland's trusted, close friends. They are forever fun, thoughtful, and generous.

✈

BY THE FOLLOWING MORNING, all thirty of Melissa and Ravi's friends and family have flown in from Canada in preparation for their wedding. Together, we spend our first day on a guided walking tour. There is a slight drizzle of rain, and it's chillier than we expected. Luckily we've had to pack for weather ranging from forty to zero degrees Celsius, so we have enough provisions to be comfortable.

We're trying to keep up with the group the best we can, but we lose them each time we stop to feed or change Kymani. Cleverly, Ravi transmits his geo-location to the group through an app on his phone, so we can always track them down.

I'm enjoying lagging behind the group. I'm less interested in what the tour guide is saying than in taking in the scenery and enjoying the views. The city is splendid, but not in a prim, clean and proper way. It has a rustic charm. Built up on a hill with the downtown running into the Douro River, the buildings appear layered on top of each other in an intricate maze. Narrow, steep streets and alleys lead to hidden cafés, restaurant terraces, and port cellars. Eventually we meet up with them again at a local café.

"Thanks very much for the tour," I say to the tour guide, offering her a tip.

"Thanks," she says with a smile. "Where are you from?"

"We're from Canada. I think the entire group is."

"Oh, you're from Canada! Nice people. Where is he from?" she gestures over at Roland who is waiting in line to grab our drinks.

"He's from Canada too," I say, wincing at her perplexing stare, knowing now where this is going. "He was born in Canada," I add.

"But where is he *from?*" she persists.

Unless you are Indigenous, you are an immigrant to Canada. Yet nobody ever asks where white Canadians are really from.

I persevere. "He was born in Vancouver, grew up in the prairies, close to me, actually. Then he lived in Montréal and Toronto before moving to Victoria. He was born in Canada and has lived his entire life there."

"Right," she says shifting a little, searching for the right words, "but where is he *really* from?"

She is not going to let this go until she defines him within a category which aligns with her beliefs of what a Canadian should look like.

Reluctantly, I let the words slip from my mouth. "Do you mean his heritage? His parents are from Barbados."

This, apparently, is an acceptable answer. She nods her head and wishes us an enjoyable trip.

I shake my head and turn away. *Why did I answer her question and give her the satisfaction?* I should have taken the opportunity to explain why it's not an appropriate question, but I didn't want to make myself or her feel uncomfortable, so I backed down from the confrontation. I resolve to be more courageous, to get comfortable with being uncomfortable, and find the words to help bring people along.

I wonder if it's too late to switch my shot of espresso for a shot of tequila.

✈

FOR MOTHER'S DAY, ROLAND arranges to have our friends watch Kymani so we can go for dinner. The restaurant's ter- race is perched on the side of a hill, and we spend the first ten minutes in silence, staring out at the cascading roofs and the calm river below.

"Thanks for this, it's really nice," I say, sincerely.

"You're welcome, baby. Happy Mother's Day. Thank you for everything you do for us, you're the best." He leans in for a quick peck.

"You are sweet, thank you." I am grateful for my forever romantic and appreciative partner. I can only handle so much gushing though, so I change the subject.

"I was thinking about our upcoming four months in France and wondering if we should cut it back." This doesn't catch him off-guard; we've both been touching on the idea for the past few weeks.

"I don't want to take that away from you, Alana, it's your dream to live in France. Plus, Jo's French will improve so much while we're there."

"I know, and we will go, but four months is a long time. What if we don't love Nice? Neither of us has been there before. Plus, I think we need to pick a place you'll enjoy as much as I anticipate enjoying France."

"I thought we would be tired of traveling and want to root down somewhere, but I'm still really enjoying it. How long do you want to spend in France?"

"Well, we have various family plans from late September to early October, so maybe if we plan to leave afterward? That gives us six weeks to explore France and two-and-a-half months to go wherever you like."

"Okay," Roland leans back in his chair, thinking of the possibilities. "Maybe we could go somewhere in Africa—South Africa maybe?"

We cheers with a smile and talk about the places he wants to see. I don't know where we'll go or what we'll do, but I'm not worried about it. Josephine and I will be in bliss in France, and I want him to have that same experience.

✈

THE WEDDING AT THE END OF OUR week with friends comes too quickly.

"Congratulations!" I hug Ravi and Melissa as we stand in the beautiful plaza of a local restaurant by the water, drinks in hand.

We found an online babysitting service and a young university student is watching Kymani so we can fully enjoy the festivities. But the time has come for me to relieve the sitter.

"The day was fantastic. See you guys soon," Roland says as he squeezes them both goodbye.

We're sorry to leave them, but our hearts are filled with the joy of eating, drinking, and celebrating. We desperately needed the invigoration that comes from being surrounded by friends. We are ready to venture off on our own again.

ITALY

Roland, about to get his mind blown by this pizza

Naples

5 months, 1 week old

May 20–22

———————◆•◆———————

"One cannot think well, love well, sleep well, if one has not dined well."

—Virginia Woolf

I NEED TO GET IN FRONT OF ROLAND before he gets to that security guard. If he goes through first, we will get "randomly selected" and pulled over. We don't have time; if that happens, we'll miss our connecting flight.

I run with Kymani in the stroller, pretending to play games with him so I can get ahead of Roland. Roland, pulling his suitcase behind him, smiles at Kymani as we zoom in front of him.

I walk confidently past the security officer offering him a smile. He waves me through. I turn my head to make sure Roland is allowed to pass. The security guard puts out his arm palm facing up and steps toward Roland, "Sir, please go to the left to have your bag x-rayed."

"Sir, he's with me," I say. "We're family."

A flash of confusion materializes on the security guard's face, but he nods, straight-faced, trying to hide his initial surprise. "All right, go ahead."

This is the way it works. If Roland goes through security before me, he, along with his traveling party (Kymani and me), are pulled out of line and forced to go through an extra layer of security, waiting in another line before hoisting our bags onto a conveyor belt to be x-rayed; however, if I go first I'm allowed through no questions asked, so that when they inevitably pull him aside, I tell them we're family and since they've already waved me through, they let us all proceed.

This year sees us on fifty-six plane rides around the world and I can now say, without a shadow of a doubt, that we are racially profiled and treated differently based solely on the colors of our skin. It doesn't matter who has Kymani, who is carrying which bags, or how many. I am not once "randomly selected" for extra security screening; Roland is, almost every time.

Roland would not be okay with me waltzing in front of him at every airport line if he knew I were doing it to "save the day." So, I usually don't, and take the punches as they come, but I'm not missing our connecting flight today.

As we speed through the airport to meet our next flight I think about the cruel irony of the world's very specific racial profiling regarding the members of our family. Because if one of us has earned the right to people's suspicion, it's me. Roland is not inclined to be rebellious; I, on the other hand, have a tendency to be a little defiant, to push back against authority, and to test the boundaries.

In high school, police officers found my backpack with a bag of weed and a pipe in it. Although legal now, at the time, it was a criminal offense. The police confiscated the drugs, gave me back my backpack, and warned me to "stay on the straight and narrow." It was never formally reported.

My First Nations and Black friend who were caught in a similar situation were not given the "teenagers will be teenagers" or "she's from a good family" pass. They were formally reported, charged, and convicted, and it affected them for the rest of their lives.

✈

NAPLES IS A BOLD CITY, FILLED WITH passionate, no-nonsense people. I can't understand a word they are saying, so this assumption is based purely on their expressive faces, their zealous yell-talk, and the way they raise their arms and jolt their pinched fingers back and forth in that classic Italian way. It's intense, fun, and slightly intimidating. I love how the back alleys have laundry strung across the apartment complexes and have kids darting between the buildings playing soccer.

We are only here for one full day before driving to the Amalfi Coast. Our kind and generous Airbnb host has sent us out for the day with a map of recommendations including coffee and pastry shops, market shopping, an old cathedral, and a tour of the underground tunnels that were used as hideaway during World War II.

"I'm starving," I say as we get Kymani settled back into his stroller after the tour.

"I could eat," says Roland, who never gets ravenous like me. I go from *Hmmm, I'm feeling a bit peckish* to full-blown hangry mode within about twenty minutes. It's not pretty. If I don't get food within about thirty minutes of the hangry stage, my body goes into conservation mode: my eyes become dull, and I walk around in a half-zombie state until I find something to regulate my blood sugars.

We walk around for a while, struggling to find anything open at five in the evening. Roland and I love that Europeans create a life balance that refuses to stay open 24/7 or fall into workaholism. They open for lunch, shut down for a couple hours, then re-open for longer, late-night dinners. If I lived my daily life here and had a regular routine, I'm sure I would applaud it even more; however, as a tourist with a baby, it can be tough to manage the timing.

"What's that place? It must be open, there's a lineup," I say pointing to an entrance with a discreet sign above: L'ANTICA PIZZERIA DA MICHELE.

"I don't know, should we go see how long it might take for us to get in?" Roland is clearly concerned about the possible wait, knowing intimately that I don't do well with not eating, like, immediately.

"We might as well try, nothing else is open." I shrug my shoulders, trying to act cool, like I'm not going to turn into a monster within the next five minutes.

Roland makes his way through the small crowd gathered at the front door to figure out what's going on. I wait on the sidewalk with Kymani in his stroller.

Roland comes back waving a small piece of paper in his hand. "Okay, we're number 84. I have no clue what that means or how long we have to wait."

"That's okay. I'll pull over here and feed Kymani if you want to listen out for our number." I quickly check the number in Italian using my Google translate app. "It's *ottanta-quat-tro*." I repeat it a few times until he feels confident he's got it. He walks over to take his place among the crowd.

Now to get the little man sorted. I pick him up out of his stroller and sit comfortably enough on the curb to nurse him. I feel a bit awkward about it, but I'm getting used to doing what I need to do when and where I need to do it. Sometimes I luck out with a nursing room in an airport, or a secluded comfy corner seat at the back of a restaurant, but most of the time I'm nursing under not-so-ideal conditions. I choose to cover up, throwing a light blanket over us. Throughout our travels, I thought I would get looks and even comments, but I very rarely do. Most everyone ignores us and doesn't seem to care at all, which is such a relief.

When our number is called, we're escorted inside the restaurant by a straight-faced, all-business host. We pass the busy cooks feverishly throwing pizzas into a large wood-burning oven. The small, basic tables are filled with people happily eating their giant flat pizzas.

We're seated and told there are two kinds of pizzas on the menu. "Margherita or marinara, so what will it be?"

"Two beers and two margheritas please," Roland says.

The plain decor and cheap tables and chairs are telling me people don't come here for the ambiance. There are only two pizza options, so they're not here for the sophisticated menu either. What's the deal with this place? Why is it so busy? Is it because nowhere else is open at this hour?

I read a quote framed on the wall and it all comes together.

"Roland, we're at the famous pizzeria in Naples—the one in *Eat, Pray, Love*! Look, this quote is from the book describing the pizza. How on *earth* did we get so lucky to stumble upon this place and not even know it?!" I'm bewildered and delighted at our unexpected luck.

Roland chuckles. "I remember that scene. No wonder it's so packed in here."

Our waiter carelessly tosses our beer and pizzas on the table without a word or a smile. I suppose the pizzeria is so famous they don't need to be polite. And the air of bubbling buffalo mozzarella in marinera sauce fired in a wood stove, is intoxicating. We grab a slice each of our giant gooey pizzas and dive in. My eyes instantly close after the first bite, and when I open them I see Roland's are closed too, as if our taste buds are asking not to be distracted by anything our eyes might have to offer.

"This is the best pizza I've ever had in my life," I murmur between warm cheesy mouthfuls. "It's so simple, and so delicious."

"I've never had pizza like this," is all Roland responds.

We don't bother with further conversation; we surrender to the pizza and let ourselves enjoy it in silence.

"That was worth the wait. It was ridiculously good," I say, in a euphoric state after finishing my entire pizza.

Roland shakes his head. "Pizza will never be the same."

"No, no it won't, but I'm happier to have loved and lost than to never have loved at all," I reply, only half joking.

✈

THE NEXT MORNING ROLAND AND our host come bursting into the apartment, disrupting my relaxed state.

"We got the rental car," Roland calls. "Our neighbor let us park the car in front of their entrance, but we've got to hurry."

"Okay, everything is packed and we're ready to go," I say, jumping to my feet and gesturing to the pile beside the door.

Roland and the host start gathering the luggage. I throw a backpack over my shoulder, grab my purse, and start rolling Kymani out the door. We quickly throw our belongings into the SUV and hand the apartment keys back to our host.

Our host crosses his arms and says, "I think I should drive you out of here."

I analyze the impossibly narrow street and compare it to our North American–sized SUV and nod conclusively. Roland agrees, handing our host the keys.

I sit in the back of the SUV with Kymani. Roland and our host roll down their windows and pull in the side-view mirrors. We wave and yell *Grazie!* to the neighbor for letting us park in front of their place, and slowly start moving. We roll cautiously down the street, the car's proximity sensors warning us we are about to hit something on all sides, at all times. I wince, worried Kymani is going to cry from the piercing, migraine-inducing noise, but his calm face has no trace of concern.

We don't make it to the end of our block before our host unrolls the window, sticks his head out along with his extended arm and pinched fingers, and makes a lively request that someone move their stuff out of the way so we can get by. He doesn't bother to shut his window and continues to passionately wave his hand or shout out at people as we inch our way forward.

By some miracle, we make it out of the narrow residential streets in one piece. We thank our host for everything as he jumps out of the vehicle to return to his apartment. It's this type of help we've received all along the way that makes such a difference on our journey.

Once we're on the highway, it's an easy cruise for twenty-five minutes to Pompeii.

"I can't figure out if Pompeii is stroller-friendly," I say, going through a number of blog posts I downloaded before we left.

"Someone needs to make an app for that," says Roland. "It's a constant struggle. Imagine if you were in a wheelchair trying to travel. How come it's not standard to indicate if a place is wheelchair friendly?"

"I guess we bring the stroller, and if it doesn't work then we can bring it back to the car?"

"Yeah, or maybe they'll keep it behind a counter for us. They've done that for me before at a couple museums. I'll put the carrier in his diaper bag in case we need to use it."

We find parking easily enough among the tour buses, a block away from the entrance to the site.

At the front gate, we hire a guide who is happy to take us around as soon as he convinces a few other people to join us.

We ask his thoughts on the stroller; if it isn't feasible, we have time to take it back to the car while he solicits other clients. He ensures us the stroller is fine to bring.

Soon we're making our way down the old streets of Pompeii. Though we stand amid this legendary place, it's still hard to imagine an entire community wiped out in one swoop, leaving a lifeless and preserved city behind.

The compound is like stepping back in time: everything is as it was. This includes the old cobblestone sidewalks and streets complete with deep grooves from the weight of traversing horses and carriages. Which are, by the way, impossible to navigate with a stroller.

Roland and I carry Kymani in his stroller around the complex like he's royalty and we are the bearers of his palanquin. Roland grabs the front of the stroller with one hand and I'm at the back, propping him up by the handle. Our guide has us on a scavenger hunt, scouring for penis engravings on the stone walls and in the cobblestone sidewalks that point us, literally, to the local brothel.

When we arrive at the brothel's front door, we realize it's too narrow to pass the stroller through. Roland suggests I carry Kymani in my arms, and he will hurl the stroller over the wall separating the street from the back exit of the brothel so we can retrieve it on our way out. The baby struggle is real today.

The narrow hallway leads us through a scattering of small rooms with beds made of stone. I was slightly intrigued at first, but the reality of this place repulses me. It makes me sad to think of all the women, mostly slaves, who had to endure their bodies being used, often under horrendous circumstances.

Our last stop before we leave is a large glass enclosure off to the side of the main square. Horrifically-preserved remains are displayed in the enclosure, including a pregnant woman, a dog, children, and men. When I see their perfectly kept bodies, the tragedy of the city and its people hits me. My imagination projects movie-reel images of ash and lava spewing down over the town. I envision the people running to escape, or accepting their fate.

The stunning town of Positano

Amalfi Coast

5 months, 1 week old
May 22–29

———————◆•◆———————

"Where we love is home, home that our feet may leave, but not our hearts."

—Oliver Wendell Holmes

THE SUN HAS GONE DOWN. I WATCH the dark, windy, narrow road, my body alert to the inches between our tire and the side of the road, which drops off in a steep cliff, to the rocky coastline and sea below. With both hands on the wheel, Roland's body is tense as he stares through the windshield, eyes glued to the road.

The bright lights of another car appear from around a bend in front of us, making me turn my head and squint my eyes. *There is no possible way both our vehicles will fit on this road. The margins are too thin.* They are not slowing down. I close my eyes, bring my knees toward my chest, and grab the dashboard as the car approaches. A squeal escapes me as they zoom past us. We didn't crash! When I open my eyes again, the dark road ahead is empty, and the other car has turned another sharp bend behind us. These roads are unforgiving, making no allowances for my nerves.

Finally our GPS tells us we've arrived at our Airbnb. The address numbers we can make out in the dark are getting closer to the one we're after—but all of a sudden the houses stop and all that's left is road and cliff. We turn around and try again, but no luck. Our cell phones only work with access to Wi-Fi, so outside of our downloaded Google maps we have to rely on old-school tactics to find our way. Roland pulls over and walks into a local restaurant to ask directions.

Kymani and I wait in the SUV. Whatever stress I would usually feel about being lost in the dark on the edge of a cliff melts away as I take in his content, peaceful little face, dreaming away with not a care in the world.

Roland comes back and points at a closed gate with no number on it. "That's the one, apparently." He shrugs. "I'll go check it out."

Kymani and I sit tight, waiting for the verdict. The gate opens. Roland stands at the entrance speaking with an older gentleman for a few minutes, then returns with a thumbs-up and a smile.

Roland drives us in through the narrow gate and is forced to make a ten-point turn to squeeze our SUV into an exceptionally narrow parking space in the corner. The owner says we can use the parking spot for the night, to unpack our things. Parking is at a premium here and we will have to move the car before the shop on the main floor opens in the morning.

Kymani and his accoutrements are always the first into the house. We hike up the steep stairs to our little apartment: a cozy one-bedroom suite with a private balcony. Even in the dark we can see it has an incredible view, which spans over the rugged coastline and the neighboring town of Positano.

✈

AT FIVE IN THE MORNING, I am on the balcony with a cup of tea, a plush blanket, and Kymani in my arms. My mind is foggy, and my eyes are puffy and stinging from the lack of sleep. Kymani, however, is wide awake—his face beams with a toothless smile and his eyes gleam with a youthful spark. He drops my bright yellow tube of mascara and picks up my soft brown leather sunglass case, quickly shoving it in his mouth. These are the makeshift toys of a traveling baby.

I smile back at him and pat his head as I shift my gaze out over the balcony. I could stare for hours at the cascade of colorful buildings from the neighboring town that crawl from the water to the top of the hill and beyond. The sky is shades of pale blues, pinks, and purples as the sun rises.

It's hard to complain with this stunning view, but I'm so tired I am not appreciating it the way I want to. Kymani is five-and-a-half months old and is still waking up every two or three hours for a quick comfort feed before going back to sleep. A part of me loves the bonding it affords, but the disruptions to sleep on top of traveling are wearing me down.

He's old enough now to be sleeping for longer stretches; it's time to make some adjustments. One of the issues with always being on the road is that our schedule requires flexibility. Kymani has been awesome at providing us with that, but it also means there's been no structure: no set naptime, no set eating or sleep schedule—so how can I blame him for not sleeping through the night?

Roland crawls out of bed to join us at a more reasonable 8 a.m., just as Kymani and I are ready to head back to bed for a nap.

"We have to figure out some sleep training," I grumble as I walk past him toward the bedroom. I suppose I'm a little resentful that he's been getting full nights of sleep since we started this journey.

Roland kisses me on the cheek and smiles softly despite my prickly greeting. "Good morning, you were up early, hey?"

"It's so hard to put any real structure in during the day, but there's got to be something we can do in the evenings." My tone has changed to desperation. "I keep ignoring it because we're too busy moving around, but he should be sleeping longer than two or three hours at a time."

"Oh buddy," Roland says to Kymani affectionately. "You've got to give mama a break. Maybe when we get to Florence we can dedicate some time to establishing a bit of a routine."

"Good idea." We have more time there, so it stands to reason we can slow things down and work on his sleep training. This is enough to give me hope: to think there will be some change in the not-so-distant future.

✈

WE'RE EATING OUT EVERY DAY BECAUSE we can't get enough of the tiny restaurants that hug the coastline and offer spectacular views from every angle. We linger on their patios for hours, perched high on hilltops or terraces hovering on the edge of a cliff. We eat fresh seafood and homemade pasta and drink rosé. We share relaxed conversation as the sun goes down. We walk around in a dreamlike state. This is the most romantic place we have ever been.

"I could stay here forever," I say to Roland, gazing out over the water as it splashes quietly against the jagged coastline. I have a glass of chardonnay in my hand that pairs perfectly with the best fungi pasta I've ever had.

"Really?" He is surprised, and I already know why. "It's so chill here."

"I know, I know," I say waving my hand dismissively. "Maybe I'd get bored at some point. But this place, it's like heaven." The exquisiteness of the whole place calms my soul. I want to lay back and cuddle with it, wrapping it around me like a warm blanket.

"It really is amazing," he agrees, and that concludes our conversation. We naturally talk less out here, comfortable in the silence and happy to feast our eyes instead.

My phone rouses me rudely from my daydreaming.

"Oh, it's Emma."

I open the message to find a photo of Savannah. She appears older than I remember; her muzzle has turned white, and her eyes are weary.

"What's wrong?" Roland asks, reading the concerned expression on my face.

"It's a picture of Savannah but honestly, she doesn't look too good." I hand him the phone.

"She's scrawny." Roland always notices details I don't.

"You're right," I agree. "Her cheekbones are protruding."

Another text comes through. I read it quickly and report back to Roland.

"Savannah isn't interested in eating and has thrown up a few times," I say, my eyes welling up as I begin to think the worst. She's eleven, old enough . . . "Emma's going to take her to the vet tomorrow." I give the phone to Roland so he can read her message word-for-word.

"I'm going to tell her to do whatever she needs to do and say thanks for watching out for her." Roland is typing into my phone, taking over the situation.

"She doesn't eat if she's stressed out. Maybe the kennel she was in while they were in England and Portugal caused some anxiety?" I am trying to think of any possible cause that doesn't involve cancer.

"Emma will take care of her. She says she'll let us know what the vet says tomorrow." Roland leans over and takes my hand and gives it a squeeze. I meet his eyes but quickly retract, trying not to cry as he consoles me.

I adopted Savannah when she was four months old, a few months before Josephine was born. They've grown up together.

I honestly don't know what I would have done without her in the darker, lonelier days of my divorce. As I worked through the emotional turmoil that comes with separating, she was by my side. She greeted me with joy, cheering me up the second I got home; she filled the house with life, making me feel less alone; she knew exactly when to come snuggle, putting her little brown and white head in my lap as I cried. I love her deeply, for many reasons, but she holds a special place in my heart as a dear friend who got me through a difficult time in my life.

I knew this time would come eventually; she will not outlive me. The knowledge doesn't make it any easier.

I go to bed early, seeking comfort and solitude. I cry and cry, soaking my pillow before I finally fall asleep.

When I wake up early the next morning, the usual refuge of sleep has provided me with no reprieve. I pick up where I left off, tears flowing down my face. I am worried about the news from the vet. My heart aches, and my eyes burn with torturous sorrow. I hate that I'm not by her side when she has always been there for me.

Although it's a picture-perfect day, I can't muster the energy to leave the house. I look ghastly, and I have no interest in pretending I'm not a wreck. As soon as it's a reasonable hour to do so, I try to numb it all away with a few glasses of wine. *This is actually helping*, I think as I coil myself into the deep patio chair with a warm blanket, on my second glass of wine and third chunk of chocolate. My head is getting cloudy with a wine fog that prevents my thoughts from moving too far in any one direction. I feel my mind and my body start to let go of the stress and anxiety. *Breathe and relax. There's nothing you can do. She'll message you the second she can.*

A text pings.

She's lost ten pounds since her last weigh-in at the vet right before you left. She has an inflamed lymph node,

*and the vet can't get a feel on her abdomen or organs,
so they want to do x-rays and blood work. It will be
approx. $450.*

For her 45-lb frame, that's a lot to lose. I reply immediately, giving Emma the green light.

*Do they know what they are looking for? Give her
lots of love from us.*

The response comes almost immediately.

*They are checking for cancer due to the weight loss.
She's getting her appetite back though. We'll get results
tomorrow morning and hope they'll know more. I'm
feeding her small amounts of wet food from the vet,
so she'll keep it down. So far, it's working.*

I throw my phone at the patio chair across from me. "Fuck!"
Roland picks it up so he can read through the messages. I push the oxygen out of my lungs with a grunt, wrap my hands over my forehead and close my eyes, mentally preparing myself for another long night.

✈

THE FOLLOWING MORNING I FEED Kymani, pass him to Roland, and go back to bed. My heart is tight, my eyes are raw, and my brain is beating a steady rhythm on the inside of my skull. In an effort to self-preserve and regain some strength, I swallow some pills and collapse back into a deep and dreamless sleep.

When I finally drag myself out of bed, I find Roland playing with Kymani on the porch. Although he can't crawl,

183

Roland has made pillow barriers around their play area. His safety-dad approach to parenting makes me crack a small smile. I love this man.

"I think we should get out today," Roland suggests delicately. "We need some sunshine and fresh air."

"Okay." I don't care what we do, as long as I don't have to be the decision-maker or the leader.

"There's a lunch spot my friend told me about. You can only access it by boat. The dock is in the next town over. We can catch the bus and walk down to the dock from there. The restaurant has a private beach and sunbeds, so we can hang out for the entire afternoon."

"Okay," I say with less enthusiasm than I intended. It does sound nice. I wish I cared more.

We're lucky enough to nab a water taxi, which are in high demand from the groups of beautiful, well-off twenty-somethings floating down to the dock in their sun hats and designer beachwear. We take a quick five-minute ride around the corner to the boat-only beach access, securing the last available reservation for the restaurant and the last two loungers on the beach. The universe is trying to be kind, and I am trying to be grateful, but I can't shake the sadness.

I take a twenty-minute nap in the sun and then guzzle two ice-cold beers. Roland is happily bouncing Kymani beside me on his lounger. Although I'm right beside them, I feel thousands of miles away. I watch Roland lift Kymani in the air and bounce him up and down to the rhythm of patty-cake. I would usually have the instinctual urge to pinch Kymani's thickly rolled legs and arms, but I don't. His little round face shrieks with joy as Roland throws him up in the air, but I can't feel the joy penetrating my own soul the way it usually does.

"I'm going to go for a dip, be back in twenty," I say. Maybe the cold water will shock me out of my depressed state.

After a quick swim in the frigid water, I plunk my shivering body on the soft-pebbled beach. I am glad to feel something, anything, even if it's vaguely unpleasant. I sit quietly, sifting through the pebbles with my hands, inviting the sun to chase away the cold. I find a small foggy-blue piece of beach glass nestled among the white rocks. I hold it in my hand, running my finger along its soft edges. Josephine loves beach glass. Ever since she was little, she would spend hours at the beach searching for it. I wish she were here to search with me. It's been almost two months since we said goodbye in Victoria, and I have another month to go before I will be able to hold her in my arms again.

What am I doing here? I am halfway across the world, with only half of my family. *Is this worth it?* I'm so sick with the pain and loneliness of missing them that I can't even enjoy the most beautiful place in the world.

Hair drips over my face. I'm sure it's doing an absolutely shit job of disguising the tears running down by cheeks, but I'm telling myself otherwise. I keep my head down and continue searching for glass, hoping nobody notices.

Because the universe is generous, it sends over two young curious girls, about the same age as Josephine. "Ciao," they both say kindly with a smile. Their beach-waved dark brown hair is lazily tied back. The taller one tucks a strand behind her ear, nervously awaiting my reply. The shorter one doesn't break her smile as she looks enthusiastically at my closed fist.

"Ciao," I say with a friendly smile.

They assume this means I speak Italian and start asking me something in high sing-song voices.

"Sorry, I don't speak Italian." I annunciate every word and speak slowly in case they understand enough English to get the gist of what I'm saying.

They nod, and one of the girls holds out her hand. It is filled with small pieces of beach glass.

"Oh!" I say joyfully. "*Bellissimo!*" I take my finger and softly examine the pieces in her hand. The colorful glass pieces, though worn down, shine like jewels in the sun. I show them my handful. With relaxed excitement they smile and put their fistfuls of glass into my hand. "Grazie!" I say, their kind gesture bringing more tears to my eyes.

"*La glass, c'est pour ma fille,*" I say in French, hoping they might be able to better understand the similar romantic language. I don't know if they understand me or not. They simply smile and continue searching for more pieces.

We spend a warm twenty minutes in the sun, combing the sand together in silent happiness. The presence of these two young girls and their willingness to share their time with me, mends my heart back together.

It's not the same as being here with Josephine, of course, but it is something—and sometimes, you just have to work with what you've got.

We spend the rest of the day eating amazing seafood, basking in the sun, and enjoying a few drinks among the happy crowd. It is a perfect little oasis and although I'm homesick, I can't think of a more wonderful place to be slightly depressed.

✈

A TEXT NOTIFICATION SOUNDS, AND I grab my phone. It's 1:04 a.m. and the text is from Emma.

Savannah has been keeping her food down and has a lot more energy today. We're putting her on a high-fat food diet and feeding her small amounts often. We will go to the veterinarian's office to weigh her every week to make sure she's gaining weight. They have ruled out the possibility of cancer. Yay! Honestly, she is acting like herself again, stealing Barnie's toys. Lol.

My body unclenches, releasing the tension it was holding. I send her my love and thanks. *Savannah will be okay. I will connect with Josephine tomorrow.* My eyes are closed before my head touches the pillow. With my heart feeling light again, I quickly drift off into a peaceful sleep.

Roland, Kymani, and Alana at the Colosseum

Rome

5 months, 2 weeks old
May 29–June 1

———————◀•▶———————

"Traveling is the ruin of all happiness! There's no
looking at a building here after seeing Italy."

—Fanny Burney

HORDES OF PEOPLE BOTTLENECK the entrance to the
Sistine Chapel, all trying to maneuver their way inside to see
Michelangelo's masterpiece. The air is thick, warm, and stifling
from the depleting oxygen in this tight corridor. I stand on my
toes and stretch to scan our surroundings: people are pressed in
and lined up as far back as I can see. We politely wait our turn,
pushing Kymani, who is seated in his stroller and surrounded
by a sea of legs. We are moving at a sloth's pace.

We're here on a specific mission for Roland. The day he
was supposed to see the Sistine Chapel, some twenty years ago,
happened to be a day it was closed. So, day one in Rome, we
are here on a guided tour to right that wrong.

When we get inside, we work our way across the densely
packed mosaic floor crowded with tourists' summer sandals.
We find an anchoring point in the middle of the floor to take
in the art around us. The altar wall floods our vision with

bright blue skies and crowded nearly naked men and women entangled atop soft clouds in Michelangelo's *The Last Judgment*. The detail in a single square foot would be enough to warrant its own piece of art; it's a thousand paintings in one. The mural is a complex mélange of bodies, the judged souls being either dragged down into hell or pulled up into the vast heavens that reach to the ceiling of the chapel.

Kymani quietly stares at the people surrounding us, moving his face from right to left to take in the buzz of everyone floating around him.

I strain my neck to take in the many Renaissance paintings, which extend across the ceiling. Above us is the famous fresco *The Creation of Adam*, in which Adam's toned naked body lies leisurely on the ground, his left arm lifted toward the sky, index finger lazily extended, waiting to be touched by God. I shake my head in amazement of Michelangelo's work; he was a genius of his trade.

We leave the busy room on a bit of a high from seeing some of the most famous paintings in the world. "Another bucket list item checked," says Roland with satisfaction. "Time for food?"

Back on the streets of Rome, I am captivated by my surroundings. The old buildings, the narrow alleyways, and the extravagant churches exude so much character and embody so much history they almost whisper the tales of the past through their ancient structure. It's a city that will never be able to escape its past. It is embedded in the very fabric of the architecture, in the culture and in the pride of its residents.

A scooter races in front of me, missing the stroller by a couple of inches. It startles me out of my tourist-gazing haze and back to reality. This city isn't only a living museum; it's a thriving metropolis. *Pay attention, Alana!*

We're in that weird mid-afternoon timeframe where most restaurants are closed. After three blocks of locked doors and rejections from serving staff, we finally come across a restaurant that is willing to make us anything from the pasta section. Any excuse to eat pasta in Italy is fine by us. We grab a table on the sidewalk and order a glass of wine. The menu has the Wi-Fi name and password on it, perfect. I wish all restaurants made it this easy.

My phone dings with various text messages.

"I got a message from Emma," I say, opening it first. "Savannah's doing great and look, she sent a picture of her sunbathing. She's too cute." I show him the photo, then return to my inbox.

"Your sister is sending us messages too." I open the texts from Tricia. "Aw, they're all together celebrating your mom's birthday, and they even brought Josephine. Your sister is awesome." I flip through the pictures of them all gathered around the table for cake, and of Josephine hanging with her cousins on the couch. "I love this," I beam, feeling happy and a little sad all at once.

"Granny is so happy surrounded by her grandkids." Roland smiles softly, scrolling through the same pictures Tricia sent to both of us. "We should give her a call when we get back to the apartment."

Later that evening, after Kymani goes to sleep, we call Nadine.

"Hello!" Nadine answers, excited as always to hear from us. She's already pulling out our travel itinerary to figure out where we are. "You're in Italy!" she informs us.

"We are," I say. "We're loving it."

"Happy Birthday, Mom!" Roland intervenes.

"Happy Birthday!" I echo.

"Oh thank you, thank you very much," she says with that infectious laugh of hers that always warms my heart and draws me in like a hug.

"Tricia sent us some photos, looks like you had a blast," I say. "It was so nice to see Josephine was able to join you.

That was really thoughtful to work things out with her dad and include her."

"Oh yes, it wouldn't be the same without her, you know," Nadine says, as if it is entirely natural and obvious to include her. I love her for that. "We had fun. We missed you three though," she says, in a loving, guilt-free way.

"We miss you too, Mom. How are you feeling?"

"Oh pretty good, my tailbone has been acting up again, so I think I might go get it checked out. See if there's anything the doctor can do about it. It's tough going up and down the stairs, you know."

"Are you still going to the water aerobics classes, or are you too sore for that?" I ask.

"I'm still going most every day. It's not as much pressure on it, so it's fine. Plus, it's nice to catch up with the ladies and sit in the hot tub afterward. It's those stairs that are challenging."

"Let us know what the doctor says. I know there's probably not much we can do from here, but if there's anything please let us know."

Nadine is already waving off the idea with her hand. "It's nothing major, it comes and goes." She says, concluding that topic and ready to move on.

"How's Pops doing?" Roland asks. "Where is he?"

"Not great, you know. Same old, I guess. He's up in his office. I don't know what he does up there. I can't get him to go out and do anything anymore." She sounds equally frustrated and defeated.

"I'll talk to him; I'll call him tomorrow." Roland knows his dad will listen to him. Roland has a way with people; he comes from a place of pure love, which tends to open people up and be receptive to his thoughts.

"Okay, okay. So anyway, how's my grandson doing? What are you three up to?" Nadine hates dwelling on the negatives.

We talk with her for the better part of an hour about everything we've seen since we last spoke with her in Egypt. We also tell her about our plans while we're in Rome, to visit the Colosseum, the Spanish Steps, the Pantheon, and Trevi Fountain. We make promises to call more often while we are in Florence for a month.

Alana, Kymani, and Roland overlooking Florence

Florence

5 months, 3 weeks old

June 1–30

———————◆●━━━━

"Florence syndrome is a psychosomatic condition involving rapid heartbeat, fainting, confusion and even hallucinations, allegedly occurring when individuals become exposed to objects, artworks, or phenomena of great beauty."

—Graziella Magherini, Italian psychiatrist

I NEED TO GET OUT OF THIS HOUSE. I can't stand Kymani crying like this. I know logically that at six months old, Kymani is capable of sleeping for longer than two hours at a time. According to this baby sleep guidebook, the crying is an expected (and acceptable) part of the process, but I can't help but want to run in there, pick him up, and cuddle him until he falls back asleep. It's torturous. I thought Roland, being the more emotional and sensitive one of the two of us, would be the one wanting to run in, but he is not fussed by it at all. *Are those sports highlights he's watching?*

Kymani is upstairs on the second floor of our Florence apartment. As we're settling in here for a month, we can afford to dedicate some time to sleep training and not worry about missing anything of the place we're visiting. The distance between Kymani's room and the living room muffles a lot of the noise, but it's still all I can hear. I feel like I might have an emotional breakdown if I have to sit here for another painful minute.

I announce I'm going to the market down the block to grab some groceries and a bottle of wine. Roland is getting a kick out of how frazzled I am. It's completely out of character for me; I'm usually the pragmatic one. I've decided this isn't even Alana reacting to the situation, but some sort of instinctual, evolutionary mama requirement embedded deep into my DNA, fueled by hormones.

The second I'm out of earshot, my shoulders drop, and my mind clears. I walk briskly to the market, because although I feel so much better to be out of the house, I also don't want to be gone too long. Mom guilt is a strong force.

When I get back to the apartment, I cautiously open the door, wincing and waiting for the sound of my wailing baby. I pause, hearing sweet nothing.

"He fell asleep?"

"Yeah, about five minutes after you left." Roland hands me the video monitor. Kymani is sprawled across his bed in a peaceful stillness. "It's getting better, he's going to sleep quicker."

"This is so hard," I sigh. "Josephine was so easy. She was sleeping through the night by two months, I never had to do any of this."

"Yeah, I don't think that's typical, Alana. The sleep training will be worth it. We need to stick with it and be consistent."

He's right. That's rational and logical. If only I could trade back this feelings-forward mama brain for my usual, pragmatic brain everything would be a lot easier. In an emotionally needy moment (*What is wrong with me?*), I start texting my girlfriends back home, soliciting moral support. As the sympathetic texts start rolling in, I feel so much better. I'm not alone, I'm just a mom trying to make it through.

Roland and I nestle in for a quiet evening of pasta, wine, and a movie. We get through supper and the movie and Kymani still hasn't woken up yet.

"Oh my, it's been more than three hours and he's still sleeping," I say. "He *never* sleeps for more than three hours at a time."

"Way to go little man." Roland says encouragingly to Kymani's video on the monitor. "We're breaking new ground here!"

He sleeps for five hours straight that night. The next night it's seven hours, and by the end of the week it is twelve hours—straight through the night. This is life-changing, for me and for us as a couple. It means I'm not sleeping with Kymani right beside me all the time and he can stay in a separate room; it means I can stay up with my husband for a few hours in the evening without worrying about sleep. It also means I can be well rested in the morning and have more energy to live. It's time to explore the city of art.

Everywhere I turn I see Renaissance masterpieces and stunning architecture. Florence's many museums and galleries are filled with pieces from some of the most famous and influential artists of the past: Michelangelo, Donatello, Da Vinci, Raphael, and Botticelli to name a few.

They say Florence holds so many treasures and is so beautiful that it could easily overwhelm a person if one is not careful. To avoid "Florence Syndrome," we take small bites every day and let each linger with us for a long while. We are in no rush and want to relish every last bit.

As we push Kymani's stroller along the very narrow sidewalks of the historical area of Florence I am enchanted. In the windows of the high-fashion boutiques in old stone buildings are exquisitely tailored suits, leather handbags, and silk scarves. We turn a corner and are met by statues of angels and saints carved into pockets of walls with detailing fit for a gallery. A woman in stilettos and a flowing black dress glides effortlessly down the cobblestone street in front of us. At the end of the block there are three quaint restaurants with terraces, their chairs filled with impeccably dressed people enjoying wine and pasta.

"I wonder which came first," I say to Roland. "Is Florence so beautiful it created, influenced, and lured magnificent artists to her, or is it that a group of artists transformed Florence into the beauty we see before us?" I am in a romantic, whimsical dream state.

"I don't know, but it's going to take us twice as long to walk anywhere because there is so much to take in on the way."

"Every day I wake up in Florence, I feel as though I am in the happiest of dreams."

We continue walking, stopping every twenty to thirty paces to take in a new piece of stunning Gothic or Baroque architecture. Roland pauses to take pictures as we make our way through small, charming alleys framed with large stone walls and hanging flowerpots. As we reach the river that runs through the city, we stop to take in the sun shining on the glistening water that flows under the ancient bridges.

We decide the view is so splendid we should go for lunch at a local restaurant with a terrace that overlooks the river. We both order homemade pasta with fresh, simple ingredients that are so high in quality I wonder if I have ever actually had a tomato before in my life. "Whatever I'm eating at home is clearly an impostor."

"Who knew something so simple could be so amazing? Kymani loves it. Look at our boy!"

Kymani is sitting in his highchair with pieces of fresh bread and homemade pasta, olive oil, and parmesan on his tray, which he grabs frantically by the fistful and shovels into his mouth.

"He's a good eater!" The waiter compliments as he pats Kymani's thick dark curly hair, lingering on it for a moment. "His hair is so unique." He pulls at a curl and watches it bounce back.

Roland's eyebrows furrow into a slight frown.

The waiter doesn't notice or wait for us to respond; he smiles and moves along.

"He's got such gorgeous hair." I say, trying to defuse the tension.

"I know, that's not the point." Roland says intently, "He will have to deal with people touching his hair his entire life. Like he's an exotic animal at a petting zoo. It's not okay."

Noted.

"Got it. Sorry."

✈

AS IS TRADITION, WE GO SOMEWHERE special for Kymani's monthly birthday. It's a fun and frivolous pursuit of that Instagram-worthy shot. Today he is six months old and we are celebrating with a day trip to Pisa. Walking through Pisa, I am delighted by how pretty it is. The town is bustling with tourists, the iconic leaning tower surrounded by busloads of people. Everyone wants that classic shot. It's hilarious watching a hundred people all positioning themselves, leaning back, and pretending to prop up the building.

I hoist Kymani up on my shoulders to give him some height above the other tourists. Roland bends down and points his camera up at us. He captures Kymani with a smile on his face, right next to the teetering building. Perfect! Now, time to find some lunch.

The guidebook we borrowed from our Airbnb suggests a pizzeria a short walk from the tower. The book is in French, so I am the designated guide. I look down at the map and then at the streets again and again, trying to make sense of it. "It's like it's missing a street, which happens to be the street we need," I say, bewildered, showing Roland the map.

"I think it's down here," Roland points down an unmarked back alley.

"Okay, might as well try. Seems odd though." It's not a street, there's no sign, and it is narrow and lifeless. "What could possibly be down there?" I frown at the map and spin slowly around like the lost and confused tourist that I am.

With no other ideas, we take the alley, which looks to be going nowhere except a possible mugging scene. We turn a bend, and the buildings angle off in opposite directions, opening up to reveal a hidden terrace.

"Amazing!"

We settle into our outdoor table, excited to enjoy a long, lingering lunch in the perfect June weather. Kymani has fallen asleep in his stroller thanks to the natural vibration of the cobblestone walkways. I love everything about Tuscany. Roland orders carbonara, a delectably creamy dish with cheese, bacon, and egg. I order spaghetti *aglio olio e pepperoncino*, a simple dish of spaghetti, extra-virgin olive oil, garlic, and chili peppers. Do not be fooled by its simplicity, it's pure heaven.

We are both in glorious moods, eating our favorite dishes and sipping on some Chianti. We are chatting about how impossible it is that half a year has gone by already. We've seen and done so much in that time, yet it still feels like it's gone so quickly. We reflect on our favorite parts of the trip so far and what we're most looking forward to in the coming months.

✈

TO CELEBRATE OUR ANNIVERSARY and Father's Day, we're spending the weekend in Venice. I personally don't have a huge interest in being here. I am aghast at the price tag and feel like it's over-touristy and doesn't have a lot of authenticity left. Roland, on the other hand, loves it. He can't get over how cool it is that the streets are made of water and wants to be in the throes of the romantic ambiance with me.

Anyway, we're here, so I should make the most of it and embrace the cheesy components of Venice. With that in mind, we take the obligatory gondola ride through the canals. Both Roland and I did this in our twenties; I came with my sister, and he visited with a friend. We both have funny, fond, and awkward memories of cruising in this romantic setting with our mismatched dates. It's nice to do it again, on our anniversary. We put Kymani's car seat in the middle of the boat, and he sits up to observe the world around him. He looks beyond his years as he gazes out longingly at the water, his floppy blue hat flapping in the light breeze. Roland and I laugh, hold hands, and indulge in a few selfies as we cruise along. I admit, it is kind of cool to float down the streets, taking in the views from the water of the buildings and bridges.

After our romantic boat ride, we walk to the Peggy Guggenheim Collection. We have seen a lot of art in Florence, but largely from the Renaissance period. The modern art collection here includes works by Max Ernst, Pablo Picasso, and Roland's favorite, Jackson Pollock.

The small museum is comfortably busy, but despite the number of people, it is dead quiet. Kymani fusses in his stroller, and I pick him up immediately so as to not disturb anyone. In my arms, he excitedly grabs for my audio guide and ear buds. I shift him to one side, put the audio guide in my back pocket, and put one ear bud in the opposite ear. Without the guide's interpretation of these abstract works, I will have no clue what I am looking at.

Despite being carried, Kymani eventually gets restless. Every little squawk and grunt fills the silent room and turns the heads of everyone in it. My arms are starting to burn as I bounce him up and down, so I make our exit with quick efficiency. I don't see Roland on my way out, but the grounds are small enough that I'm sure we'll find each other later.

Outside there's a lush garden with benches to sit on. It's a relief to be outdoors where I'm not anxious every time he makes a noise. I nurse Kymani and continue to listen to my audio guide, learning about Peggy, who I'm completely impressed by. She made this amazing gallery from an inheritance equivalent to a million dollars. She found artists she believed in and continued to invest in them, slowly building her collection. What she accomplished is inspiring.

"Ah, there you are!" says Roland walking toward me. "Are you finished, or do you want me to take Kymani so you can go back in?"

"I'm good," I reply. "We should probably make our way to our supper reservations. It's a bit of a walk from here. Hopefully Kymani will fall asleep on the way."

The streets are lined with high-end stores, ready to capitalize on my travel high. I am romanticizing the idea of getting a black Chanel purse I see in the window, despite the fact that the price tag is completely out of my reality right now. Roland is not taking my little fantasy seriously at all, declaring it absurd to even contemplate a purse at that price. I sigh, let the idea go, and continue on.

We walk by half a dozen men displaying fake knockoff purses on the sidewalks. I avoid eye contact; I don't want to give them any false hope of a sale. Roland does the opposite. "Hey man," Roland greets one of them. The man smiles at Roland and extends his hand, lighting up as if Roland is the first person today to great him in a friendly manner. I instantly feel guilty. *What would have been the harm with giving them a smile and saying hi? Why did I treat them like that?*

"Where are you from?" Roland asks.

"Senegal," the man responds, with a nod and smile that I reciprocate. He turns back to Roland. "American?"

"Pretty close," Roland says laughing because we get that a lot. "We're from Canada." Roland glances down at the man's merchandise. "Wait, isn't that the Chanel purse you were looking at earlier?" asks Roland, pointing to the faux black leather and silver chained purse I had been admiring.

"Yes," I say hesitantly. I never buy fake anything. I don't like the idea of it. If I can't afford it, fine; I'm happy to buy something I can. However, my eyes linger on the purse that is exactly like the one I saw in the store.

"How much, man?" asks Roland and before I know it, he's deep in negotiations. The man wants twenty euros for the purse that was two thousand euros in the store. Roland holds the purse up and asks without a word, *Do you want it?*

"Okay, sure." I nod. If nothing else, I can test drive it— try it on with different outfits and see if I love it as much as I think I will.

Luckily, Kymani is asleep by the time we arrive at the restaurant. It's getting more difficult, as he gets older, to ask him to eat and sleep wherever we happen to be.

At our table, I place the fake Chanel on the table beside me. Our waiter greets us affectionately, boisterous, and quick to smile. After taking our order, he stops abruptly and cocks his head. He grabs a fork off his tray, pokes at my purse, and dramatically sniffs with his nose. "*Hmmm*, smells Moroccan to me!"

He throws his head back, laughing hard at his own joke. Roland is doubled over in equal amusement. I join in, but my rouged cheeks give away my mortification.

✈

ON A ROAD TRIP FROM FLORENCE, we pull up to a large stone castle nestled into the soft rolling hills of the Tuscan countryside.

"Hi," I say quickly to a petite woman who has scurried over to greet us. I glance and gesture toward Kymani. "I need to give him a quick change and then put him in a carrier before we get going. It's okay if you start without us. We don't want to hold anyone up."

"I'm sorry, we would wait but there's another couple—" the woman says kindly with a thick Italian accent.

"It's completely fine," Roland tells her. "Please, go ahead. We will be right there. No need to keep them waiting."

With that, she heads off toward the entrance of the castle.

A few minutes later, we join the other couple for the remainder of the tour. The guide is in the middle of explaining the history of the property and kindly gives us a quick recap of what they've covered so far before continuing. The Medici family ran Florence for a long time and their fingerprints are everywhere in the city's history. This estate belonged to a family that plotted to kill some of the Medici family members. After the plot failed, the family was run out of town. What drama!

After our history lesson and tour of the grounds, we enter the kitchen where our chef has started the prep work for our gourmet lunch. He shows us how to make pasta dough with the simplest of ingredients.

"The ingredients should be of the highest quality. And most importantly, it's all about technique," the chef says in his thick accent with a sly smile on his face. Given his smirk, I demise he is suggesting his culinary technique does have *something* to do with the outcome of the food.

He shows us how to knead the dough effectively, roll it out and cut it to the correct size. We have a blast cooking up a storm with the other couple, who are from California and are here on their honeymoon. Once we finish all the prep work we are escorted to the dining room where the sommelier greets us and presents the various wines we will be indulging in with our meal.

We eat and eat and drink ourselves into a utopian bliss, surrounded by the gorgeous castle walls. Afterward, we wander around the grounds, taking in the vineyard-filled landscape. How lucky these people are to live in such a place! In the heart of Tuscany is it easy to understand why the Italians revel in *il dolce far niente* (the sweetness of doing nothing). Here, busy doing nothing, we take in the best of everything—the culinary ingredients, the delicious wines, the fairy tale landscapes of rolling hills and ancient cities. There are few places we have visited I would be even remotely interested in moving to, but Tuscany has captured my attention.

"I could retire here," I say to Roland, letting the daydream dance in my head.

"We don't speak Italian," Roland says pragmatically.

"Everyone in Italy under forty speaks English anyway. I'm not saying move here permanently, but maybe for three to six months a year. Like how my parents go down to Arizona, except it's *Italy*!"

"That *would* be amazing . . ." he concedes, "but expensive."

He's far too worried about the details for my liking. Oh well, I've got about twenty years to work on this idea; no need to push it too hard right now.

"I can drive us home if you want, so you can enjoy the view," I offer, but he says no thanks and opens the door for me, as he always does. I adore this little romantic gesture, which unfailingly makes me feel special and loved.

✈

OUR NEXT DAY TRIP IS OF A SLIGHTLY different variety: first the Museo Ferrari then the Museo Lamborghini, in Modena and Bologna respectively. Roland is so excited to bring his boy to these museums he's practically vibrating in his seat.

To the credit of both museums, they do an excellent job of portraying the cars in interesting ways, providing historical context and the stories behind their making. I especially appreciate Lamborghini's creative displays of the cars that have featured in movies. For Roland, these cars are like masterful works of art. I can appreciate where he's coming from and so I work extra hard on being patient. I give him all the time he needs to wander through the galleries and take a ride in the simulator.

Once we leave the Lamborghini museum, we search for a local Italian restaurant to eat at before we drive back to Florence. We come across Pizzeria Maggi, which has decent reviews online and a high convenience factor, being right around the corner.

I have been on the hunt for the best tiramisu in Italy, a fun and exciting mission, since we arrived. I rarely have sweet cravings and most desserts don't appeal to me. However, tiramisu is one of my favorites and since I'm in the motherland I will not waste the opportunity. When the waitress brings it I can tell this particular homemade batch has potential by the color of the whipped mascarpone, which has a brighter yellow to it than most.

I dip my fork into the soft, spongy dessert and take my first bite. In an instinctual reaction, my eyes close, and I inhale softly, then exhale with a long *mmm*. The sponge is so thoroughly soaked in the espresso that it dissolves in my mouth, and the whipped mascarpone spun with egg and sugar is smooth and full-bodied.

"Oh my, that good is it?" Roland asks. I open my eyes to find him staring at me yearningly—well, at the dessert actually.

"You have to try this."

"Do you want to try mine?"

"No thank you. I don't want to disturb what's happening in my mouth right now."

"Oh my word . . ." he murmurs at the first mouthful. "This is incredible. I love all tiramisu, but this is next level."

Just then, the waitress comes by to check on us. The short, sturdy woman smiles with pride as we gush about how this is the best tiramisu we've had in all of Italy.

"Can we please order two servings to go?" I request. "Is it possible to pack it up? We need to drive back to Florence today, but this cannot be the last time I taste this."

"*Si, si,* of course." She smiles, her apple cheeks flush with joy.

With miraculous self-control, we savor our to-go desserts over the next three days, wanting to indulge in it but also trying desperately to save some, wishing the dish would never empty.

✈

ON OUR LAST DAY IN FLORENCE, we walk into the Galleria dell'Accademia di Firenze, excited to visit one of the most famous statues in the world. Once we pass through security, we walk briskly down the short hall, turn the corner, and stop. There he stands: Michelangelo's *David* in all his magnificence. We stand for a long moment, enraptured by the godlike presence of the statue as sunbeams stream from the skylight onto his perfectly carved figure. His naked, off-kilter stance is deeply sensual despite the sculpted muscles and determined glare.

We approach and circle, inspecting him from all angles. He is perfect, from the veins in his hands, to the muscles in his calves, to the length of his second toe. Seeing this sculpture feels for me the opposite experience of seeing the *Mona Lisa*: it's so much more impressive than I thought possible.

After we finish examining in bewildered awe, we back-track to Michelangelo's sculptures of the slaves. These unfinished works give us a rare glimpse into the artist's process. It is inconceivable how the large hunk of rock is transformed into a man. Although unintentional, the sculpted bodies appear trapped, as if they are trying to break out of the rocks.

After an hour of taking it all in, we hit the streets of Florence for one last lunch out.

"I know this is sacrilege, but I'm getting kind of sick of Italian food," I say, grimacing at my own remark. But I'm used to eating a wider variety. Back home we eat different ethnic foods all the time, there's so much variety.

"Have you seen any restaurants here that aren't Italian?" asks Roland.

"Surely they must . . ." I pause to reflect. "Actually, I haven't—interesting."

"Is there no Chinatown here? Every city has a Chinatown, don't they?"

"I don't think so. We've been wandering these streets for the past month and, now that I think about it, there hasn't been much diversity of any kind here."

"Well, except for the African guys selling knockoffs," Roland points out.

"Yes, true. It is weird though, the general lack of diversity, yet everyone's been nothing but wonderful to both of us. You haven't encountered anything since you've been here, have you?" I'm self-conscious of what I don't notice, although I am desperately trying to be more perceptive.

"No, it's been great. That is weird. The only exposure they have is maybe a few tourists and the hustlers, yet there's been no negativity since we got here."

"It's official! We should retire here." I give Roland a sly smile.

Alana and Roland overlooking the town of Vernazza

Cinque Terre

6 months, 2 weeks old
June 30–July 6

———•———

"The future belongs to those who believe in the beauty
of their dreams."

—ELEANOR ROOSEVELT

MY MOM HAS THIS THEORY THAT when you're down-and-out you should make a big purchase. It needs to be something you will keep for a long time and that costs a scary sum of money given your situation. When you do this, it will tell the universe you are not worried, that you believe in yourself and your dreams. You are manifesting that things will turn around quickly.

Eight years ago, before I left Saskatchewan to move to BC, I was going through a hard time. I had given up my job, had little savings, an almost two-year-old daughter, a failing marriage, and I was leaving all my friends and family behind in search of a different life. I gave up everything to try and make it in beautiful Victoria. This seemed like the perfect time to invest in a large piece of art, just like mama taught me.

I came across a young artist at the market selling a huge 3 x 5-foot painting of a gorgeous seaside town. I loved it the second I saw it and wanted to know more. She told me she did a semester of her fine arts degree in Italy and painted this scene while visiting Cinque Terre. I had never heard of the place, but something drew me to the painting. I bought it on the spot with the little money I had left in the bank, leaving me only $350 to move my family halfway across the country. It has hung proudly in my home ever since, through the failing of my first marriage, my days alone, and into my new life with Roland.

When we decided to come to Italy on this trip, I desperately wanted to see this town. The painting has been a symbol of hope for me; a promise to myself, fulfilled, that things would get easier. Those better days are here.

When I finally take in the view of the town from the same angle that my painting depicts, my eyes well up with emotion. I have finally made it. The buildings are the same pinks, yellows, peaches, and greens as the canvas hanging on my wall evokes: stacked atop each other and cascading downhill to meet the rocky steep cliff above the sea. The calm water flickers in the bright sun underneath it all.

I wipe the tears from my eyes and close them. I let the sun's warmth soak into my skin. I listen to the water's rhythm and slow my breathing to match. The salt in the air reminds me of home. I open my eyes and indulge in the moment. Mom, I made it.

Milan

6 months, 3 weeks old
July 7–9

"Life is all there is. And if that's true, then we have
to really live it—we have to take it for everything it
has . . . "

—JAY-Z

LIGHTS FLASH, THE BASS PUMPS, and the entire stadium
is on its feet. The beat is in my body to its core, making me
bounce up and down as I sing at the top of my lungs along
with Jay-Z's easy flow.

Beyoncé and Jay-Z concert

I turn to Roland, wide-eyed with excitement. "Thank you!" I mouth to him.

"You're welcome," he smiles back, then returns his attention to the stage, his hand bouncing up and down to the beat.

The crowd erupts in screams and clapping as Jay-Z finishes rapping. I throw myself into Roland's arms yelling in his ear, "That's my favorite song, I am so glad they played it!"

The crowd explodes in an even more frenzied shrill, and I turn to the stage to see what is happening. Beyoncé is walking down the stage, her long flowing hair blows behind her, making her look every ounce the goddess she is. Her voice hushes the crowd. Everyone stops to listen. She has us all eating out of the palm of her hand.

When Jay-Z talks and sings about racism, I feel like I'm listening with new ears, and my heart hurts with new layers of comprehension. I tear up reading the feminist words of empowerment and strength that fill the massive screen on stage. This power couple is doing so much more than dazzling and entertaining us. They are delivering powerful messages about life and love.

We fall into bed that night with our ears ringing, so tired, but still giddy, delighted to be leaving Italy with such a bang.

GREECE

*Carley (bottom left), Alana, Josephine,
Kymani enjoying the Greek sun and beach.
Photo credit: Carley Schriml*

Chania

7 months old

July 9–August 6

———————— •◆• ————————

"Because there's one thing stronger than magic: sisterhood."

—Robin Benway

I'M WAITING IN FRONT OF THE arrivals door at the airport. I have butterflies in my stomach. My eyes dart back and forth through the open door looking for my sister, Carley. She has graciously traveled with Josephine from Canada to the island of Crete.

My hands are fidgeting, my fingers flickering against my thighs, playing an old piano song from when I was a child. I do this when I'm nervous. I play the song over and over, moving my fingers up and down as if they are gracing the keys of my grandparents' old piano in my parents' living room.

"Oh!" My hands shoot into the air. Josephine locks eyes with me, smiles, and waves both hands frantically. Her tall, slender ten-year old body comes quickly toward me and into my arms.

My eyes fill with tears as I hold her tightly. I lower my head and press my cheek against the top of her light brown hair. I close my eyes and take her in, squeezing her even tighter against me. Her little body quivers, overcome with emotion.

217

She pulls away slightly and looks up at me with her big brown eyes. She is a personal fountain of youth; she's the mirror image of a younger me. She can only hold my gaze for a moment before she collapses back into my body, squeezing her arms around me.

"I missed you. I am so glad you're here," I say.

"I . . . love . . . you . . . Mom," she manages between starts and stutters and sniffles. She backs up slightly, keeping her hands attached to my waist and smiles. "I brought you a Mother's Day card."

She swings her backpack around and pulls out a handmade card and a little gift. Light, happy tears wet my face. I love that it was so important to her to have this ready for me when she arrived.

After thanking her and taking her in for another long hug I ask, "Baby, where's Aunty Carley?"

"I don't know," Josephine replies, peeling herself away and turning toward the door.

"Oh, there she is," I say, waving to my sister as she peeks her head out from behind a portly couple at the luggage carousel. "Jo, I think you better go back in there and help her with the luggage." I'm assuming the security guard won't be bothered given that she's a kid; so far Greece is pretty laid back.

"Okay," she says, and runs back to join her aunty. I giggle, watching the charms on her backpack bounce up and down as she hurries over to help retrieve her luggage.

The two of them come walking out a few minutes later. I see others watch my tall, striking sister stride toward me. It's impossible for her to come into a room unnoticed. She has a magnetic energy that beams out of her wide, genuine smile, and disarming openness.

I take her in my arms for a long hug. "Thank you so much for taking care of Josephine and coming all this way. You're a rock star."

"Are you kidding? We had so much fun! Didn't we Josephine?" My sister says wrapping an arm around her niece and flashing a smile. She turns to me, "It is so good to see you!" She pulls me in for another quick hug. "I can't wait to try on this jumper you're wearing. I bet it will look great on me." She bursts out laughing. We're both giggling like it's a joke, but we both know she'll be wearing this outfit within forty-eight hours.

"All right, let's hit the road!" I say, clapping my hands for emphasis. "I can't wait to show you the hot ride I picked up for us."

"*Oooh*, what did fancy Alana get us, Josephine?" Carley asks, and they are both hook, line, and sinker because they would fully expect me to have indulged in a champagne-caliber ride. Little do they know our ride is more cheap draft beer.

We walk up to our compact brown European hatchback, which is at least fifteen years old. "Et voilà!" I say, pulling out my key to open the trunk.

"Where did you find this poor girl!?" Carley asks, exploding into a laughter so strong tears escape down her cheeks.

I return the laughter. "I didn't even know they rented cars this old. She's got some hard tourist miles on her, for sure. . . . Jump in." I grab my sister's luggage, followed by Josephine's, and stuff them miraculously in the trunk. "I promise, our villa is a slight notch up from the car. Not much, but a bit." I say it in a joking tone, but I'm actually kind of serious. They slump into their seats with an expression that tells me they aren't sure what to believe.

"Does our place have a pool?" Josephine asks, getting straight to the point.

"Yes, baby, it has a great pool right outside," I reassure her.

"Okay, let's go!" she says satisfied, excitedly clapping her hands.

Twenty-five minutes later we're driving up the steep hill that leads to our villa. Once parked, Josephine gets out and streaks across the dusty loose dirt parking lot toward the villa's main gate. I instinctively go to call out for her but stop myself; there is no need. There's no traffic and everyone here is very friendly.

Carley and I go through the main gate and to the pool at the back of the complex. The view from here is lovely, as the villa sits atop a hill overlooking the ocean and the strip of hotels and restaurants along the main road below us.

"Wow, this is all right." Carley steps to the farthest edge of the veranda, taking in the scenery.

"The sun sets right in front of us. It's a delightful way to end the day," I tell her. The pool and the view are by far the best parts of the villa, so I'm glad she's seen them first.

"Carley!" exclaims Roland, breaking our lingering gazes at the ocean. We turn to see Roland walking toward us, one arm around Josephine and the other inviting Carley in for a big hug. "So glad you're here, this is awesome!"

Roland and Carley embrace in a sincere, warm welcome. It means so much to me that Roland gets along famously with my family. After the opposite experience with my ex-husband, I don't take this for granted.

"Hi babe," Roland says, turning his attention to me. He leans in to give me a peck. He does this religiously, always giving me a kiss hello and goodbye whenever we part ways and come back together.

After an inaugural dip in the pool followed by a hearty supper, the kids are tuckered out and ready for bed. With them down, we adults gather on the patio with our glasses of wine to watch the sun go down and get caught up.

"Josephine is amazing, honestly, she was so well-behaved the entire way here," Carley offers without me asking. "Her manners are impressive, and she never asked me for a thing the entire time. We never had one bad moment. She listened to me without issue."

It's kind of her to tell us, but I honestly hadn't considered any alternative. There was never a doubt in my mind she would be anything but gracious.

"I'm so glad to hear that," I say, proud of my girl. "Did you have fun in Ireland on your way over? I guess it was a bit quick. What did you have, like thirty-six hours or something?"

"We had a blast. The hotel was great, thanks for booking that. It was right in the middle of everything. We made the most of it, doing a bus tour and getting fish and chips in the evening at a local pub." Carley pulls out her phone to show us some pictures.

"Aw, Josephine would have totally loved that, some solid Aunty time." Roland smiles at the thought of the pair running around Dublin together. "I'm looking forward to a weekend in Dublin with my sis. Sorry I'll miss you for a few days Carley."

Roland's sister Tricia is flying to Dublin for work this week. Her brief time in Europe happens to land smack in the middle of when Carley is visiting. I encouraged Roland to meet up with his sister in Ireland while I keep the kids with me in Greece; it's too rare an opportunity to pass up. It's not often he gets alone time with his sister, and it gives me the opportunity for some one-on-one time with my sister too. As we get older, time with our siblings is usually shared with spouses, kids, parents, and even friends. I love the big get-togethers too, but once in a while it's so nice to catch up alone with our life-long, DNA-sharing best friends.

✈

I TAKE KYMANI WITH ME and drive Roland to the airport. We give each other a heartfelt goodbye. "Please send my love to Tricia and tell her I'm sorry I couldn't come with you to see her."

221

"I will," he says, and it's not lip service. He will diligently pass the message along to his sister. "Have fun!" He gives me one last hug. "I love you."

"I love you too. Safe trip!"

By the time I get back to the villa, Carley and Josephine are poring over some tourist pamphlets and planning our itinerary. I love Carley for this. It's so nice to have a fellow planning-happy travel companion. I've been doing the lion's share of the organizing since the trip began. I didn't think much of it, continuing to work away at it because it is important to me to make the most of our trip and see as much as possible. It's only now, as Carley takes over, that I realize how nice it is to have someone else take the wheel—and how much I needed a break.

Carley has a beach day planned for today and has scheduled various train tours for the rest of the week. It's not a strenuous agenda, just enough to keep us busy so we don't waste away in the sun by the pool.

"Great, we're set. After lunch, on the way to the beach, we can stop by the tourism office and book all our tours. If we book them all at once we get a 10 percent discount."

I giggle and roll my eyes playfully. Carley is so frugal. She's always hunting for a deal, using coupons, searching for sales, reusing things until they fall apart, and even then she finds a way to use the parts to make something else. The lady is in heaven in a thrift shop. I wish I had a bit more of that in me. We saved enough money over the past four years to travel with relative ease because the last thing I wanted to do on this trip was to miss out on things because of a tight budget. However, a little more money-consciousness would go a long way to help us ensure our money stretches comfortably to the end of the trip.

In anticipation of Josephine and Carley's arrival, I put together some beach-themed care packages for them. It's my welcoming gift, and my humble thank you to Carley for taking time away from her husband and two young children to come spend time with us. The four of us are set. We have beach bags, towels, ridiculous pineapple blow-up floaties, pool noodles, sandcastle buckets, and a racket game. We are ready for a great week of fun in the sun.

We walk out of our small villa, down a steep hill, and across the street to the beach. We find three lounge chairs on the sand and plop down in them. We leave Kymani in his stroller, under the large umbrella firmly planted between us that provides a large canopy of shade. Josephine dumps her dress on her beach bag and goes running straight for the water. She is a strong swimmer, having taken lessons since she was three, so Carley and I lie back in our loungers and order two large draft Mythos beers, keeping an eye on her as she splashes in the water. It doesn't get much better than this.

✈

THE FOLLOWING AFTERNOON WE go on our first train tour, visiting a winery and the oldest olive tree in Greece.

We hop on the train with our gear, including Kymani in the car seat. The guide is not sure what to make of the baby in the seat, but we reassure her we're fine and he's been on more tours around the world than most of the adults on this train. Once we figure out how to lodge the car seat securely on the train bench, I lean back, enjoying the cool wind coming through the open convertible roof.

The little train meanders its way through the soft, sage green hills dotted with orange groves and olive orchards. Below, the water sparkles under the bright sun like a long diamond bracelet across the horizon. We pass small villages, which seem trapped in a time long since passed. Each village has a large stone church and a handful of humble houses with verandas and carports covered in grape vines. Children wave at us from the street on their way home from school, and older women look up curiously from their chair on the porch.

As we get deeper into the interior of the island, the land gets dryer and the hills steeper. We search for goats that like to hide in the shade along the dry rocky canyon walls. Josephine jumps with glee when she spots a mom and her kid enjoying a grassy midday snack toward the bottom of the canyon.

The train stops at the old olive tree, and we are amazed at the size of it. The tree is between two and three thousand years old. It has a large, twisted trunk that belongs in a Harry Potter movie, and you can walk right into the hollow middle of it. The tree exudes an old and wise dignity with its wrinkles, cracks, and large bony knots protruding like arthritic knuckles. I try to imagine all the changes this tree has witnessed and the secrets it must hold. With the constant battles and wars, it's a miracle there is anything this old left living. Josephine, Carley, and I gather around and give the tree a big hug, sending it some love energy to keep it going, and hoping that maybe some of its own energy will rub off on us.

We arrive back at the villa late that evening. I get Kymani settled into bed straight away. He is exhausted from all the stimulation.

My sister's company is like having an extra set of arms. She's a mom, so knows exactly what to do and is always helping, eager to cook or clean when needed. She knows me so well I rarely need to explain myself, and honestly she does a better job than I do most of the time. All of this is a huge relief and a nice break. She energizes my soul. Carley has a glass of wine waiting for me when I emerge and already has Josephine showered and tucked into her bed reading a book. We regroup outside on the patio for some much-anticipated sister time.

I scan my phone for the first time all day and see some messages from Roland.

"Uh-oh, I better give Roland a quick call. It's the first time he's flown without Kymani and I this year. Sounds like things didn't go well at the airport."

"No problem. Maybe I'll call home, see if I can catch the hubby and kids."

Roland answers on the third ring. "Hey babe, how are you doing?"

"Hey, yeah I'm okay. I'm at the hotel, waiting for Tricia to finish up a meeting."

"That's a relief. What happened?"

"I was at the security line in Chania, and they pulled me out of the line. The only other group that got pulled over was a South Asian family of four. Security brought me to a counter and two officers came to see me. They were flipping through each page of my passport over and over again. Meanwhile, a constant flow of white people walked through the line with their passports barely being glanced at."

I can hear the mix of anger, frustration, and sadness in his voice.

"The officers kept asking me the same questions over and over: *When did you arrive in Europe? How long are you staying in Europe? Where have you been so far? Where are you going now?* I answered them the best I could, trying to be polite and consistent.

"I have no clue what the issue was. I asked them if there was something wrong, thinking I could help them if I better understood what they were looking for. They ignored me. After the first two officers left, two different officers came and asked me the same series of questions. I reiterated the same answers over and over again. I told them I was worried about missing my flight.

They finally let me go with no explanation. I sprinted to the gate. I only managed to make it because my flight was delayed."

I feel so angry I want to march down to that airport and demand an explanation.

"That's bullshit. If it had been me instead of you flying alone to Dublin, this wouldn't have happened."

"I know," he lets out a long sigh. "I can't let it get to me though. I want to enjoy this weekend with my sister."

"For sure. Enjoy your time with Tricia. Go have a Guinness in a cool old pub. Enjoy traveling without the kids and have a great time. I love you."

Carley and I return from our respective phone calls. She's ecstatic and my gray-white complexion looks like a vampire has drained all the blood from my body. I take a swig of wine, hoping it will bring some rosiness back to my pale cheeks. My sister asks me what happened. We talk for a few hours, not only about Roland's airport encounter but about the other incidents we've experienced on our travels. She is shocked and frustrated too. Whenever I tell my white family and friends these stories, I get a similar reaction.

Our days naturally find a pattern, an easygoing schedule. We wake up early, have breakfast outside on the veranda, then jump in the pool for an early-morning swim. Kymani has a morning nap, and we enjoy that time reading, talking, and preparing lunch. In the afternoon we either head on another train tour or go down to the beach. We're sure to sneak a few happy hours in and mix up dinners out with dinners at home. After the kids go to bed, Carley and I enjoy some alone time, talking and catching up.

Before we know it, we're saying goodbye with tears in our eyes and heartfelt promises to see each other soon.

✈

ROLAND RETURNS FROM IRELAND, thankfully with no airport incidents. He flew through Germany and said they were the friendliest airport staff he has encountered yet. He is feeling rejuvenated from the visit with his sister. They enjoyed going to Dublin's big tourist destinations during the day and staying up late each night catching up.

The four of us have two-and-a-half weeks left in Greece. We planned this long period in Greece partially so Roland could enjoy some relaxation time, but also so we could regroup as a family and enjoy each other's company instead of being busy rushing around. We thought this would be especially important for Josephine after not being with us for months. However, our plans are going sideways quickly.

We begin bickering. Tension is rising and everyone is annoyed with each other.

Josephine is having a tough time adjusting. Partially, she is bored, but mostly she's not enjoying the new family dynamic with Kymani in the mix. She has been my only child for ten years, so having to share the attention with a baby is throwing her off. From Josephine's perspective, the baby never gets disciplined and never does anything wrong (despite being annoying) and gets all the attention, not only from Mom and Roland but also from total strangers. I tell myself it's just an adjustment period and that things will improve with time. I ease the transition by carving out quality mom–daughter time, hoping some individual attention and love will help. Roland does the same.

Roland and I work on being kind, gentle, and patient with her because we know she's going through a lot. It's tough when she's acting out and goes from happy to mad to sad in an instant. Nothing is good enough for her. She doesn't like any of the activities and the only thing she will eat is spaghetti bolognese.

Spending this much time together and coming off time with our siblings is also amplifying the differences between Roland and me. His sister is kind, gentle, and thoughtful in a way I can never be, and with my sister, there was a natural flow. Our energies matched.

Roland tries relaxing, and I am irritating him because I'm bored out of my skull and itching to do something, anything.

My inability to chill out, combined with my expectations of him (expressed in not-so-delicate a form) to do and be more, is creating tension. If Roland and I were cars sitting at a red light, Roland would be a hybrid that happily shuts down and enjoys the break in a quiet and peaceful state. I would be an old muscle car that grumbles and spits in loud fits because it was not built to stay still.

We leave Greece completely out of sorts with each other and ourselves. I'm not sure if the next few weeks blitzing through central Europe are going to kill us or make us stronger.

POLAND

Portraits, prisoners of Auschwitz

Kraków

7 months, 3 weeks old
August 6–11

———————•———————

"What is done cannot be undone, but one can prevent
it happening again."

—ANNE FRANK

WE HAVE COME TO KRAKÓW on a pilgrimage to Auschwitz.
We are in a van, watching a documentary about the death
camps as we drive there. As a family, we want to pay our
respects, and to honor the terrible losses and atrocities
that remain our global inheritance. I feel it's important to
teach Josephine, and remind ourselves, of how fear can be
manipulated, and result in monstrous outcomes that we might
assume are inconceivable. The Holocaust is one of the most
tangible and recent examples of humanity's dark side, and I
want my daughter to see, and understand, something of this
crucial piece of our shared history.

Our week here also includes a visit to Oskar Schindler's
enamel factory; Kazimierz, the Jewish Quarter of Kraków, the
inhabitants of which were forcibly relocated in 1941; and the
Płaszów labor and concentration camp. Each place we visit

is rooted in the same terrible history. It's a hard, emotional week. Every day we listen to horrific, heartbreaking stories that represent a tiny, tiny fraction of the atrocities committed.

Nothing in the countless movies I have seen or books I have read prepares me for what I see at Auschwitz and how it affects me. We walk under the iron sign at the entrance that reads WORK WILL SET YOU FREE—a perverse symbol of the kind of double-speak and psychological torture that the Nazis were so adept at. The heavy electric barbed wire fencing directly contradicts the sign and is stark evidence that no prisoner who came through these gates was free. My body clenches and I can hardly breathe as we proceed. The threat, though decades passed, still feels real here.

Inside the buildings are various display cases containing mounds and mounds of people's hair, shoes, bags, and prosthetic limbs. My hands shake, and my eyes prickle with tears. We pass a display cabinet of wallets, fabric, and bookbindings made from human skin and hair—everything was repurposed and reused here, including prisoners' remains. Everything done out of need on the one side, and with cold efficiency on the other.

There are pictures of prisoners on the walls: adults, teenagers, kids. These faces are not those of actors or actresses playing a role, or characters described in a book I'm reading: these are the eyes of real people, most of whom did not survive even three months in this terrible place. I want to honor each soul as I pass, look each one in the eyes and tell them they are not forgotten and their story lives on. But I can't. There are too many of them.

We walk through a gas chamber, following safely in the footsteps of so many people who never walked back out. Inside I smell the cement, I see the hole in the ceiling, and I imagine the fear. I feel trapped, tense, and claustrophobic. I force myself to stay—stay long enough to pay my respects. I touch the walls, tears running down my face, placing my hand where so many would have desperately clawed to get out. The tour guide is explaining how the chamber, and the crematorium in the next room, works. His speech is a muffled blur. I am too overwhelmed to listen. All I hear and understand is that this is an efficient operation for murder, the engineering of which was a source of great pride for those in charge. It makes me sick and angry.

Josephine stays close to the tour guide, soaking up everything he says. She is attentive and quiet, her face somber and respectful. I catch her eye from the back of the group where I stand with Kymani. *Are you okay?* I mouth with an exaggeratedly inquisitive face. She nods and gives me the thumbs-up.

Across the road, we enter the larger Auschwitz-Birkenau Memorial: a massive complex with rows upon rows of living quarters and multiple extermination sites. The scale of the operation makes the numbers real. I can see and feel how millions of people died here.

Our visit to Auschwitz changes us.

We stop bickering. Josephine stops complaining about food she doesn't like, stating that it's a lot better than the watery broth the prisoners received. She recognizes that even if she doesn't like the taste, it at least has nutritional value and makes her full. For that, she is grateful.

CZECH REPUBLIC

Roland, Alana, Kymani, and Josephine in front of
Vltava River, Charles Bridge, and the Prague Castle

Prague

8 months old

August 11–16

———◆•◆———

"Travel is my favorite kind of drama."

—Alana Best

JOSEPHINE SCRATCHES HER HEAD feverishly through her ponytail.

"Are you okay?" I ask.

"I don't know. My head is really itchy."

I walk toward her, lifting my hands to take out her ponytail. I freeze. A small bug crawls over her hairline.

"What's wrong?" Josephine asks.

"You have lice, darling."

"What? I do?" Her frightened eyes water.

"Yeah, I saw one. It's okay," I say confidently to calm her, "we'll get it sorted."

We quarantine Josephine in the bathroom and give her a movie to watch on an iPad. We check Kymani; thankfully he is clear. Roland boils pots of water and disinfects every article of clothing Josephine and Kymani own since they've been sharing the same suitcase. We do the same for all her linens, all his soft toys, and anything we think she might have touched.

I'm not usually one to be paranoid, but the last thing we need is a family outbreak of lice. I can't imagine the nightmare of trying to treat Kymani's curls with those chemicals. We would have to shave it all off.

I can't help but laugh at the situation as I painstakingly comb through Josephine's hair. We're in one of the most gorgeous cities in Europe, and here we are locked in our apartment treating lice and disinfecting everything we own. I've purchased enough chemicals to re-do the treatment two more times. I insist we also blow-dry her hair on the hottest setting and burn through her hair with a scalding hot straightener.

The things I never thought I would have to deal with while traveling the world.

The following morning, we get ready for our six-hour walking tour around Prague. We're excited to take in this exquisitely preserved city, which managed to make it through both world wars with minimal damage.

I check my email before we walk out the door and there's a message from the tour company informing me they don't allow infants. Fuming, my thumbs race over my phone's keypad, explaining that there was nothing on the website indicating this policy, that we booked this tour over a week ago so telling us fifteen minutes before we leave is not appropriate, and that we don't have time to book another tour.

"I say we go talk to them in person," I say to Roland. "It's always better in person, maybe they'll let us join them. If we stay here and wait for a reply, we'll definitely miss the group."

Roland is hesitant. Sometimes he likes my powerhouse attitude, but other times he can't believe the things I try to pull off. He sees I'm not taking no for an answer. With little choice he says okay, and we're out the door.

When we arrive at the tour there are six other tourists already there. We discuss the issue with the guide. He calls head office to let me speak to them directly. I am determined, but calm and polite. I explain we only have today to go on this tour and their last-minute cancelation is putting us in a difficult position. If they had informed us of their policy a week ago when we booked it, we would have understood. Given the timing, the only acceptable alternative I see, is to send a private guide to tour us around today for the same price.

They explain they don't allow children because of the strenuous amount of walking, and the stairs involved. I tell them we understand the physical requirements and are completely capable of handling it. If we can't, we will leave, and it will be our responsibility. I also say, voluntarily, that if the baby is creating a negative experience for anyone else on the tour, we will leave. We've been on countless tours over the past eight months and are fully aware of the realities of bringing an infant with us.

They reluctantly agree to let us join the group. We thank them for their flexibility and understanding. I pass the phone back to the tour guide so he can hear it directly from them. The entire group's attention is directed at us; they heard everything I said. I can tell by their expressions they are not excited to have an eight-month-old on this tour with them, but I'll show them.

Our guide is fantastic, walking us through Prague's rich history and culture. He tells us about some of the pivotal historic events, including the rise and fall of communism. The cobblestones of Old Town put Kymani to sleep, giving us the opportunity to admire the Gothic, Renaissance, and Baroque architecture.

We stop and stare when we arrive at the scenic Vltava River, running under the famous Charles Bridge with the Prague Castle behind it. This is the perfect backdrop for Kymani's eight-month-old picture. We gather as a family and ask a fellow traveler to take the picture for us: another one for the books.

We finish our wonderfully exhausting day at the Prague Castle. As we say our goodbyes to the other members of the group, several make a point to say how great both the kids were throughout the day. They commend us for traveling with them and are impressed how well they managed. I could not be prouder. My work here is done.

AUSTRIA

Josephine and The Kiss, *by Gustav Klimt*

Vienna
8 months old
August 16–22

———◆•◆———

"The greatest legacy we can leave our children is happy memories."

—Og Mandino

"SIGMUND FREUD, JOSEPH STALIN, Adolf Hitler, and Leon Trotsky were all patrons here," I tell Roland and Josephine as we walk up to the entrance of the sophisticated Café Central, in downtown Vienna.

We open the door, and in front of us is a large, decadent display case fit for crown jewels. Encased inside is a wide variety of cakes, tarts, and pastries. In the room at large, beige pillars turn into gold and green arcs, which peak at the vaulted ceilings which support cast-iron chandeliers. Scarlet seats are filled with smiling faces, enjoying coffee and treats.

We are escorted to a booth in the middle of what could easily pass as a castle's grand ballroom. My curious eyes sweep over the tables, investigating our neighbors' food and drink choices.

I'm nervous to be here and worried how we will be treated. I see no other infants, children, or Black people. Given the general snobbery that oozes out of every crevice here in Vienna, I expect not to be served in a welcoming manner.

A waiter in a crisp white shirt, black vest, perfectly pleated black pants, and a large white apron moves swiftly toward our table.

"Good day," he greets us with a warm smile, handing me a menu. He gestures to Kymani, "And who is this young prince? What a delight." When he hands Roland a menu he nods with a respectful but kind "Sir." He turns to Josephine and hands her a menu. "Miss. Have you had a chance to look at our pastries? Please feel free," he offers kindly, gesturing toward the display case at the front of the room.

Once the waiter leaves the table, I breathe a sigh of relief and peruse the menu. I feel guilty for my assumptions. It's not often, after all, that we are treated poorly in a restaurant. However, it's not common that people are warm and kind either. I've been telling myself it's the culture here, but I can feel the eyes from strangers as we pass by. I hear the confused sound in people's voices when we tell them we're all together.

"That was amazing!" Josephine exclaims as we walk out the door after our breakfast. She wraps her arms around Roland and me. "Thanks for breakfast."

"That was top notch," I agree. "Delicious down to the last drop and crumb." I have a happy buzz from the caffeine and chocolate as we stroll through the city's streets, admiring the immaculate, white-stoned buildings that tower around us on our way to the Natural History Museum. The former glory of the Austrian Empire is apparent in the pristine, intricate buildings that is fit for nobility.

"Is this the museum or a palace?" Roland asks.

"I wonder how disappointing it must be," I laugh, "for them to travel and realize the rest of the world's cities do not possess the same beauty they're surrounded with every day. I hope if they come to Canada they appreciate the outdoors."

After our museum tour, we walk a few blocks to the city hall to eat and see the free outdoor showing of *Les Misérables*— the musical theatrical show, *not* the movie.

"Vienna is Europe's best kept secret," says Roland appreciatively. "It should get the same hype as Paris or London."

I agree; it is deserving of it. The city comes across as so self-assured and poised, I wonder if it prefers not to be in the spotlight. Perhaps it has no desire for the fame, publicity, and the tourists that come with it.

"Even Vienna's street food scene is classier than ours," I say as we arrive at the large square filled with street food vendors.

"Is that a beach?" Josephine asks in disbelief.

I follow the direction of her pointed finger to see a fake beach on a wood platform, with people lounging in chairs with a spritz in hand.

As we walk, the smells shift and change with every couple steps. There are so many options we don't know where to start.

We seek out a table and swoop down upon it quickly, claiming it before someone else does. Roland volunteers to go out and get our food with Josephine while I hold the table with Kymani.

Some excellent Mexican food and two spritz cocktails later, we make our way to the outdoor theatre.

We're early enough to get some fantastic seats, and we soon discover that the technology behind this free production is as incredible as the setting. I'm impressed with Vienna's philosophy that everyone should enjoy music, no matter their economic situation. The richness and diversity of the city's music scene, past and present, acts like its pulse. Home to some of the most famous composers of all time, including Mozart, Strauss, and Beethoven, it remains a cultural hub for developing music and offers an abundance of prestigious live events ranging in genre and form, from classical and opera to jazz, modern rock and pop.

It's an ideal night: the air is that perfect temperature where you could comfortably sleep outside under the stars. Roland and I sip our beers as we all nestle into our seats. It's Josephine's first time seeing this iconic show, and I'm excited for her to see it in such epic circumstances.

Two-thirds of the way through I tell Roland I'm taking Josephine to the washroom to avoid any of the long lineups afterward. We rush quietly through the crowd, which has grown thick since we first sat down. People sit on the grass, and rows of people stand at the back behind the benches provided. Ours is the perfect plan: there are no lineups to use the washroom and we're in and out in a flash. When we get back to our seats I whisper to Roland that he might want to do the same, but he says he's fine.

When the show finishes, the crowd erupts in applause. We all stand, clapping feverishly, smiles wide and eyes twinkling with the delight.

The thunderous noise wakes Kymani from his sleep. It's a bit late, but he fell asleep for half of the show, so at least he had a nap. If we race home now, we can get him into bed within twenty minutes.

"Everyone ready to go?" I do one last check under the bench to make sure we haven't left anything behind.

"Yeah, I just need to run to the washroom first," says Roland.

There are swarms of people heading to the bathrooms. "Are you kidding me? Why didn't you go before?" My anger rises quickly, fueled by a few cocktails. How can such a lovely, kind, and thoughtful man be so selfish sometimes? "No, I'm not waiting for you. If you had to go, you could have missed two minutes of the performance like the rest of us and gone while the show was on. Look at how many people there are, Roland. It'll take forever. It's well past Kymani's bedtime and Josephine needs to get home too. You are not holding everyone up while you wait in that mile-long lineup to use the bathroom." I am furious with him. "You're a dad now, your own wants and needs no longer come first!"

He is angry too. "I didn't have to go during the show but now I do. It will only take two seconds. Why do you have to get so angry so quickly? You're being dramatic and completely unreasonable. You're overreacting."

"It will *not* take two seconds, Roland. I'm leaving. I'll take the kids home and get them into bed. Do whatever you want and make it home when you can." My body pulses with fierce indignation. I turn and walk away, not even waiting for a response. I know very well he doesn't have the best sense of direction. I also know I've planned everything for this trip so it might take him awhile to even figure out the address for the Airbnb. I'm being mean, and I know it. *Serves him right,* I think righteously. *Maybe if he actually planned something now and then he wouldn't be so clueless about where we are.* My mind is rapidly conjuring every tiny annoyance I've felt since the beginning of this trip. *When he gets all turned around on his way back, that's on him.*

I can't let my face show the rage swirling inside. I have Josephine with me and that wouldn't be fair. For her, I'm smiling and asking what her favorite part of the show is. We are skipping on the cobblestones and giggling our way home. It's like my mind is split in two: half of me furious at Roland, the other half joyously enjoying the walk home with my excited ten-year-old. This is motherhood.

I confidently find our way back to the apartment. I ask Josephine to get in her pajamas and brush her teeth while I get Kymani tucked into bed. I slowly close the door to Kymani's little nook to find Josephine waiting to say good night. "I had such a wonderful night," I say truthfully, having cooled down enough to start feeling a bit regretful for blowing up on Roland.

"Me too, Mom, thanks for everything." Josephine comes in for a big hug. "Good night. I love you."

"I love you too." I pull her in closer.

To my surprise, Roland comes walking in the door soon afterward. He didn't get lost and if I'm honest, the bathroom line clearly didn't take as long as I thought (hoped?) it would. *Damn.* However, in true Alana fashion, I show no remorse. After all, there's a bigger picture to consider here. He should have thought of everyone else.

"I'm sorry," he says, eyes wide and sincere.

I take a deep breath. "Me too." Whatever residual anger I feel melts away. I know he means it, and I am sorry too. It was a perfect night, suddenly hit by a flash flood of emotions. I can see now that it had been building since our time in Greece. We needed to vent and get it out of our systems.

✈

THE FOLLOWING DAY IS MOTHER–daughter and father–son day. Josephine and I are going to the Spanish Riding School and a café. Roland and Kymani are chilling out at the apartment and venturing out only to find some grub. To each their own. Off we go.

We are escorted to the top balcony of the Spanish Riding School where we are left to find the best unassigned seats we can. Josephine and I walk around the oval room filled with people who have arrived early to secure their seats. It's difficult to find a place that isn't blocked by the large white pillars that surround the arena where the white Lipizzaner stallions and their riders will perform. Finally Josephine squeezes into a small space against the railing that only a child will fit in. Unable to join her, I sit on the slightly less advantageous bench above her, my view blocked in a couple of places. I enjoy watching her reaction more than the horses themselves anyway.

I think we're turning a corner with her. She's excited, happy, and enjoying the sites. I've been catching moments where she helps put Kymani's bottle back in his mouth or dangles a toy in front of his eyes. The second Josephine walks in the room Kymani erupts in laughter, clenching his entire body with excitement. Watching them interact is the sweetest thing.

After the show, we find a quaint café on the edge of a busy plaza with an assortment of gelato. It's nice to talk with her without the interruption of a baby. She tells me she's worried about not being in school this fall and about missing her dad. She tells me she is excited about her uncle, aunt, cousins, and grandparents coming to visit us in France, and that she can't wait to see the Eiffel Tower in Paris. I listen, and ask her a ton of questions, mixing serious ones with silly ones.

When there's a pause in the conversation she sincerely asks, "So, how are you doing?"

Josephine has always asked me that since she was little. A rare characteristic in most children, she is aware the entire world doesn't revolve around her, and she genuinely cares how everyone else is doing. She has an uncanny ability to know how I'm feeling before I realize it myself, especially when I'm stressed out. I am age- and relationship-appropriately honest with her. I never pretend everything is fine if it's not; there's no point, she can see through it anyway.

I tell her I'm glad we got some alone time today and I think it's important to do it more often. I tell her I was worried about her when we were in Greece, but glad things are getting better. I express my gratitude for this trip and my excitement for what's coming up—I too am eager to being in France for six weeks and can't wait for my parents and my brother's family to visit us there. It means a lot when the people you love can be a part of these major moments in your life.

✈

AT THE RISK OF REPEATING MYSELF, the Belvedere Museum is a palace of wonder. I ponder if the locals are desensitized to being surrounded by so much decadent beauty. Do they stare in awe and amazement like I do? Are they proud to be from this splendid city filled with culture and history? I imagine they know exactly what they have here. The outside world must seem terribly unrefined in comparison.

We weave in and out of the rooms and corridors until we turn the last corner, and there it is.

"Is that the real one?" Josephine asks, her eyes wide in amazement, her jaw dropped.

"Yes, that's it. That's Klimt's *The Kiss*," I say. Josephine's astonished encapsulates the entire reason I wanted to travel with my children. This painting is to her what the pyramids were to me. She studied this artist in class, she knows about his life and his works. Now, like magic, the pictures, and words she saw in her schoolbooks have come to beautiful, golden life.

HUNGARY

Széchenyi Chain Bridge at night

Budapest

8 months, 1 week old
August 22–28

———◆•◆———

"Well-behaved women seldom make history."
—Laurel Thatcher Ulrich

"LISTEN JOSEPHINE, STAY CLOSE to the door and if I say to get off, we have to exit the train immediately. Okay?" I am sweating through my shirt as I stand at the train station without a ticket. *What am I teaching my ten-year-old daughter?!* This is not exactly what I had in mind when I thought she would get an education through her experiences traveling the world.

I wait for Josephine to nod her head attentively, to be sure she understands I'm being serious. "I would buy a train ticket if I could figure out where the heck they sell them, but I can't and the train is here, so we've got to go," I say, convincing myself as much as her that I'm not intentionally being a bad guy.

It's a late, warm August evening in Budapest. It was the perfect night for a stroll along the Danube, crossing the famous bridges to see the sites lit up along the waterfront. Josephine and I wanted to enjoy some alone time, talking, walking, and taking silly selfies. We walked to Elizabeth Bridge from our Airbnb and decided the chain bridge wasn't too far away.

When we got there, we thought we could handle walking to one more bridge, then take a cab or train back home.

The walk was breathtaking, the tiny lights strung along the buildings and bridges glimmering against the dark sky and reflecting off the still river, engulfing the view in little bright lights as if we were in the heavens, surrounded by stars. We were laughing and talking, enraptured in a dreamlike trance, not noticing our feet beginning to get weary and the time passing Josephine's bedtime.

We peered over Margaret Bridge for a long while, letting our eyes indulge in the luminous landscape. Our pictures could not capture what our eyes were seeing: the photos are flat in comparison to the multi-dimensional spectacle before us. We put our phones away and relaxed into a long glance instead. Some things can't be captured in a photo.

When we crossed from Buda on one side of the river to Pest on the other, to our surprise, we found hardly anyone around. The streets were silent, the shops all closed, and there were no cabs in sight. We managed to use a store's guest Wi-Fi, sitting outside their front door, to figure out how to take the train home—however, nobody is present to sell tickets, so here we are: ticketless and sneaking on the train to get home.

"Okay, hop on."

We slink onto the train and stay close to the door. "We're two stops away, we'll be home soon." I hope we can make it the whole four kilometers back downriver to our Airbnb without getting busted, but even if we only make it one stop, we'll be halfway closer.

The train lurches forward with a high-pitched screech and I exhale a deep sigh of relief that no transit officer gets on before we get going. Every meter we pass I am grateful for, knowing it would have been a tough walk home for Josephine. We arrive at the first stop and my palms are sweating. I'm watching every person that gets on the train, gauging if we are safe to stay on. My nerves are getting to me, and I keep glancing at the train door, knowing we might have jump off at any moment. A kind gentleman offers us his seat, but I want to stay close to the door. I politely decline, explaining we are off at the next stop. The train hiccups, then moves slowly forward again. I pray I didn't miss a transit officer getting on because now we are stuck on here and we can't get off. My breath shortens and my chest grips. Why do I get us into these situations?

The train comes to the next stop. I take Josephine's hand and fly out the door as quickly as it opens. Several meters later I realize we are running, for no reason. I stop.

"Jo, we're here, it's okay."

She grins from ear to ear. "That was fun!" she says, giggling, her eyes wild with excitement.

I laugh a little too. "Yeah, well, let's not try that again."

✈

THE NEXT DAY ROLAND GRACIOUSLY stays home with the kids for the morning so I can explore the famous Budapest baths. The constant needs of being a mom, spouse, and travel planner can take a toll. I'm excited for a time-out and a morning to myself. I leave the apartment at 8 a.m., later than I had wanted but I can't complain about the extra sleep. I walk the fifteen minutes across the bridge to the Gellért Thermal Bath.

As I walk inside the intimidating beauty takes me aback. Tiled floors surround the large aqua blue pool and thick, sand-colored, carved pillars spring up like trees on either side, extending to a second-story balcony. The ceiling is a large domed arc of glass that lets in the pale early-morning sunlight.

There are a number of rooms to explore, both inside and outside, all with different and stunning features. In the early morning, there are only a few older ladies and myself. I walk into a smaller side room with warm pools on either side. Large blue tiles decorate the bottom half of the wall, bordered by a gold trim that leads your eye to a sculpted fountain of a child pouring forth therapeutic water. The grandiose, aristocratic surroundings make me feel warm before I even dip my toe in.

I step slowly into the pool and close my eyes, letting my body sink into the warm water, which holds my body with what feels like tenderness. I breathe. There is nobody who needs me, nobody depending on me, and absolutely nothing for me to do but float. I want to linger here for hours.

The tourist crowds swarm in by mid-morning as I exit, making my way to my massage. The masseuse doesn't speak English. Perfect, no idle conversation necessary. I lie on my stomach and close my eyes. The subtle smell of lavender oil fills the air. I drift as she begins to roll her palms over my back, kneading out the stress. My muscles surrender to the suggestion of her hands and melt into relaxation.

By noon, I'm in a euphoric state. I feel completely rejuvenated and ready to meet the family for our afternoon outing.

We head to the local art gallery, which is located in a stunning castle complex. Frieda Kahlo is the subject of a special exhibition. I know of her work, and the work of her husband Diego Rivera, but I have never seen it in person. It feels a bit odd to be seeing things that aren't from Hungary, but this is an exception I'm willing to make, especially because I'm excited to expose Josephine to this pop-culture and art icon.

The exhibit chronicles her dramatic life, most strongly influenced by her passion for art, a debilitating accident, and her love affair with her famous husband. In true Frieda style, the works depict bold, bright colors, flowers, and wilderness infused with deep sorrow and celebration. Her life and her work move me deeply. She was strong, fearless, and unforgiving in her decisions. Despite her many hardships, she created art that is so honest it continues to reach millions of people and dance with their very souls.

FRANCE

*Alana and Jo eating (ridiculously good) macaroons
along la Promenade des Anglais*

Nice

8 months, 2 weeks old
August 28–September 11

———◆•◆———

"Having children is like living in a frat house—nobody sleeps, everything is broken, and there's a lot of throwing up."

—RAY ROMANO

KYMANI THROWS UP ALL OVER HIMSELF for the third time. Giant tears are streaming down his face as he holds out his arms, desperately wanting us to pick him up and console him. We strip off his clothes and gather the once more soiled linens.

"Is it the Tylenol making him throw up?" Roland suggests, in the parental guessing game of *What's Wrong with You?*

"Is this syringe jetting the medicine to the back of his throat triggering his gag reflex?" I ask.

"Maybe. Should I clean him or make a new bottle?"

"Hey, do you think he's allergic to this formula? We've never used this one before. I think I have a bit of the old stuff left; I'll go grab it."

I'm only nursing Kymani three times a day now, and the rest is being supplemented with formula. However, we are forced to switch brands every time we change countries.

After Roland cleans him in the shower I feed him the old formula. He keeps down and drift off to sleep.

I'm on Google translate comparing the labels from our new formula, which is in French, to the old one in German. "The same ingredients are in both; I don't know what's wrong."

Roland shrugs. "Maybe he's just sick."

"Yeah. I hope he recovers soon. He's having a rough go." And so are we. He's throwing up multiple times a day, he's tired and cranky, and waking up in the middle of the night, crying, and sweating.

While Kymani naps, the three of us head to the backyard to assess the above-ground pool. I use the net to retrieve the plentiful number of leaves and dead bugs floating on the sur-face like a layer of cream. I may have gotten a bit too cheap on this accommodation. Once clean, we dip our feet into the ice-cold water. My feet go numb while sweat drips down my back.

The old house has poor air circulation making Josephine and Kymani's upstairs rooms unbearably hot. We've placed fans beside their beds, which blows air directly on them all night to keep them cool. We don't open any of the windows because of the insatiable mosquitos that attack our defenseless children in their sleep. Even with the house sealed, they both wake up with bites on their faces, arms, and legs.

As a new school year has started in Canada, I try diligently to homeschool Josephine. Math, we are told by her teacher, is the subject we should concentrate on. After an hour, we are on question three. Her cheeks are beet red from anger or frustration or shame, I can't tell. Her ears redden and fat tears land on the paper, making translucent blobs around her pencil markings.

I leave the table to give her some space to work through her emotions. I grab my phone and scroll through Facebookland, distracting myself from my own life.

A text comes through. It's my childhood best friend, Kim, though to call her my sister would be a more accurate description.

John and I broke up. I don't want to talk about it. I'm not ready.

My heart wrenches. *Shit.* He seemed like such a great guy. There were issues, of course, but what relationship doesn't have those? She's anticipated my desire to call her immediately; it takes all my willpower to respect her wishes. I want to reassure her, but will it be okay? I'm too old to believe everything will be all right, all the time.

Kim and I have gone through the thick and thin of life since the age ten. From childhood crushes to adolescent rebellions, through family dramas, university, marriage, divorce, and finding ourselves single again in our thirties, she has been a rock in my life.

I met Roland a little over a year after my separation, but Kim has not had the same luck. She's had casual and serious relationships come in and out of her life, and she's tired. She wants to be settled and have children.

When I went through my divorce, she was my sister-friend and my counselor. We texted a dozen times a day and spoke all the time. We relied on each other, even though we were three thousand kilometers apart.

We've traveled frequently together over the years, and I thought for sure she would meet us on this journey, but money is tight.

I want to do something to help. For everything she has done for me, for everything we always do for each other. I couldn't let my sister-friend sit in heartbreaking agony halfway across the world. This will not do. So I type.

I'm sorry Kim. You need a vacation, come visit me in Europe. I can use points for your ticket, and you can crash with us wherever we are.

I would looove to, but I'm not sure this new job will give me the time off. Maybe in October?

It's EUROPE! Tell them you won a free trip (which is basically true). How can they say no!? We are in Spain in October and Jo will be with her dad for two weeks so you can take over her bedroom. You deserve this, and frankly, I can't imagine doing this journey without you being a part of it.

The wheels were in motion, and they would not be stopped. Within the week, her tickets were booked.

After lunch, Josephine comes around and is ready for math again. I sit down next to her and re-explain the lesson, thinking *This isn't worth it.* I can't spend half a day several times a week going through this emotional-spiral-of-death. We had great intentions, but it's not working. I will hire a tutor when we return to Canada if she needs it.

✈

ON OUR FOURTH DAY IN NICE, it's my birthday. Kymani has sufficiently recovered, so we jump on the train to downtown.

Armed with a list of the best places to go in the market, we navigate quickly, finding everything we need for a picnic under the perfectly clear blue sky. Our menu consists of potatoes dauphinoise, roast chicken, a baguette, several kinds of cheeses, a chocolate torte, and a bottle of bubbly. We carry our scrumptious plunder down to the water and trot along the Promenade des Anglais until we reach Castle Hill. The park, high on the hill, overlooks the sea. A couple of other families and lovers sprawl on the grass with their picnic baskets and blankets.

This is one thing the French do best: they take the simple pleasures in life and enjoy them in the most luxurious way, like wine, sex, food, family meals, art, a bike ride, or a picnic. I love this uncomplicated, balanced approach to life, which ensures a high caliber of excellence in all basic life categories.

We eat, drink, laugh, and play. It's my perfect, simple, French birthday.

✈

I DROP JOSEPHINE OFF AT A cooking class, and the teacher insists I go about my day and come back to pick her up in a few hours. On the rare occasions I find myself alone, the world and I seem to enter a new dimension. Everything slows down. I hear, smell, feel, and see things I normally would not notice—like the slight breeze coming off the sea and rustling through the leaves of the trees. I breathe in the fresh sea-soaked air and note the flowers planted delicately in the windowsills of the French apartments, and the long streaks of pale clouds in the very blue sky.

I relish in the mental break, to stop thinking and strategizing about the baby: Does he need to eat soon? Does he need to be changed? When will he need to nap?

About Josephine: Is she getting enough attention? Is she hungry? Is she worried? Is she happy?

About Roland: Should I translate this into English for him? Does he feel included? Am I meeting his needs?

About traveling: What bus do we need to catch? Did I book the next tour? How much is this costing in Canadian currency?

Nobody needs anything from me right now. I can walk, absorb my surroundings, and decompress.

I meander up the hill to the Marc Chagall National Museum, relishing the idea of wandering through the exhibit at my own pace, without distractions, my senses and my brain entirely dedicated to enjoying the art.

The Chagall paintings, I am familiar with, are filled with whimsical people floating through the air like a dream (*Over the town*, 1918, or *The Birthday*, 1915), or surrealist and cubism paintings that fused his Russian upbringing and his French surroundings (*I and the Village*, 1911). This gallery, however, is dedicated to an entirely different set of work in which he attempted to paint scenes spanning the entirety of the Old and New Testaments.

The thick, brightly-colored works maintain the whimsical style I associate with him, but their contents are very different. I enjoy observing them from a few inches away, where the strokes are indecipherable, and then backing away until the ingenious image comes into focus.

I leave the gallery, walk through its garden and down the hill. A woman sets a chair on the sidewalk terrace in front of a small café, looks up and smiles at me. I take this as a sign. I order a glass of wine and relax in my sunny spot. I don't have a functioning phone, and I am glad for it. All I can do is sit, people-watch, and bath in this glorious southern French sun. I sip on the chilled, buttery-smooth, oak-infused chardonnay as the breeze brings a sweet and salty smell of flowers and sea.

I cheer at the reminder that tomorrow Josephine and I will paint together at a class. The teacher told us to come with some ideas of what we'd like to paint. There is a reason why Provence and the Côte d'Azur have been residence to so many famous artists. There is inspiration everywhere. The clouds softly blur streaks across the impossibly blue sky as the sun emits the perfect pale yellow onto sparkling seas. If you go for a drive to neighboring towns, you'll pass golden fields of sunflowers and bright stretches of lavender that burst into vibrant view. There are castles and century-old houses hidden behind crumbling stonewalls. I find myself constantly wanting to capture its beauty and preserve it in my memories.

When I arrive to pick Josephine up, I have a soft buzz from the glass of wine, the sun, and some quality time to myself. Josephine moves toward me, beaming a youthful smile yet mature in her full-length apron. She stretches her arms out to give me a big hug. With pride, she tells me about the French dishes she's prepared and is especially excited about the poached pear crumble tart. She is glowing, and this above all else is what makes today special.

✈

ROLAND EMERGES FROM THE HOUSE, and we go to the Matisse Museum together. Roland has not liked Nice so far, although I'm not sure he's giving it a fair chance as he has spent more time at home than exploring the city. He seems happy enough though, so I give him his space.

Josephine, enthusiastic about teaching us something for a change, shows Roland where we catch the bus. One of the things we appreciate about Nice is the ease and simplicity of their transit system. The city has universal tickets that can be used on the train or the bus, and one ride is the same cost no matter how far you go. These small things make for a tourist's dream.

Kymani manages to stay gallery-acceptable quiet for all of half an hour.

Roland takes Kymani out of his stroller and hands him to me. "This used to be a lot easier."

At almost nine months, he's becoming more independent, and he's awake for longer stints during the day. Gone are the days when we could push the quiet sleeping baby through galleries for hours without a care in the world. Now he makes funny noises, intrigued by the sensations of forming his lips, tongue, and cheeks into different faces while simultaneously exploring vocal ranges and decibels.

We take turns holding Kymani and, with a little patience, see the entire gallery.

✈

ROLAND HAS BEEN GONE FOR three hours and I'm worried. After our discussion in Portugal, we decided to spend six weeks in France spread between Nice, Provence, Dijon, Paris, and Bordeaux. He went to pick up the rental car we will use to travel from now until we get to Paris.

Neither of us has cell phone service, so we can only reach each other when Wi-Fi is available. I've sent him a text, but he hasn't responded. How long do I wait before I pack the kids into a cab and go searching for him? What could have happened for him to be this long? I pray he didn't get into an accident and is now lying in a hospital bed, alone.

Another half hour goes by. Every minute is an eternity. With the anticipation that we will have to go search for him, I change Kymani and pack his diapers, bottles, water, and formula. Josephine runs up the stairs to change and brush her hair. I strap Kymani in his stroller and put a bottle in his mouth, which he holds for himself and sucks contently.

Where are the baby wipes? I am rummaging through the bags trying to find them when I hear the door open. I drop everything, turn, and walk briskly toward the bedroom door. I peek my head around to find Roland at the end of the hallway, closing the front door.

"Are you okay?" I ask.

"I forgot my passport."

"Oh no. What happened?"

"There was a massive lineup and one guy working. He was so slow—it must have been his first day, or I hope it was. Anyway, they have a rule that they won't let you rent a vehicle without your passport."

"I imagine they take that rule pretty seriously after that man in a rental van bulldozed through the Promenade Anglais. I thought you kept a picture of it on your cell phone?"

"I think I do, but my phone died. I tried to use their computer to access my email, but I couldn't find copies on there.

The guy was really nice and ended up giving me the car, but I promised I would email him pictures of my passport as soon as I got home."

"Wow, that was very kind of him. We were about to head out on a search party for you." I gesture to Kymani in his stroller. "Since we're almost all packed anyway, should we go to the beach?"

Josephine leaps up from her chair at the kitchen table "Yes!" she exclaims, leaving her half-eaten croissant on the cheap blue plate.

Roland is in deep concentration on the computer, passport in hand.

"Roland, are you okay with that?" I ask again.

"Sure." He doesn't take his eyes off the screen. "Just let me send this email first."

Despite us being 'almost ready,' it takes us forty minutes to get out the door. I remember the pre-kids days when it took less than ten minutes. What did I do with all that extra time?

By the time we drive into the parkade, Roland is substantially more relaxed.

Josephine runs into the water before we finish laying out our towels on the soft, round pebbled. Kids and families condense along the beach. These warm days in the September sun are especially precious, taking in the last of the summer days before autumn descends.

I plunk myself on the shoreline and place Kymani down in front of me. The sea rolls gently around our legs, giving him a few inches of water to splash in. I rest my eyes over to the brilliant blue green vastness while the waves lap against my skin. The southern French sun reflects off the water like mini crystals. The heat on my face turns my mouth up at the corners and eases my shoulders down.

Kymani's floppy hat bounds up and down as I bounce him on my knees. He splashes the water over and over bringing on explosions of giggles and shrieks. His laughter is contagious, and I join him, absorbing his youthful joy.

Josephine and Roland are deep in the water playing games, both with smiles that challenge the immensity of the sea. Whatever lingering stress there was from the rental car mishap has been washed away. Their heads bound in and out of the water in a playful dance. Squeals spill out of Josephine as Roland throws her in the air and she lands, nose pinched, and eyes shut, in the salty water.

This moment is imprinted in my memory. Like old video footage on an 8 mm camera it has a nostalgic patina and conjures in a flickering display that will put a smile on my face whenever I choose to dig out the old box from the attic of my mind, turn on the projector light, and let it play.

Saint-Rémy-de-Provence

9 months old

September 11–25

"I am not an adventurer by choice but by fate."

—Vincent Van Gogh

TO ENCOURAGE ROLAND OUT of the house, I book a photography class in the neighboring town of Arles. This town was home to Van Gogh for a short while before his death. While Roland and his guide walk around together, indulging in their shared passion, Josephine, Kymani, and I take our own self-guided tour.

Our first stop is the ancient Colosseum. The Romans conquered Northern Africa, Greece, Spain, France, and up to England and Wales, leaving legacies like this one behind. It is a mini version of the one in Rome, with a fraction of the tourists.

Next, we are off to a museum and a gallery, stopping at cafés and a local park to get some kid energy out. I am shocked, even still, at the ease with which we travel with the kids. Of course, there are moments, like when we arrive at the gallery and no strollers are allowed, so I'm stuck carrying Kymani's twenty-pound body as we move through the rooms. When my arms give out, I sit down on a bench with him on my lap

Josephine in Provence

and take in the pieces from where I am. Sometimes I plop him on the immaculate floor to give my arms a break. Although the rule seems arbitrary and inconsiderate, it's a small inconvenience I would take any day to be walking around the old, castle-like dwelling of a noble painter in the South of France.

At the end of our day, we meet Roland on the outside veranda featured in Van Gogh's painting *Le Café de Nuit*.

"How was the tour?" I ask eagerly.

"It was fantastic. I think I've seen almost every inch of this town."

"How was your guide?"

He fills us in on the new settings he's learned and turns his camera to show us a few shots he took in emulation of Van Gogh's paintings.

"Oh, I know that one!" says Josephine, excited. "That's *Starry Night*."

"Good job, Jo!" Roland pats the top of her back lightly in encouragement.

"Fate is such a funny thing," I say. "This painter, under-appreciated, sick, sad, and self-tortured throughout his life has left a legacy to which this whole town owes its fame and new identity. And nobody saw it coming."

"No kidding," Roland agrees, picking Kymani up out of his stroller and placing him in a chair.

Josephine stands behind Roland, singing Kymani's favorite song, enticing him to smile for his nine-month-old picture. I hover just outside of the frame in case he decides now is the moment he'll start becoming mobile and leap out of the chair. Roland quickly snaps a few pictures and voilà, *parfait!*

✈

THE FOLLOWING DAY, JOSEPHINE and I visit the asylum Van Gogh was admitted to after he cut off his own ear and

271

sent it to his friend. I've always been intrigued by this man, who was haunted by the dark shadows of mental illness and plagued with challenges, yet created works that look like products of a beautiful dream.

A slender staircase leads us to the second floor. We walk into Van Gogh's room, pausing at the front door. His room is exactly like the painting.

A small single bed with a wood frame is made with a simple red woolen blanket and white sheets. A wooden chair sits empty beside the bed. The framed window offers a view of a walled garden filled with lavender. Beyond are the rolling hills of Provence, with their tall, pointed cypress trees, and above, that brilliant sun and wispy clouds. Next to the window, a canvas sits on a wood easel, inviting us to imagine him painting the view.

"I remember this chair," Jo says, stepping past me.

"I'm sure he never thought his time here would turn it into a place people would travel thousands of miles to see."

As we walk back downstairs, we examine the reproductions of the paintings he did while residing within these walls. Outside, the lavender garden is calming and offers a picturesque landscape for the patients of the mental health facility. The haunting energies linger in the halls and between the walls.

After our walk, we drive to a restaurant in a small French town twenty minutes away.

This girl across from me has grown into a chic young lady. Her golden sun-kissed hair is tied lightly on the top of her head in a very French bun. She wears a loose button-up blouse tucked into black denim pants. The earrings she picked out compliment her outfit perfectly. Her lips glisten with the light layer of the peach-tinted gloss. Josephine and I indulge in crème brûlées the size of salad plates, infused with lavender. Josephine thanks the waitress in French after ordering an espresso for me and another water for herself, and I am astonished and proud of the woman she is becoming. I enjoy every moment of her company, loving that I have a friend, in my daughter, as wonderful as her.

✈

JOSEPHINE HAS BEEN ENJOYING a daily routine of walking by herself to the bakery down the street to pick up croissants for breakfast and a baguette for supper. Kymani is as thrilled as his sister with the local baked goods. He stuffs fistfuls of croissant into his mouth, spilling the flaky crumbs all over himself and the floor. We decide eating outside is more enjoyable for many reasons.

"The market in Saint-Rémy-de-Provence is on this morning," I say, assessing interest. "Our Airbnb hosts have invited us for dinner tonight and insist we bring nothing, but I thought we could find some flowers and pick up a bottle of wine for them." Their neutral expressions inform me they need more convincing. "Please—it's only fifteen minutes down the road, and we will take the entire afternoon off to play in the pool."

"Okay, great," says Roland. We both turn to Josephine, who gives us a reluctant nod. I've clearly been wearing her out with our outings.

We're lucky to find parking, even in the early hours of the market's opening. The small surrounding streets are already packed with cars and people. We squeeze our stroller and large basket in and around the eager crowds. I encourage Josephine to speak French to the vendors, who are kind and patient with her. She can carry on a French conversation, but when she gets nervous it takes her longer to find her words. The vendors are interested in where we're from and how we know French.

"*Nous sommes de Canada,*" we say, and they either smile and say, "*Oh, oui, oui, nos cousins!*" or they frown in slight confusion and say, "*Mais, pas de Québec?*" To which I explain that people speak French in Canada outside of Québec, though not as often, and the accents are different.

My dad grew up in a rural French community near Winnipeg. His first language was French. My mom, who was born in Montréal, Québec doesn't speak French at all. My siblings and I learned from my dad, and from a variety of schoolteachers from rural French communities, as well as Québec and France. This combination of influences is what makes it difficult to nail down our dialect and accent. The locals love that we try and that we continue to teach our children French. They are open and friendly, consistently contradicting the many rumors I've heard regarding the French's patience for foreigners.

We weave in and out of the bustling market, picking out a variety of cheeses, cured sausages, olives, fresh vegetables, and flowers—in fact, we indulge in this delightful activity every second day by attending the market days in the surrounding towns to replenish our stocks. Within an hour, our bags are overflowing. We head back home for an afternoon picnic and some pool time.

I open a text on my phone from Tricia and turn toward Roland, who is lounging beside me at the pool with his headphones on. "Hey babe, your sister wants to chat with us."

He pulls his headphones down, and I repeat myself.

"Yeah, she called earlier, I need to get back to her. We can call her tomorrow morning so she can see Kymani too." He turns to put his headphones back in.

We should be doing a better job communicating with people back home. "I should check in with my family, too. I can't believe we'll be seeing them in a week."

I send a short text on the family chat then lay back with my cold glass of chardonnay in hand, enjoying the sun and relaxation by the pool while Kymani naps and Josephine remains nose deep in her latest book.

✈

THAT EVENING WE HAVE EVERYONE dressed in their finest for our dinner upstairs with our hosts. François and his partner Claude purchased this old house to spend their summer months here in Provence. To our delight, they've taken up cooking as a serious retirement pursuit. Their kitchen is professionally equipped with an impressive array of gear, including an island with heat lamps.

Upon arrival, a glass of champagne is poured for us. They offer a *comfit* appetizer that melts in my mouth. François's English is as proficient as my French, and both of our partners are monolingual in the opposite language. We do our best to tell stories and ask questions in both languages, pausing to allow for translation.

They tell us they're going to sell their house here. As a gay couple, they've not felt welcome, and even unsafe at times. They don't disclose the details of the number of incidents over the past few years, but they tell us they now keep weapons by their beds.

Roland says he has received a lot of looks in these small towns but has been surprised how friendly everyone has been.

François says the locals are kind to tourists; they depend on their business after all. However, living here and being accepted as a local is impossible unless you're a fourth-generation Provençal.

As they explain all of this to us, my dreamy rose-colored glasses start to crack. It is easy to romanticize a place and maintain the illusion while playing tourist. I can't help but wonder, is none of the world what I thought it was?

✈

THE FOLLOWING MORNING, WE SLEEP IN a little later than usual. Roland and I try to shake the dull, wine-induced ache out of our heads with some fresh baked croissants, fruit, and coffee. Once we've woken up sufficiently, we gather on the couch to call Roland's sister.

"Hi!" the four of us exclaim, hands waving to Auntie Tricia through Roland's phone.

"Hi! How are you?" she asks, politely but without the generous smile and enthusiastic energy she normally has.

Roland, Josephine, and I take turns telling her what we've been up to the past few weeks since we last spoke with her. We flood the conversation for far too long with talk of our travels and adventures.

"Kymani got his first tooth, and I lost a tooth!" Josephine opens her mouth to point out the gap.

I sigh, she speaks more excitedly about her tooth than her time in France.

Jo's comment puts a smile on Tricia's face. "Really? Let's see! Did the tooth fairy come?"

"Yeah, I got five euros!"

"Wow, the European tooth fairy is generous. I hope you find a keepsake to remember your trip."

A natural pause in the conversation allows Roland the opportunity to change the subject. "How are you? How are the boys? What's going on over there?"

"Well, things aren't great," Tricia says with a nervous laugh as she turns her head away from the camera. "Dad's in the hospital."

Oh no. I have a million questions, but I pull myself back to give Roland the space to speak to his sister. I gesture to Josephine that she can go inside and read a book.

"What happened?" Roland asks.

"He had a stroke, we think. They're still running some tests. He went to bed early Saturday evening a bit confused and disoriented. Mom thought he was just having a bad moment and was tired. But the next morning he was worse, so she took him to the hospital."

"How's he doing now?"

"He is confused about where he is and why. He remembers Mom and me but has a hard time with other people. I'm not sure how much of it is short-term versus long-term effects. They should have more results for us in the next day or two."

"How's Mom doing? How are you?"

"Mom has been at the hospital every day. I'm taking some time off work to bring her back and forth and to attend doctor's meetings with her. I have also been cleaning her house and cooking, so she can spend more time at the hospital. She's worried and not sleeping much."

"I'll give her a call. Thanks for helping with everything, Tricia. Thank goodness you are there. Is there anything we can do from here?"

"Thanks. I can't think of anything right now, but I'll keep you updated as we learn more. They'll be keeping him in the hospital until we receive the results."

"I'm sorry Tricia," I say sympathetically, wishing I could think of more to say than this. "Send love to Ed and Nadine for us."

Roland and I say goodbye to Tricia and turn to comfort each other with a long hug. We call Nadine, but she doesn't pick up. She must be at the hospital.

"Do you want to go home?" I ask Roland.

"I don't know. I don't want to leave you here by yourself with the kids, and I'm not sure what I could do to help if I were there."

"Don't worry about us. My family is visiting for the next few weeks, so there'll be plenty of help around. Go if you need to go, Roland."

"Okay, I will speak to Mom and wait for the test results before making any decisions."

We knew this was a possibility, that his dad could take a turn. His health has been fading over the past four years. Even though we made the conscious choice to be here despite this possibility, we're riddled with guilt. We wanted to be here for us, but now we want to be home to see Ed, to comfort Nadine, and to help Tricia.

We spend the day at the house, none of us with the spirit to do much of anything other than be close to each other.

That afternoon, while we play with Kymani on the floor, Kymani moves onto his hands and one knee, shuffling himself forward in his version of a crawl. Roland and I burst into smiles and laughter. Our hands clap wildly, encouraging his first move. If he's trying to cheer us up, he's doing a marvelous job. Roland scoops him up and flings him in the air, showering Kymani with love.

✈

ROLAND SPENDS THE NEXT FEW days at home. He calls his mom, gets updates from his sister, and visits his dad on a video call. I give him the space he needs to speak with his family, taking Josephine out with me, and offering to take Kymani as well, but Roland wants him to stay. Kymani provides a positive distraction.

Josephine and I explore the surrounding towns by car. We roll down our windows and let the September breeze blow through our hair as we drive through some of the most breathtaking scenery we've ever seen. We attend markets, explore cobblestone alleys, and visit small castles.

As we arrive at each town, I tell her its claim to fame: this is the town where the author of *A Year in Provence* lived; this was the castle of the man whose name coined the term *sadist*, and so on. I love every minute of these road trips through Provence; I can't think of a better way to bond with my girl.

I hope she remembers even a tiny bit of this when she goes all teenager on me.

Roland updates us when we arrive back home. Ed is stable, and the doctors confirmed that he did have a stroke. The stroke has left him physically weaker, shaking, and having trouble walking and getting in and out of chairs or his bed. He has a hard time remembering anything short-term, and even has gaps in his long-term memory.

"You should consider going back," I urge Roland. I want him to know he can return whenever he needs to. I don't want to be pushy, but I do want to make it easier for him to go.

"Part of me wants to go, but to serve what purpose? They said he is stable, and he'll likely be the same when we return in four months."

"What do your mom and your sister say?"

"They haven't asked me to come back, and they say that I should continue traveling."

"Would they ever ask, or would they leave it to you?"

"They would ask if it was really bad . . . I think."

I'm not convinced, but he knows his family better than I do, so I let it go. "How are they holding up?"

"Tired and stressed but okay, I think. I'm glad Tricia is there. I keep asking if we can help in some way, but they keep telling me there's nothing."

We continue gallivanting across southern France in a guilty haze for leaving Canada on this trip. I want us to fly back tomorrow, until I think of my family—my parents who have never flown overseas, and my brother and his wife with their two young boys, who are helping my parents travel. How could I do that to them?

A whirlwind of emotions runs through us every day. I tell myself to enjoy the moments we're in, after all, if we're going to stay, there's no point in being miserable about it. We focus on the kids, who are a happy distraction. I find myself laughing with them and being taken in as we visit the castle at Baux-de-Provence and the Carrières de Lumières art show, just to feel terrible for enjoying myself when our loved ones are not well. There's no winning this battle, of course. No matter what we choose to do, we're going to feel a certain degree of awful because it's simply an awful situation.

Dijon

9 months, 2 weeks old
September 25–October 2

———————•◦•———————

"Traveling—it leaves you speechless, then turns you into a storyteller."

—Ibn Battuta

I PACE AND TINKER UNNECESSARILY with the napkins as we wait for my family to arrive. I've cleaned our apartment, dressed the kids in adorable outfits, prepared an array of appetizers from the market, and opened a Chateauneuf-du-pape, we brought from Provence, and let it breathe. There's nothing else to do but wait. They've flown into the closest airport and are making their way here in rental cars. My mom (Marg) is with my dad (Aurèle) in one car, and my brother (Miguel), his wife (Billie-Jo), and their two young boys (Sam and Louis) are in another. Anticipation of their arrival has me jittery and restless.

A text comes through.

Hi, Mom here. We are a few minutes away from Dijon. We've lost Miguel and Billie-Jo. Where do we park and how do we find you?

*From bottom left, clockwise: Miguel, Aurèle,
Alana, Roland, Kymani, Marg, Josephine, Sam,
and Billie-Jo enjoying brunch on the terrace*

I giggle; of course they lost each other. I send them the address of two parkades nearby hoping they'll figure out how to punch it into their GPS.

Text me when you're close. Josephine and I will walk to the parkade and help you with your bags.

Within twenty minutes Josephine is running gleefully into my parents' arms. They made it. Neither of my parents have traveled oversees before (though what they lack in experience they make up for with determined spirits) and my dad is the first in his family to come back to their motherland, where his ancestors left over three hundred years ago to start a new life in Canada.

Josephine and I take their suitcases and escort them back to our apartment. My mom is moving slowly, her ankles swollen from the flight and her joints aching from sitting too long. My dad interlocks his arm in hers and keeps pace with her along the narrow sidewalks. Their bodies are weary from the journey, but their eyes gleam with the excitement of children. My mom points to the church's yellow terracotta tiled roof with the black, red, and green triangles on it. She traces the iconic pattern of the Burgundian polychrome roof with her finger. "How beautiful."

At the apartment, Roland greets my parents with arms stretched wide. The wine begins to flow, and we dig into the delicacies with reckless abandon. We talk about the trip and the town we are in and what we want to do this week.

Soon, Miguel and Billie-Jo walk through the door, their adorable golden-haired sons cautiously hiding behind their legs. When the boys see the familiar faces of Grandma and Granddad, they abandon their posts and run into their arms. Josephine goes in to hug them hello, and they gladly welcome the attention from their older cousin. Roland and I will need to put in more time and effort to win them over.

My brother and sister-in-law are calm and collected, as always. Billie-Jo, despite the international flight and drive, is perfectly put together in her fashionable mustard colored skirt, long-sleeved black top, thick scarf, and earth-toned bangles. She is poised and relaxed, giving off an air of I-woke-up-looking-this-fabulous.

Of all the people I thought might meet us on this yearlong journey, I was the most confident in these two. My brother and I are stubborn and proud, which leads us to do whatever we've committed to. Once, after a few too many cocktails on New Year's Eve, we declared a shared resolution to run a half-marathon. I had a one-month-old and neither of us had run five kilometers straight in our lives. Despite these challenges, within a month we were signed up for a running group, and we completed our first half-marathon that spring.

After a couple of hours of chatting and catching up, our party winds down early. Everyone is excited to reunite but also tired from the trip. We say our goodbyes for the night and make plans for an early-morning market meet-up.

That evening, as we cuddle on the couch and settle into a Netflix show before bed, I receive a text. "What time is it? Ten? What does Miguel want?" I say, half to Roland and half to myself. "He's wondering if I want to come out with him and my dad." I look down at my leggings in bewilderment. I forgot people go out this late in the evening.

"You should go."

"Are you sure?"

"It's a rare opportunity to have a drink with your brother and dad in France."

"Well . . . okay. You're the best, thank you!" I change quickly and head out the door.

When I arrive at the restaurant, I find them seated at an outdoor table. They are halfway through a bottle of wine and diving into a burger and frites. My dad gestures politely to the waiter and asks in perfect French for another wine glass for me. The tall man scurries inside and returns promptly. He pours my wine without once looking at me, he is smitten with my dad. This is easily done, given the amount of charisma that oozes out of the man. His genuine smile, generous laugh, and playful demeanor charm everyone he meets.

Dad glows, relishing the opportunity to converse to the man about his ancestor's origins, which has ties near Dijon. I'm grateful I get to see him in this moment, sitting across the table from his children at an outdoor restaurant in France, enjoying fine wine and speaking his first language freely. This is the good life.

✈

TRAVELING IN RURAL FRANCE IS best done at a relaxed pace, which makes it easy for our three generations to travel together. We cruise in a convoy across the vineyard-drowned hills of the Burgundy countryside. We stop at an old castle and wander through the ancient stone building. The adults are interested in the history and the wine. The kids are in awe of the catapult.

"They have so many old things here," Josephine marvels from the backseat, as the castle gets smaller in our rearview mirror. She writes a few words in her travel journal and reflects, "Nothing in Canada is old like that castle."

I'm delighted by her insight and ask if she'll read parts of her journal to us as we drive. I am clinging on to hope that she is being positively influenced by this year of travel, though sometimes I wonder if the importance is lost on her.

At the local park of a neighboring town, we unpack fresh bread, veggies, fruit, preserves, cheeses, and truffle butter from the market onto our shared blanket. Lying in the grass, we eat while Sam, Louie and Josephine run and dance around us. The

October sun is shining through the sparse clouds, giving us a comfortably warm fall day.

"How's your dad, Roland?" my mom asks.

"He's in the hospital still, but he's stable. Things have gotten slightly better over the past couple of days. We're hopeful his memory and physical strength continue to improve."

"Are your mom and sister there?" My dad asks.

Roland nods. "They are with him the majority of the day, to keep him company, but also to catch the doctors when they're doing rounds."

"We were so sorry to hear about it," says Billie-Jo empathetically.

"Do you think you'll go back home?" Miguel asks.

"I'm going to stay, for now. I don't want to leave Alana with the kids. My mom and Tricia are doing a great job over there and don't need me. Plus, Pops would be happy we are here together."

✈

THE FOLLOWING DAY, EVERYONE needs time to themselves. My parents have come down with a cold and spend the day in their rooms recovering. Miguel and Billie-Jo go to the park with the kids and indulge in some boutique shopping. Roland, Josephine, Kymani, and I go to the local grocery store to pick up some baby provisions and a few other essentials.

I have an oversized bag and a basket to carry our goods back home in. I place some diapers and wipes into the bags and move toward the formula.

Roland turns the corner with a shopping cart as I place a container of formula in my bag. I hand Roland the bag, "Can you hold this for me, for a second? I want to check that this is the same formula we used last time."

"What are you doing?"

His hushed-yell startles me. "I'm putting it in my bag, so I know if we have enough space to carry our groceries back to the apartment."

"I'm not touching that bag!" His hands are raised, and he takes a step back

"Why?"

"You know a security guard has been following me since we got here, right?"

"What?" I glance behind Roland and spot him. "Oh . . . well, we aren't doing anything wrong. I do it all the time. If he accuses me of anything, I'll sort it out with the manager."

Roland shakes his head. "This is white privilege at its finest. I'm using the cart. I'll go get the bread if you want to grab the cheese." He turns to leave, then stops when he sees Josephine drinking from a can. "Where did Josephine get that?"

"I gave it to her," I pause, waiting for him to say something. He stares at me in disbelief. "She was thirsty," I defend. "Don't worry, I'll pay for it later. Obviously."

"Unbelievable."

Roland turns the cart toward the bakery section. As he walks away, the security guard trails behind him. If anyone should be followed, it's me; I'm putting unpaid items into my bag and have given an unpaid item to my daughter to consume, and nobody minds.

Josephine finishes her drink and hands me the empty container. Growing up, my nanny did that for us all the time. I had never thought of these actions as white privilege before. I didn't recognize what I was doing as anything different from what other people would do. Maybe this is why the concept of white privilege can be hard to grasp. We so often use it to our advantage unknowingly because we've always had this privilege as part of our daily state of being. It has been part of our experiences for our entire lives.

As I walk through the store, I reflect on my reaction with Roland. I acted as though I have inherent rights. If anything were to go wrong in this situation, I would speak to someone with authority to straighten it out. I would have asked for an apology. I have no reason to believe the conversation would escalate, that the police would be called or that anything negative would happen to me. Roland would not be guaranteed the same respectful hearing if he were to complain about such a misunderstanding or false accusation. And so, he avoids the unnecessary conflict.

✈

OUR BABYSITTER IS A COLLEGE student who does not speak much English. This is an excellent opportunity for Josephine to practice her French and Kymani can't understand any language, so no worries there. I give her instructions and tell her we'll send her a message when we arrive at the restaurant and have Wi-Fi. I also provide the information for Miguel and Billie-Jo's babysitter, and my dad's cellphone number. She is much less fussed about everything than I am, practically shooing us out the door *"Ne t'inquiète pas! À bientôt."*

We venture twenty minutes out of town to an old estate winery with my parents, Miguel, and Billie-Jo. We are encouraged to wander through the cellar, which dates back hundreds of years and could easily be used as a stage set for a period movie. A stone fireplace separates two great rooms. Wild boar heads are mounted next to shields engraved with family crests. Each room has thick, ancient-looking wooden tables, intimidating throne chairs, and medieval battle gear resting against the walls.

As we walk toward the stairs we pass a room filled with old wine bottles and barrels made of French oak.

Upstairs, an enthusiastic gentleman pours our chosen wine samples, one by one. After the tasting, we each purchase a few bottles of our favorite wines. We've spent more money on wine this week than on our apartment, but these bottles would be at least twice the price at home, so technically we're saving a fortune.

We walk with a happy buzz to the Michelin-star restaurant around the corner. My brother orders two bottles of grand cru pinot noir for the table. The wine is exquisite in complexity with a smooth finish. I relish every sip, especially knowing I'll have to eat Kraft dinner and cheap beer as soon as everyone leaves to make up for this period of indulgence.

My parents tell us Josephine's favorite places so far are Provence and Vienna. Billie-Jo and Miguel tell us she spoke to them at length about her experience visiting Auschwitz. I'm happy she's talking to people about the places she has been in a meaningful way.

The conversation shifts as we discuss the next leg of our trip together, and what we want to do in Paris. Roland and I are here to spend time with family, and therefore willing to go with the crowd. We have an extra three days there, after everyone flies home, so we can see anything we missed then.

"We've seen more this year than I ever thought we would in a lifetime," I smile, happy to reminisce on how far we've come.

"What an incredible journey," says Billie-Jo. "You should write a book. It's not every day you meet someone who treks across the world with a newborn. Plus, everything Roland has experienced."

The idea shocks me. This year was for us; I hadn't thought about sharing it. Me? Write a book? Who would read it?

Billie-Jo planted a seed and watered it with encouragement. She tells me our story is worth telling and reassures me I'm capable enough to write it. Her confidence gives me the strength I need to pursue this new dream. We all need more of this kind of nurturing.

Roland, Miguel, Marg, Alana, and Aurèle at the Louvre Museum
Photo credit: Josephine Rosseker

Paris

9 months old
October 2–9

———————◂•▸———————

"We travel for romance, we travel for architecture,
and we travel to be lost."

—RAY BRADBURY

WHY DID I PLAN ON RETURNING the rental car we have had
for a month, in Paris? I did not think through the logistics of this
decision, that this would require us to drive through the hectic
city, find our apartment, unload, and park. As this was my (not
so) brilliant idea, it's only fair that I am the one driving. I pack
the car nervously, imagining the narrow streets, the six-lane
roundabouts, and the passionate drivers who are all in a rush.

"Have you ever been to Versailles?" Roland asks, breaking
my spiraling thoughts of driving doom.

"No."

"I haven't either. It's only about forty minutes outside
Paris. Should we go on our way? It's supposed to be awesome."

"Great idea." This will at least delay my driving-in-Paris-
anxiety for a few hours.

We pull into the parking lot of the Palace of Versailles with
all our car windows down in an attempt to dilute the smell of
Kymani's diaper. I pray the poo is contained and hasn't seeped
onto his clothes and car seat. Once parked, I lay him down in

the backseat to change him. Thankfully, it smells worse than it is. I hand Josephine the wrapped-up dirty diaper and point her in the direction of the trashcan.

Roland gets the stroller, diaper bag, and snacks out of the car as it begins drizzling. Ensuring Kymani doesn't roll off the seat, I keep one hand on him and use the other to grab our cheap umbrellas from the floor. I hand one to Roland and one to Josephine. We all throw on an extra layer to protect ourselves from the chill before strolling up to the decadent, gold-embellished palace.

Josephine, Kymani, and I go through the typical rigmarole of taking off purses and backpacks to go through security. I scoop Kymani out of the stroller and Josephine collapses it, so it fits through the scanner. On the other side of the metal detector, I turn back to tell Roland I need to pee. He is nowhere in sight.

"Where did he go?" I ask Josephine, but we both already know the answer.

"He's probably taking pictures." Yep, Josephine knows the deal.

Some days I want to throw his camera in the trash.

"I need a washroom; do you need to go?"

"No, I'm okay."

"Can I leave you with Kymani? Roland should come through security soon, and I'll be right back. Don't move until one of us comes to you."

She nods. I race to the building.

Of course, there's a long lineup for the ladies' room and none for the men's. With all our worldly knowledge, how have we not figured out that the women's washrooms need to hold twice the capacity of the men's? Even better, can't we make them all gender-neutral, and move on? With every passing minute, I grow more anxious. For one, I might pee myself. Second, I fear leaving Roland to go through security on his own. And third, I worry Josephine will leave her post.

I finally get into a stall and pee faster than I ever thought possible. Once out, I dart toward Josephine.

"Alana!"

I stop in my tracks at Roland's deep voice. I scan the horizon for them. There he is! He's standing with Josephine and Kymani, waiting for me. The anxiety drains out of me. All is well. I should have had more faith; of course they're fine.

It's late in the afternoon and the tour buses have all gone, leaving the grounds quiet. Roland takes advantage and starts taking pictures. The decadent beige and red u-shaped building is adorned with urns, busts, and a gilded balcony overlooking a marble paved courtyard. The dark rain clouds swirl dramatically overhead above the blue and gold roof.

With no strollers allowed inside, I lift Kymani into my arms and start touring through the room of mirrors, the sleeping chambers, and various other formal rooms. The lavish palace, draped in thick luxury, pays tribute to the wealth and glory that was the French monarchy. Its extravagance is a symbol of the vast inequity that fueled the French Revolution.

After our tour, I drive us into Paris.

Twelve years ago, right before I left with my little sister on our inaugural twenty-somethings-backpack-through-Europe trip, my dad told me a story that stuck with me. On his friend's visit to Paris, he rented a car. He thought it would make it easier to maneuver between his hotel, his business meetings, and the sightseeing he had planned both in and outside of Paris. While attempting to make it from the airport to his hotel, he got so frustrated with the intensity of the traffic that he parked the car on a boulevard and left it there. He called the car rental company and told them where they could pick up their car. The image of this frantic man leaving his car in the middle of a Paris roadway median has been burned in my memory ever since. Now here I am, attempting to do what my dad's friend wouldn't do: navigate a car through Paris.

I drive along the Seine toward the 2nd arrondissement. It's a picturesque drive—or would be, if I had the confidence to take my eyes off the road for more than a millisecond to enjoy it. The driving isn't as bad as I imagined, except for the motorbikes that weave in and out of traffic through blind spots, coming an inch from our vehicle before disappearing again into the crowd of cars.

"Mom! It's the Eiffel Tower!" Josephine shrieks with delight from the backseat, clapping her hands and pointing. "Do you see it Rolo? It's right there!"

I suppress my immediate urge to tell her to pipe down. She doesn't get this excited about many things. I should be encouraging her.

Roland is quicker than me, already expressing his enthusiasm "Oh, awesome, Jo!"

"That's so cool," I say, and it is. "We'll make sure to go see it up close this week," I promise.

It's dark by the time we make it down the last few streets to our Airbnb. In the end, we only had three missed turns and a construction re-route to deal with: not completely smooth sailing, but nothing catastrophic either. It's funny how a fear-based story can get into your head and take over.

The apartment is on a quiet back street, two blocks from a busy restaurant and retail area. The one-way streets are extremely narrow, with no parking available on either side. We have so much stuff, there's no way we can unload unless I can get us near the front door. I think of my dad's friend and wonder if I can hop the car up on the sidewalk for a few minutes, but concrete pillars guard them against opportunists like me. We arrive at the front door, and I pull over the best I can, urging everyone out of the car as quickly as possible. I hope we can unload before a car comes cruising along.

I can't believe the amount of stuff we have accumulated since we've had the luxury of throwing things into a car. Our bags and luggage cover the entire sidewalk. I help Roland get things into the lobby before the anxiety gets to me and I tell him I have to move the car. Two cars have already tried to come through, but graciously backed up and went another way. I'm not sure how long our luck will last and I'm feeling rude for taking up the space.

"I saw a parking lot four or five blocks back," I say to Roland. "I'll park the car overnight, and we can return it to the car rental tomorrow."

"Okay, I'll leave Kymani with Josephine upstairs and come back for the rest of the things in the lobby."

"Great, see you soon. Hopefully nobody takes our stuff as you're going up and down the elevator."

"Good point. I'll take the valuable things up first."

Two wrong turns later, I make my way into the parking lot. I'm a few blocks away from the apartment, and I'm excited about the brief walk back. It's rare that I'm out this late, and it's a luxury to be by myself.

Young lovers and friends make their way to and from the surrounding restaurants, bars, and cinemas. I've always favored fall fashion and Paris, of course, is on point. The women breeze by in elegantly loose trench coats, their heeled boots clicking against the cobblestone. Their hair pulled in a loose bun or left to delicately frame their faces. Men adjust their hats and re-wrap the scarves around their necks.

What a wonderful city to live in, especially for the young and beautiful.

"Clever," I giggle as I enter and survey our apartment. "So, by a two-bedroom apartment, what they mean is one bedroom and a living room that has a door."

"Yeah, not exactly what we thought." Roland shrugs it off. Neither of us get fussed over such things anymore; mishaps like this happen so often that if we worried about it, our travels would be a miserable experience.

"Is Kymani in our room?"

"Yeah, I put him down in there, so he doesn't wake up Josephine. She's on a pullout in the living room."

"I got a message from my mom" I update him. "They're settled with Miguel's family in their apartment down the street from us. We can meet them at the gallery in the morning." The kids occupy the bedroom and the living room. There is nowhere to sit in the *petit*—the word the French use to describe everything tiny in a way that sounds luxurious and charming—area that doubles as the entryway and kitchen. "I guess we should get some sleep. Unless you want to sit in the bathtub and watch a show," I laugh.

"There is no bathtub."

"Well, I guess that settles it."

✈

THE FOLLOWING DAY WE VISIT the Musée de l'Orangerie to indulge in some of Monet's famous lily pond paintings. My nephews, who are four and six, are done with the gallery after about thirty seconds, but impressively keep their composure for an hour. Kymani also gets restless and is ready to go down for a nap, but he isn't being his cool and calm self about it. Maybe he's teething.

The museum is on the edge of a long rectangular park that extends to the Louvre on the other side. The park is equipped with a playground for the kids—the perfect way for Josephine, Sam, and Louis to get some energy out. We unpack some snacks and let them run, jump, and play. Billie-Jo is not interested in going to the Louvre, having been to Paris a few times before. The crowds are off-putting to my parents, but they decide to join Roland, Josephine, Miguel, and me, who want to make the ritualistic visit.

Kymani finally falls asleep in his stroller, making it easier to jet around the art museum. Josephine and I share a set of earphones, which are plugged into my phone. The free audio guide efficiently tours us through the labyrinth of rooms, showing us the most celebrated paintings and sculptures. The *Mona Lisa* is Josephine's must-see, as it is for the other thousand tourists gathered in front of the small painting. I could spend days meandering through the halls, but given the circumstances, we are happy to zip through, seeing the highlights within an hour.

Josephine, Kymani, and I reunite with my parents, Miguel, and Roland at the front entrance. While we have Wi-Fi, we connect with Billie-Jo, who has brought the kids to another park with carousels a few subway blocks away. I call an Uber for my parents, Roland, and Kymani. My brother ushers them outside to find the driver while Josephine and I remain in the Louvre to stay connected via Wi-Fi to the Uber app.

Fifteen minutes after the app indicates it has picked up everyone, Miguel has not returned. Weird. I send him a message telling him we're going to go look for him outside, and if we don't see him, we will hop on the subway and meet him at the park. It's annoying not having functioning phones to communicate with everyone. Josephine and I head outside to where the Uber was and stand on cement pillars to get a better vantage point, searching the crowd for my brother. There are tons of people, but Miguel's six-foot-eight frame is usually easy to spot. We search around for ten minutes before deciding he must have left.

At the subway entrance, there are no ticket booths or electronic dispensaries. I throw my hands up in exasperation.

A gentleman approaches me and asks in French if I need a ticket.

This is sure to be a scam, he is strategically waiting for desperate tourists leaving the Louvre.

"*Oui, s'il vous plaît.* Two tickets, how much?" I respond in French.

To my surprise, he sells us two tickets at the proper rate. There is nothing about his attire that indicates he works for the city transit services, but to my further surprise, the tickets

297

work, and we get in. I scold myself for my negative assumptions; against all intentions, I've become a bit jaded.

The announcement of the next stop doesn't sound right. "Oh no, we're going the wrong way. Come on Josephine."

I instinctively jump off the train and turn around, expecting to see Josephine doing the same, but a middle-aged woman with a short brown bob blocks her way. The woman sees my panic, looks behind at Josephine, and realizes she's in the way. She moves to the side, putting one foot on the platform, and keeping one on the train.

An alarm rings and before Josephine can get out or the woman can move, the doors to the subway close. The doors are unforgiving, and the woman is slammed between them— she's stuck. I stand on the platform, darting my eyes between the woman screeching in pain and the scared expression on Josephine's face from inside the train. The door repeatedly opens slightly, but not enough for the woman to move, then slams shut on her. A man from inside the train pries open the door while another pulls the woman into the train. The doors finally release her from their grip, opening fully. She is inside the train, in shock, clutching her chest. I reach inside the subway, grab Josephine's arm, and pull her out quickly. The train doors shut again.

"I'm sorry," I call out as the train speeds off to the next stop.

"Are you okay, Josephine?"

"Yeah. That was freaky."

"I hope she's okay." Flashes of the woman's winced expression and squeals echo in my head. "If we ever get separated like that again, get off at the next stop and I will come find you. If you get off, and I am the one stuck on the train, then stay where you are, and I will find you. Okay?"

"Got it."

I repeat the instructions one more time and quiz her on the new protocol. When she passes, I take a calming couple of breaths and look around to see if there's a way to get us onto the other side of the platform. We head for the stairs, at the top of which is only the street exit. *Weird.* Stations are typically designed to allow you to move between platforms without leaving. When we reach the other side, we try to use our tickets to get in, but they don't work.

There's no electronic ticket vendor and no random person selling tickets. Great. A teenager in a hoodie walks through in front of us and Josephine slips in behind him. Although it's technically *wrong*, I am immensely proud of my streetwise kid. A man in a trench coat holding a briefcase comes forward, sees what's going on, and gestures for me to go through with him.

I turn to Jo, "It's only three stops away, let's go." I'm relieved we are on the right track again.

We find Roland, Kymani, Billie-Jo, the two boys, and my parents waiting at the park gates for us. No brother to be seen. "Where's Miguel?" I ask, worried.

Roland shrugs. "He was supposed to be with you."

"We waited and waited, but he didn't come back. I left him a message that we were coming here. I hope he got it."

What a mess. Miguel is savvy enough to make it here on his own or figure out a way to contact us, so I'm not panicked, but I do feel guilty for leaving him behind.

A few minutes later he comes waltzing through the gates, looking at me with a smirk on his face that says *You jerk!* I wince in an apologetic guilty-as-charged expression. "Sorry!"

We manage to walk five blocks without losing anyone—a small miracle for this group. The restaurant is a tiny nook in a mostly residential neighborhood. As we take over the eating area with our North American–sized strollers, purses, backpacks, and diaper bags I am painfully aware of our touristy presence in the quaint, elegant space. A waiter kindly offers to take our excess belongings to the back, restoring the ambiance.

With bellies full of wine, duck, roast potatoes, and crème brûlée, taxis are in order. Two of the three cars come right away. Roland, Kymani, Josephine, and I crawl into one and my parents take the second.

"Can I go with Grandma and Granddad?" Josephine asks me.

"Sure, they're right behind us. Go hop in. I'll pick you up from their place after Kymani goes to bed." My parents are sharing an apartment with my brother's family a few short blocks away.

My eyes follow her as she walks behind us. When her cab door shuts, I tell the driver we can leave. Josephine's cab pulls out after us and follows but we are soon separated by the heavy traffic.

After we put Kymani to bed, I walk to my parents' apartment to pick up Josephine.

When they open the door for me, there's frenzied energy. I immediately look for Josephine and spot her. She isn't lost.

I do a quick headcount and see everyone but—"Where's Granddad?"

Sam, my brother's oldest boy, giggles, "Grandma left him behind!"

"What? *Where*? At the restaurant?"

"When Josephine came in my cab, I thought he was trading spots with her and going in your cab, so we left," my mom says, not looking worried at all.

"We were freaking out," says my brother. "We didn't think Mom had the address or any euros. We thought her and Josephine were gallivanting around Paris, lost, with no money or phone." I can picture this entire scenario easily: my dad has overseen the phone, money, and logistics since they arrived. "Dad had to wait for another cab because there were too many of us to fit into one," my brother continues. "He should be here soon."

"Wow! How is it possible to lose so many people in one day?" I ask perplexed.

Dad walks in a few minutes later, giving my mom the same *You jerk* smirk I got from my brother a few hours before. Mom laughs and declares she's off to bed, hoping to medicate herself out of this cold and into a better state in the morning.

✈

MY PARENTS ARE DRAINED. Whatever virus they picked up is getting the best of them. They opt to stay in the house today and relax. We keep bringing back different medications from the pharmacist in hopes that something will help them, but it's not getting better.

The rest of us spend the afternoon at the Centre Pompidou. The modish contemporary glass building is equipped with escalators that run up the outside of its walls: it's an art piece of its own.

Beside the museum, a small plaza with the pool-sized Fountaine Stravinsky which offers Josephine, Sam, and Louie some space to be kids after enduring an hour and a half of quiet art contemplation. Sam playfully smacks his younger brother on the back, yelling, "You're it!" sparking a flurry of quick-stepping feet. The kids begin to chase each other around the fountain in a game that looks closer to *run around in circles* than *tag*.

Mid-game they stop in their tracks when some street performers erupt into a breakdance. Sam is staring in awe at the young man who is flipping himself upside-down in one-handed handstands. Louie, his younger brother, yells "Whoa, Josephine, did you see that?" Josephine smiles as she bops her head to the beat and watches the group twirl, flip, and spin in choreographed unison.

Despite dusk sneaking upon us, we decide everyone has enough energy to do a quick trip to the Arc de Triomphe on our way home. We're excited to show the kids where Miguel and Billie-Jo got engaged over a decade ago.

"I thought there was an elevator?" I ask Roland as we are herded up the stairs in single file like cattle, with people directly in front and behind us. There is no room to turn around and I can't stop, so, with Kymani in my arms, I make my way up the 284 steps. Roland offers to take him, but I give him the baby bag instead and tell him we can switch when I get tired.

Within a few minutes, my strained muscles are forcing a self-motivating pep talk. *Okay, Alana. If you can hike the 75 km West Coast Trail pregnant, you can do this. Keep going.* My arms ache from holding Kymani up, and my legs are shaking, but Kymani has fallen asleep. I don't want to wake him up by transferring him to Roland. (Although it's likely that even if Kymani wasn't sleeping, stubbornness and pride would prevent me from giving in.)

It's worth the climb: the view is as spectacular as I remember it, with the bright lights of the city casting a glow over the dark night's horizon. From above, the arc feels like the beating heart of Paris, pumping the flow of cars through the arteries of the roundabout and into the veins of the streets that make up this magnificent city.

I collapse in relief on a stoop, a few feet back from the edge. I am content to watch the tourists who are trying to find the best camera angle to capture even a fraction of the beauty before them. Josephine and the boys are ecstatic about the Eiffel Tower, which although far away, commands attention as it glows and shimmers.

Paris, you never disappoint.

✈

MY PARENTS TOOK A TURN FOR the worse last night. My dad didn't sleep and was feeling pressure in his chest. I urged them to call a doctor, but my dad refused. I fear one day his stubbornness will be his demise—that he won't get the help he needs when he needs it. My mom is also struggling with this horrible cold, but her symptoms do not include night sweats and heart palpitations like my dad, so we are less worried about her.

"Please call a doctor tomorrow if he's the same," I say to Miguel who has just told me they are still sick and won't be joining us. "Do *not* ask them or give them a choice. It's covered under their medical insurance, and someone will come to the apartment."

"Yeah, I think we'll have to. We'll see how he's doing tomorrow." Miguel agrees, but he's not looking in my eyes, which makes me question how committed he is to the strategy. Clearly, he's worried my dad won't let the doctor in the door.

This irritates me to no end. Why is Dad so stubborn about getting help? (We don't know it while we are in Paris, but we find out later, through medical tests in Canada, that Dad suffered a minor heart attack.)

I need a distraction. I pull out my phone. A text has come in; it's Roland's sister. My heart sinks.

"Roland, you need to read this. She said she sent you a message yesterday." I pass him my phone. I can't be the one to tell him, it has to be his sister.

"I'm sorry, Roland," I say after he finishes reading the message. I give him an engulfing hug. "Do you want to go back to the apartment and check in with your family?"

Roland stands in silence. His contemplation indicates this is hitting him hard. "He isn't coming home."

"I know baby. I'm sorry." I give him another long hug, and he shakes, tears running down his cheek.

The admission of Roland's dad into long-term care confirms the doctors do not expect him to get better and, that this is his new normal. His short-term memory is limited, and his mobility weakened. Ed, as we once knew him, has changed. Permanently.

"Do you want us to come with you?" I ask. "We can go back."

"No, no. Thanks. I don't want to ruin Josephine's day. She'll want to see the science center with her cousins. Plus, I need some time alone. I'll call Tricia to find out what's going on. Actually, why don't I take Kymani? It's nice to have the little guy around and it will make it easier for you."

"Whatever you want."

✈

THAT NIGHT, JOSEPHINE AND I take an Uber to see the Eiffel Tower light up. The two of us find a bench to cozy up on under the tower. We count down the time like it's New Year's Eve: *ten, nine, eight . . . three, two,* one! The tower explodes into flashing lights. Josephine, cuddled up to me, with wide eyes filled with wonder. It's magical to her, seeing this iconic structure up close and flickering with thousands of dancing lights.

After the show, Josephine walks down the street and picks out some key chains and memorabilia for her and some close friends. She's so excited that she's bounding more than walking, a smile permanently spread across her face. She turns toward me and gives me a hug. "Thank you," she says, the words so sincere it melts my heart.

"Well, this is a lot easier without Kymani and the stroller," Josephine observes as we maneuver quickly through the crowds to the subway.

"I know it is, baby, but without Kymani, we wouldn't be here at all. The maternity leave is what's helping us finance this trip and have the time off to be here. He won't remember any of this, but we will. We owe him, big time."

Josephine gives Roland a hug when we walk into the apartment and asks how he's doing. In hopes of cheering him up, she shows him all the memorabilia she picked up from the Eiffel Tower. Her ears are red, a telltale sign of her exhaustion. Like a firework, she goes from beaming to fizzled out within seconds. She collapses on her bed and is asleep before we turn off the lights and close the door.

Roland spoke with his sister and his mom. For being in his midseventies, Ed's vitals are strong and, he's physically stable. However, after a number of assessments, they determined that his cognitive impairments require twenty-four hour care. He is frequently unaware of where he is, has limited short-term memory, and gaps in his long-term memory. Despite the changes, he's in good spirits. He's a star patient, and the caregivers appreciate his positive, friendly, and kind nature.

Nadine is relieved he will receive the care he needs but is strained, worried about affording her home with her prized garden along with a quality care home for Ed. Her insomnia has gotten far worse. Despite her exhaustion, she goes to the gym every morning before tending to Ed at the hospital for the rest of the day. You would never guess she's in her midseventies. She is extraordinarily strong, with an energetic spirit and a generous heart.

Roland's eyes are heavy from the emotional weight of the updates. He leaves long pauses between thoughts then squints hard, creating a watery barrier between himself and the world. The realities are sinking in, and he is mourning the change.

✈

AFTER SAYING GOODBYE TO my parents and brother's family, the four of us have three more days in Paris. Josephine and I take advantage of the last day we can use our museum access card to visit the Musée d'Orsay. The art gallery is chock-full of some of the most influential artists of the twentieth century including Degas, Monet, and Van Gogh. Josephine is excited to see the original paintings by Van Gogh that we saw in reproduction in Provence, such as *Bedroom in Arles*, the self-portraits, and *Starry Night Over the Rhône*.

After, we walk along the waterside, passing the bridges that gracefully arch over the Seine river like ballerinas, perfectly poised. On this cool fall day, our noses and cheeks turn rosy with the light swirling wind. Halfway to Notre-Dame we duck into a café to warm ourselves with some French onion soup. As we order, we go back and forth with the waiter, who insists on speaking English to us, while we insist on speaking French to him. Although we both could switch at any time, we both decline and continue to speak in the language of our choice in a tenacious act of defiance.

Having spent too much time lingering in the café, we decide not to wait in the lineup with the hundreds of tourists to get inside the Notre-Dame; instead, we listen intently to our audio guide as we tour the outside. We walk with our heads angled upward and our mouths open slightly in admiration of the carved gargoyles, apostles, and saints. We pause for a long while, taking in the intricate, round stained-glass window that blossoms like a rose in the heart of the cathedral.

As we head toward home, we stop and turn to get one more glimpse of the cathedral from a distance. At the time, we did not know how lucky we were to have seen it before the fire that would soon devastate it in April of 2019. I put my arm around Josephine and hold her as she takes a final picture of the elegant cathedral, standing watch over Paris.

On our way back to our flat, we pick up some comfort food for Roland. When I open the door and announce our arrival, I hear a low-energy hello from the living room.

Roland is lying on the ground, absently rolling a car back and forth in front of Kymani.

"My mom was admitted to the hospital today."

"Wha—wait, what?" I close my eyes and shake my head, unable to process what he's telling me.

"She's been in a lot of pain the past few days. At first, she thought it was her sciatica, but it moved from her leg to her chest."

"What is it? What's wrong? It was bad enough to go to the hospital?"

"She could barely walk—you know Mom, it had to have been awful for her to call an ambulance. The doctors think it might be an infection."

"But . . . she, she was so healthy," I finally mutter. "She's a powerhouse. How could this happen?"

My mind races with possible explanations. I wonder if his mom's heightened levels of anxiety, insomnia, and stress are the contributing factors. Maybe she picked something up at the hospital and is having trouble fighting it in her exhausted state.

"I can hardly believe it either. She's strong, though, I'm sure she will be fine."

"How are you? What do you want to do? Maybe you should go home . . . ?"

"I need to talk to Tricia first. I don't know what the diagnosis or prognosis is. What if it turns out to be exhaustion, and she's back on her feet in a day or two?"

"Roland, even if your mom will be fine in a few days, I think you should go. This shows how stressed and exhausted she is. I'm sure your sister is going through a lot, too. They seem like they could use some help and you would have the luxury of not working and not having the kids with you."

Roland doesn't utter a word, just sits, gazing at nothing.

I thought he needed permission to leave, but given his vacant expression, I'm not sure I'm taking the right approach. "I would come with you, but I'm hesitant because Josephine's dad is meeting us in Spain in a week and Kim is also flying out for a visit. Plus, honestly, I'm not sure how much help I would be with the two kids there."

"No, no. I know."

Am I saying anything right, or am I making things worse? I keep trying. "It's our last day in Paris tomorrow. We can book your flight out from here."

He doesn't respond. I don't know what else to say, so I grab the computer and start searching for flights.

"We can get you home the day after tomorrow without breaking the bank. I'll book them right now."

As I wait for Roland to find his passport, I check how many points we have left.

"I can't find the passports. Do you remember where we put them?" His head hangs and his hands lay heavily at his sides, palms up in surrender.

I jump up and look in the typical spots: the diaper bag, the backpack, and my purse. Nothing. I go through my luggage. Nothing. Now I'm getting nervous. The last time we used them was to get into France over a month ago. This is our fourth Airbnb since then. Roland goes through his suitcase as I scour Josephine's. Nothing.

My face is feverish, and my palms are clammy. I go through every bag again. Nothing. I look at my phone; it's 1:30 a.m. Exhausted and strung out, I grab the laptop and email the three previous Airbnb owners to see if they were left behind. The car rental would have contacted us by now, so I rule that out. The only other possibility is that they were stolen or lost along the way.

I've been in charge of the passports since we started this journey. I am stunned at how calm Roland is. He continues searching without once blaming me or getting mad that he can't go home to see his sick parents because I lost all our passports.

"Babe," I say finally, "they're not here. I'm sorry, I've got nothing left in me and I don't think there's anything more we can do tonight."

"Okay," is all he says before giving me a hug. "Let's go to sleep."

In the morning, we pack all our belongings, purging what we can't carry with us on our train ride to Bordeaux, which is booked for the following day.

I get a text from François, our host-extraordinaire from Provence.

I'm shaking and can hardly breathe. Hopelessness gets thicker and stronger with every possible solution that is ruled out. I'm worried this will be another one.

I open his message and start to read it aloud to Roland. A dry sob escapes. "They found our passports in the night table." My eyes close, I exhale slowly, and my body shivers from my head through my torso, releasing the built-up stress. *Everything is going to be okay. Roland will get home, Josephine will see her dad, and I will meet my friend in Spain. We're not stuck in Paris for weeks trying to deal with the bureaucratic mess of replacing passports. Breathe.*

When I'm calm, I read on. "François can send them by express mail to Bordeaux. They will arrive before our last day in France."

With the mystery of the lost passports solved and the luggage packed, we go out to enjoy our last afternoon in Paris. We take the subway to Rue Cler and have lunch at a picturesque café before meandering to pick up wine and chocolates. The park nearby offers an excellent view of the Eiffel Tower. It's Kymani's ten-month-old birthday and the tower is the perfect backdrop for the photo ritual.

In a few days, Roland will go back to Canada and Josephine will be off for two weeks with her dad. We will no longer be together. However, all our problems temporarily melt away as we sip wine, eat fine chocolate, and watch the sun go down behind the Eiffel Tower. We stay in this moment as long as we can, holding on to the romantic, carefree charm of the city around us, deeply aware that it won't last forever.

À bientôt Paris!

Alana, Kymani, and Roland at the Cité du Vin,
Bordeaux's wine museum

Bordeaux

10 months old
October 9–12

———————◆◆◆———————

"You may encounter many defeats, but you must not
be defeated. In fact, it may be necessary to encounter
the defeats, so you can know who you are, what you
can rise from, how you can still come out of it."

—Maya Angelou

"MADAM, THESE TICKETS, THEY ARE not valid," the train
agent says politely with a smile, shrugging and handing them
back to me.

"*Pour quoi? Comment?*"

"They're expired," she explains in French. "They were
purchased for September 9, and today is October 9."

Shit, how much wine did I have when I was booking these?
We move to the side and let the next passenger in line through.

"Wait here. I'll run and get us new tickets as fast as I can,"
I say to Roland and start sprinting down the corridor before
he can answer me.

I arrive at the ticket booth but there are six people in line.
We have less than five minutes before our train leaves. I race to
the back of the station where I thought I saw a ticket vending

machine on our way in. Yes! There it is, and no line. I punch at the screen in a frazzled frenzy. It's taking forever to process. I finally get my credit card to take and can hear the printing of the tickets. I look at my phone: two minutes.

With tickets in hand, I fly back to the platform. The agent sees me and waves me over to scan my tickets.

Josephine hops on the train. Next, we carry Kymani up the steps in his stroller. I stay on the train while Roland passes me our bags. I'm piling one piece of luggage on top of another feverishly. My eyes dart from the door to Roland as visions flash through my mind of the train door closing between us, half our luggage and Roland, left goodbye-less on the platform. By now the vestibule of the train is completely blocked by all our things. Finally, the last bag is lifted, and Roland jumps on the train. We are both out of breath, our foreheads beaded with sweat. But we made it.

✈

MY COUSIN SARAH AND HER new husband Joel arrive with arms open wide for big, enthusiastic hugs. Roland and I were disappointed to have missed their wedding in July, back in Canada, but are grateful to be able to see them for a few days on their honeymoon. We uncork a bottle of wine we've been saving for the occasion, carrying it with us from Dijon, and lay out our various market goodies.

"Cheers! Congratulations Sarah and Joel!"

We drink and listen to stories from their wedding. They show us pictures and videos, reminiscing over their favorite memories of the day. It was everything they wanted.

The conversation naturally moves on to our experiences traveling. The newlyweds have come from the Côte d'Azur and Provence as well. We share stories about what we've loved, what we would do again, and what we would skip.

Roland's phone dings. "Babe, Tricia is at the hospital with Mom. They can video chat for a minute," He turns to Sarah and Joel "Sorry, I'll be back. I haven't been able to reach her, so I better take this opportunity."

Roland steps out and I give them a rundown of what's been happening with Ed and Nadine over the past few weeks. I also tell them about the passports and how we're trying to get Roland home on Friday. As I explain everything out loud, I become even more aware of how stressful and upsetting it has been.

I excuse myself, leaving Sarah and Joel on the balcony with their wine, to visit with Nadine.

"Hi Nadine! Nice to see you!" I say, avoiding *How are you?* "We miss you terribly."

"Oh, hi!" Nadine says with enthusiasm, looking clear-headed and present. "How are you making out in your travels? You're with your cousin now?"

"Everything's great over here. We celebrated Kymani's ten-month birthday in front of the Eiffel Tower yesterday. We'll send you some pictures. Now we're enjoying some exquisite wine with Sarah and Joel, congratulating them on their wedding."

"That's nice." Nadine looks down instead of at us. She's not her usual self, but better than I thought she might be.

"I'm sorry Josephine, Kymani, and I can't come home too. I wish we could, but with Josephine's dad's coming to pick her up from Spain next week . . . If anything changes or you need us there, we'll be on the next flight home."

"Oh, no, no, no," she waves it off, shaking her head from side to side.

"I'll be home on Friday, Mom," says Roland. "You hang in there. I'm looking forward to seeing you."

"Oh, such a bother. I'm sorry." She hates that we're going through all this trouble to get Roland home. I hope it's a sign that she doesn't think her condition is too serious, and that she will be okay.

"I'm happy to come home. It will be great to see you and Pops, too. It's all good. How are you feeling, Mom?"

"Well . . . I'm not doing so well," she says, rubbing her eyes as tears start to stream down her face. "I'm in a lot of pain. It's my hip. I can't really move very well."

Tricia interjects and tells us we need to wrap things up, Nadine needs to get some rest.

"Goodbye, Nadine. We love you so much. We miss you." I wave and blow her a kiss.

"Bye, Mom. I'll see you soon. Say hi to Pops for us. We love you so much."

Tricia reappears on the phone as she walks down the hall, out of Nadine's earshot, to give Roland an update.

I thank Tricia for organizing the video chat then let her and Roland talk.

Roland informs me later that Nadine has been diagnosed with bacterial meningitis. It can be fatal for the young and the old, but they caught it early and are expecting a full recovery. She is otherwise healthy and strong, so it's a matter of waiting for the antibiotics to do their work. Tricia is working with the doctors on pain management for her hip.

✈

EVERYONE SLEEPS IN A LITTLE THE following morning. Our lazy start drags on for over an hour as we drink coffee, eat croissants from the bakery downstairs, and recalibrate from last night's wine. At 10:30 a.m., I send François a message. No mail has come, and the passports have yet to arrive. He responds immediately, telling me he is walking down the street to the post office to ask them what they have done. I didn't think it was possible for someone else to be more concerned than we are, but he might be winning.

"Hello," I say, picking up the call.

"Allo," he says in a quick, panicked tone. "I cannot believe it. They say it will not be arriving today. What does the word *express* even mean? Unbelievable, this is unacceptable. . . . I'll send you the tracking number. They assure me it will arrive tomorrow morning."

"Thank you for walking down there, François. All your help means a lot. Hopefully they will come tomorrow, and everything will be fine. We don't leave until the following day, so we have time."

There is nothing more we can do, so we venture out to enjoy the day. We walk toward downtown along the river, enjoying the view. It's hard to believe that after nine months of traveling side by side, we only have today and tomorrow left with Roland. This reality makes us cherish the time we have.

Roland plans to rejoin Josephine, Kymani, and I in Spain at the beginning of November, in about three weeks. We hope by then Nadine has recovered, Tricia will have had a break, and his dad will be in a temporary home. We'll then continue our trip on to Malta, India, and South Africa.

We arrive at the Miroir d'eau, a water feature the size of two hockey rinks that reflects water like glass. The sunny fall day offers a clear blue sky with a few cotton-candy clouds. Behind the mirror is a horizon filled with thirteenth-century architecture. It's a gorgeous view on its own, but the double take of the reflection makes it that much more spectacular.

A pleasant lunch awaits us in a nearby plaza. The warm October day is comfortable enough that we can sit outside on the terrace in the cobblestone square. We cheers, smile, and laugh in the ambiance.

After indulging in our midday wine and gelato, we decide some retail therapy is in order. Promenade Sainte Catherine is an impressive shopping street for the size of the city, and we explore the boutique stores, excited to make some rare purchases.

The wine flows freely that evening as we enjoy a late, adult-only dinner after the kids go to sleep. We laugh and talk, dressed in some of our new apparel. It's the perfect, quintessential European day.

✈

REFRESH.

I have been pressing the refresh button on the computer every thirty seconds to see where the postal truck is carrying our passports. It's so close, only a few blocks away, moving toward us. In another block, I'll give Roland the signal to head downstairs.

Refresh.

The truck turns south instead of continuing east toward us. *Ugh.*

Refresh.

The truck is circling the block and heading back, north, toward us. I take a sip of coffee.

Refresh.

The truck continues north, past our street. This is annoying.

Refresh.

The truck circles the block north of us and is heading back toward us.

Refresh.

The truck isn't moving.

Refresh.

Not moving.

Refresh.

Refresh.

Refresh.

A message pops up. Our package could not be delivered. What the hell!? I gather my purse and tell Roland I'm going down to the post office to find out what is going on. Joel offers to come with me: he has a functioning phone and is proficient in French, so I appreciate the company.

I am sweating, nervous and anxious. We absolutely need those passports today. Without them, Roland won't be able to fly home tomorrow morning and the rest of us won't make our flights to Spain.

I try to explain the situation to the post office clerk, showing her the tracking number. My French is failing me; I'm a nervous wreck. I can't think straight, and nothing is coming out right. I exhale, exasperated, when the woman doesn't offer anything but confused looks.

Joel attempts to explain in his own words as I call François. He answers immediately and I pass the phone to the clerk so he can speak to her. She suddenly understands, nodding her head and speaking rapid-fire French back to François.

The postal clerk frowns at her computer for a minute, turns to me, and says in French, "The message says you did not answer the service call and gave permission for the package to be brought to the warehouse for pickup."

I tell her, "We have been waiting the entire time at the apartment and the truck never came. We certainly did not give anyone permission to drop it off at a warehouse."

"I apologize, madam, there is nothing I can do; you will have to wait until the truck finishes its deliveries for the day to find out which warehouse the package has been dropped off at."

I thank the clerk as politely as I can while François curses the French postal service enthusiastically. I'm glad it's him and not me. He apologizes a hundred times and says if he hears anything, he will call us right away. I thank him for everything he has done and hang up.

With a wave of hot sweat, I realize how ill-equipped we are to deal with any sort of emergency while traveling. I don't know the systems here, the second language is a barrier, and often we have no friends or family to help us out. An uncomfortable swell of vulnerability takes over me. It's like we've been walking on thin ice this entire year, and this is the first time I've heard the gut-wrenching sound of a crack underfoot.

Sarah and Joel take Josephine and head out for the day to explore some sand dunes nearby. I am strung out and exhausted. My body wants to shut down and go to sleep. There's nothing I can do until the truck stops, so I might as well lie down and have a nap with Kymani.

I wake up in a panic, knowing instantly that I've been in a deep, coma-like sleep for far too long. It's five minutes to three and I've missed two phone calls and half a dozen texts from François. Shit. I sit up and read the messages quickly. Our package has arrived, and they've provided an address for the warehouse where we can pick it up.

I scramble to get the blankets off me and rush upstairs to tell Roland. I grab the computer. The warehouse closes at 4:00 p.m.—an hour from now.

Google Maps says the warehouse is on the other side of town, about forty minutes away. I quickly call an Uber as Roland gets Kymani and ready.

The driver sends us a message.

I can't park in front of your building. I will be at the IBIS hotel.

I respond, trying to keep calm.

The app will say I am disconnected from Wi-Fi when we leave the apartment. Please wait for us. We are two adults and have a baby in a stroller.

We rush out of the apartment, descending as fast as we can down the five flights of stairs (the elevator is broken) with

Kymani in his stroller. We run down the street to the IBIS hotel. There's nobody there.

I have no Wi-Fi here and we're not going to make it if I have to return to the apartment and call another one. Mercifully a cab pulls up to the hotel. I wait for the passengers to disembark.

"Bonjour Monsieur, êtes-vous disponible?"

He indicates he is free, and we hop in.

It's now forty-five minutes before the warehouse closes. I give the driver the address and tell him where we are going and why. He tells us we won't make it. There is too much traffic this time of day. I tell him to go anyway, we have to try.

The traffic builds, the taxi slows and the minutes add up. I slump lower into the backseat, tears running down my cheeks. We're not going to make it. My heart sinks and my head races with all the things I'll need to arrange now. I rub my forehead with my index finger and thumb, trying to massage out the stress coursing through my brain. I'm not sure why I'm torturing us by continuing the journey, but we're already this far.

We arrive at 4:15 p.m., fifteen minutes after the warehouse is closed. It's dark inside and the parking lot is vacant. Defeated, I drag myself to the doors. They're locked. I ring the buzzer. No answer. I try again. Maybe there is someone still there. Nothing. I try one more time, in desperation. "Please, please, please answer," I whisper in agnostic prayer.

Click. The door unlocks. I open it. The man behind the counter waves his clipboard apologizing in French for not answering the buzzer as he was in the back. I thank him for letting me in and explain to him the importance of the package. I don't stop until I get the entire story out, hoping if he hears it, he might show me some mercy and help me out.

"Madam," he says, when I finish, "it's okay, we don't close until 5 p.m."

My first emotion is anger. I take a deep breath, counting my blessings instead of my grievances. He checks my tracking number on the computer, smiles, and heads to the back. A few excruciatingly long minutes later, he comes back and asks a colleague a question. I take careful breaths, trying to manage my panic. They retreat to the back of the warehouse together. Another few minutes go by. I am praying again. "Please, please, please let them find it."

The man appears holding up the package triumphantly. "Oh!" I exclaim and throw my hands in the air. *"Merci! Merci, merci beaucoup."*

I sign, pay, and walk swiftly out the door. In the parking lot, I wave the package so Roland can see it from the car window. I jump into the backseat and tear open the plastic flap. All our passports are there. I hold them close to my chest, hugging them, breathing in deeply.

✈

ROLAND LEAVES FOR THE AIRPORT at an absurd four in the morning. We said our goodbyes the night before, so he could slip out of the house while we slept. Our flight doesn't leave until early afternoon, so we have time to get up, check-in online, and clean up before we head out.

"Oh no!" I throw myself away from the computer, face-palming my forehead.

"What's wrong?" Sarah asks.

"I booked our flights for the wrong day. Well, the right day, but the wrong month. I did the same thing for the train tickets on the way here, I must have booked them both at the same time."

"How much did the flights cost?"

"Not *that* expensive, maybe two-hundred or so."

"Can you book new ones?"

"Let's see . . . well, there are flights available for a reasonable price that depart late tonight. I guess I'll book those, and we'll have to wait at the airport until then."

It's going to be a long day.

I'm frustrated and feeling anxious.

It's okay. You are strong and resilient. You are capable. Worst-case scenario: you have a brutal eight hours at the airport, a horrific flight, and then you'll be in Barcelona, where you don't have to do anything if you don't want to. The time will pass soon enough.

We say goodbye to Sarah and Joel, scrambling to get all our gear into the Uber. We have an eight-hour wait before our plane leaves. It's going to be a trying day, but it's not just this 24-hour period, it's the accumulation of the hard week behind us, pounding down on me. There is no sense in complaining, though; it won't help. We have to move forward. I smile at Josephine "Here we go!"

SPAIN

Kim and Alana at the Parc de la Ciutadella
Photo credit: Lautaro

Barcelona

10 months old

October 12–November 1

———◆•◆———

"How do I love thee? Let me count the ways. I love thee to the depth and breadth and height my soul can reach."

—Elizabeth Barrett Browning

"WOULD YOU MIND WAITING here a minute?" I ask the cab driver who I think understands English well enough to grasp what I'm saying. "I want to make sure we can get into the apartment."

He nods then helps unload the trunk, placing our bags on the sidewalk. I tell Josephine to wait in the car with her brother.

It's almost midnight; the streets are dark and quiet. The tall apartment building looks old, weary, and rundown, with doors and windows secured by steel bars. The main street beside the building is blocked off due to construction. A few young men linger outside a corner store across the street. I keep my eye on them, without drawing their attention.

The entire scene makes me nervous.

I do not like that my kids are in the back of a cab alone while I am at the front door of this apartment. I do not like that all our possessions are sprawled on the sidewalk for the taking. I do not like that I am standing outside a sketchy-looking building in the middle of the night with no cellphone service. I especially do not like that I feel vulnerable as a woman and a mom out here on my own.

I nervously scan my phone for the instructions on how to get into our Airbnb. I continually glance back at the cab and at our bags, making sure nothing has moved or changed. I read and re-read her message, trying to decipher the broken English. I punch the buttons on the intercom, praying I have this right, and I don't wake up the wrong person in the middle of the night. I press enter and wince, dreading angering the wrong person at the other end of the line. Or worse, nobody answers.

"Hello," a friendly woman's voice comes through the speaker; I relax and let out more of a sigh than a hello. "I'll be downstairs in a moment," her voice rings cheerfully through the speaker.

I run back to the cab and start gathering the kids. I thank the driver and tell him he can go. He nods, smiles, and then moves our luggage closer to the front door. He doesn't leave; instead he stands with us, waiting until the Airbnb host comes down to let us in. What a wonderful man!

Josephine and I greet the host with friendly handshakes before escorting us inside, helping me carry the stroller and bags up the steps and into the narrow lobby. The slim, creaking elevator comfortably fits three people standing: not enough room for all of us, let alone our luggage. I am again left with the unpleasant task of dividing up the family and our belongings to reach our destination.

I send Josephine up the elevator with Kymani in his stroller while the lady showing us to our apartment takes the stairs with one of our suitcases. I wait for the elevator to come back down and ride up with the other suitcase, the Pack 'n Play, and the baby bag.

I walk into the apartment and am instantly relieved. Josephine, Kymani, and all our things are safely inside. The apartment gives off a completely different vibe to the exterior: it's modern, clean, spacious, tastefully decorated— it feels like home.

I make a bottle for Kymani and put him to bed. I whisper my thanks to him for being such a star, and I also tell him, if he wants, that he's welcome to sleep in tomorrow morning. It's worth a shot.

I give Josephine a big hug good night, thanking her for everything she's done to help me today. I don't know how I would have made it through without her. In the past few months she has transformed from upset, jealous sister to helpful third parent. I'm so thankful for her maturity and for being there for me when I need her most.

I like to think of myself as a strong, independent woman who is capable of handling things on my own, but I would be lying if I didn't say I was scared tonight. I felt like I had a neon target on my back.

✈

THE NEIGHBORHOOD LOOKS MORE inviting by daylight. We discover a fantastic bakery and café across the street, which continues to fuel our croissant habit. I smile at the other moms we pass, strolling with our children down the sidewalk. Josephine, Kymani, and I walk to the grocery store and load up on as much as the two of us can carry back to our flat.

Back at the Airbnb, I put on Spanish cartoons for Kymani when I get a text from Roland.

Hey babe, I hope you and the kids are doing well. Granny sends her love. I'm with her at the hospital, she's doing great. It's mind-blowing going between the sixth floor where Pops is, and the seventh floor where Mom is. Tricia is spending the first day in over three weeks with her family. It feels good to be here.

This puts a smile on my face. I'm glad he is there. I miss him already and traveling with the kids is certainly easier when he is here, but his family needs him.

In the afternoon, I gather the strength to take the kids sightseeing. We find the subway station close by, and by some miracle it's equipped with an elevator. This makes single parent–traveling with a stroller so much easier. Thank you Barcelona!

Our first stop is Barcelona's Arco de Triunfo. The grandiose redbrick monument is adorned with crowns, and angels perch on large carved pillars below. The arch is the entrance to a luscious park in the center of the city. We stroll through, listening to our downloaded audio guide. Josephine is interested to learn that there are parrots in the palm trees that flank the promenade and is staring up at the noisy calls of the birds to get a glimpse. I'm interested to find out that the arc was developed as part of the 1888 Barcelona World Fair.

What happened to those? They used to drive the creation of the some of the world's greatest and most creative architectural feats—Paris's Eiffel Tower, Montréal's Biosphere, Seattle's Space Needle, and Barcelona's Arc and Magic Fountain of Montjuïc. I try imagining what it would have been like to see the arc unveiled. Men dressed in black suits and top hats offering a hand to their wives as they stepped out of horse-drawn carriages. The women extending a gloved hand and striding onto the street in long, constructed dresses cinched at the waist, fascinator adorned with flowers or feathers, and lace parasols to shade them from the sun.

We continue down the promenade, where Josephine gets caught up chasing bubbles a peddler has ingeniously brought to entertain the kids and get a little money from the parents.

Kymani and I park in the shade and watch Josephine glee-fully jump, chase, and poke the bubbles, darting in and out of the dozen other children in a wild chase. The laughter, shrills, and shrieks fill the air as the bubbles tumble around them in big wobbling spheres, catching the light creating a psychedelic rainbow glow. These small, unexpected joys are a traveler's bliss.

Upon Josephine's insistence, we visit the chocolate museum. I have a few days left with Josephine before she goes with her dad, bonus mom, and sister (technically her stepsister) on a two-week whirlwind tour of Barcelona, Naples, northern France, and Belgium. She's excited to see her dad, and it will be fun for her to travel with her sister, who is a year younger than her. I'm impressed that we've come together to pull this off.

As we leave the museum, I am proud of myself for navi-gating Barcelona successfully with the two kids on my own. I have one more venue in mind before we head home for dinner. I look up at the dark clouds rolling in, warning us with their swollen, heaviness. I pause, nope—I'm not ready to push my luck and add bad weather to this mix. It's time to call it a day.

✈

BACK AT THE APARTMENT, WHERE there's Wi-Fi, my phone is blowing up. What's everyone in Canada doing up so early in the morning? It's 6 a.m. in BC where Roland is, and 7 a.m. where Kim is in Saskatchewan.

I get Kymani and Josephine situated on the couch and put on *Moana*, Kymani's favorite movie. Snacks and bottles are handed out; shoes, stroller, and bags are put away. I crack open a cold beer, take a healthy swig, grab my phone, and plop myself into a comfortable gray club chair to read Roland's texts.

Hey babe, call me back when you can.

Not good. That's the shortest, bleakest message I've ever received from him. Usually his messages are lengthy and filled with love and humor. Something is wrong. I wonder if his dad has had another stroke. I call back; nobody answers. I try one more time, still no answer. I send him a message instead.

Hey love, sorry I missed your calls and message. I took the kids out for the day. We're home for the rest of the evening. I'll call you back when Kymani falls asleep, in about three hours. Love you. xo

"What's going on, Mom? Are you okay?" Josephine watches me with a concerned look on her face, clutching a throw pillow. She has the instincts of a jungle cat.

"Yeah, I don't know. I think something happened back home, but I can't get ahold of Roland."

With not much more to say, she nods and turns her attention back to the TV.

He must not be answering because he is at the hospital. I close my eyes and send him some supportive love vibes from 8,685 kilometers away.

There has to be something I can clean or cook. My nervous energy has my body lifting me off the chair before I consciously choose to. I look toward the kitchen, eager for the distraction, but my beer sitting on the coffee table catches my eye. I relax back down and take another big swig. Maybe I'll finish this beer first.

I respond to Kim's message quickly. She's organizing a tour or two for when she's here and wants my blessing.

A few hours later, the apartment is spotless, the kids have eaten, and it's time for Kymani to go to sleep. I place him softly in his pack 'n play, singing the same lullaby I used to sing for Josephine when she was a baby. *Hush little baby, don't say a word, mama's going to show you a hummingbird.*

If that hummingbird should fly, mama's going to show you the evening sky. . . .

I touch his face and run my fingers through his hair. "Good night little one. I love you. Sweet dreams. We'll be back with Daddy soon. He misses you and loves you very much." I look at him stretched across his bed and wonder how he got so big.

I look at the clock on the microwave in the kitchen. It's 7:15 p.m. I put my super-mom face on as I walk into the living room to chat with Josephine. We go through our tentative plans for the next two days and decide the Barcelona zoo and the aquarium are the top priorities.

I tell Josephine I need to call Roland back. I give her permission to read a book in my room, which is the furthest bedroom from the living room. She's excited about the idea of curling up in my bed and bounds out with no complaints.

"Hi baby," Roland answers. I'm relieved to reach him, but my heart sinks at the somber tone of his voice.

"Hi babe, how are you? Is everything okay?"

"It's Mom." He pauses and takes a deep shaky breath. "She's gone." He chokes up, unable to get another word out. I can hear his tears through the phone. I can feel the anguish of his heart breaking.

"What? When—but how?" My mind races, unable to reconcile what I have heard. *Like gone, gone? What does that mean? How is this possible? They caught the infection early. I spoke to Roland last night, and he said she was doing great.* I wait for Roland to gather himself so he can tell me what happened.

"I was with my mom all day; we had such a great day together. Tricia came over after supper, bringing me a roti. I left Mom's bed to go heat it up. Of course, Mom had an earful of instructions: 'Rogie, make sure you put a wet paper towel around it, so it doesn't dry out in the microwave.' When

I returned, she looked at the dried-out roti shell. She already knew but asked anyway, "Did you put the paper towel over it?'"

I listen to him as he accounts for this day that has turned so unimaginably. "'No mom,' I said, 'I'm sorry.' Teasing her, I said 'Isn't it time for your nap?' She sucked her teeth and said, 'You know, you're lucky I'm stuck here in this bed, otherwise I'd cut ya ass!'"

I let out a weak laugh to show him I'm following.

"We laughed. It felt good to laugh together. I shared my roti with Mom. She hadn't been eating a lot, but, you know, it's her favorite. We spent the rest of the evening talking." He takes a deep breath, bracing himself. "Just as Tricia and I were about to leave for the night, Mom asked me if I would stay with her. She never asks for things like that. Maybe she knew and she didn't want to be alone . . . ?

"I woke up in the middle of the night, in the hospital chair next to her bed. Mom was breathing heavily. I told her to slow down. I got worried 'cause she wasn't calming down, so I ran outside to the nurse's station to tell them what was going on. A nurse came racing in, but after looking at her chart, she didn't seem very concerned.

"'She has anxiety, she must be having a moment,' was what the nurse said. She grabbed the oxygen mask and put it over mom's mouth, telling her to calm down and breathe in and out, deeply, and slowly. She sent for the doctor. Mom kept getting worse." His voice is breaking.

"This young doctor came in and started running around me as I held Mom's hand. Then Mom stopped looking at me. Her gaze moved to over my shoulder, like she was looking beyond me, but nobody was there. She whispered, 'Jesus, I'm ready.' She took one more breath, then slipped away."

I close my eyes, still not believing this can be true.

"The doctor yelled 'Code Blue!' and within seconds there were people streaming in out of nowhere. They made me leave the room as they tried to bring her back. I called Tricia to tell her what was happening, and she rushed over. They worked for half an hour, trying to bring her back.

"I thought she would come back . . . but, she didn't."

✈

THE NEXT MORNING, I PULL the covers over my head, willing the world to leave me alone. My eyes are swollen and burning from sobbing. My heart is shattered, and my spirit is dimmed to a shadow of its usual self. I bury my head in the pillow of a strange bed, so far from home, and weep again.

Kymani's cries pierce through our dividing walls. I wipe my eyes but it's pointless, the tears won't stop. My body moves like a puppet, mindless and spiritless, toward Kymani's bedroom. I pick up my boy and hear a "Hello, baby," come out of my half-smiling mouth. I change, feed, and clothe him without being present.

I am reunited with my body as the day goes on. The kids are a positive distraction, not giving my mind time to wander too far down a sorrowful path of grief. Their neediness keeps me present, and even manages to occasionally make me forget about the piece of my heart that has been ripped from my chest.

At ten, Josephine is old enough to understand what is happening, but the sadness does not linger. She looks at me knowingly throughout the day when my gaze drifts off into the distance or a tear rolls down my cheek. She is likely spending more time worrying about me than mourning the loss of her granny right now. It's a good time for her to go visit with her dad and their family.

The days go by uneventfully. I force myself to take the kids out of the house every day and explore. I worry that if we stay in, I will bury them alive with me under the weight of this heavy grief that's piling thicker and thicker, until we can no longer breathe. No, I can't let them suffer too; we must keep moving.

The sadness catches up to me at night, after I've tucked the kids into bed. I try distracting myself with planning Kim's visit or reading a book, or to console myself, and Roland, with a phone call, but I can't escape it. I pour a glass of wine, trying to calm down and relax, but it only makes things worse. The wine opens the valve of sadness in me, leaving me utterly depleted, a puddle in the corner of the couch.

I send Josephine off with her dad.

Then, I let myself go.

I wallow for an entire day and an entire night. I tend to Kymani, but otherwise I feel free to let my feelings take over, knowing it won't impact him the same way it would Josephine. I'm too scared to let myself go on like this for long, so I restrict it to twenty-four hours of 100 percent guilt-free, raw crying and screaming.

I look at pictures of Nadine holding Kymani, of her hugging Josephine, of our wedding, of Roland's fortieth birthday, and of family suppers gone by. I think about our traditions: every year she would come to our house in spring to help us pot flowers. I reminisce over the conversations we had when we went out for dinners and to the movies. I try filling my heart back up with the memories of her smile, her cheeky sense of humor, and her contagious laugh.

✈

A WEEK AFTER NADINE'S DEATH, my sister-friend Kim flies to Barcelona. I'm supposed to be taking care of her, lifting *her* spirits after a hard breakup. Now, we'll be taking care of each other, as we have, countless times, over the years.

Kymani and I hop on the subway to go greet her at the airport. I navigate the stroller through the crowds of people, following the signs to arrivals. I'm waiting for less than a minute when I see her walking across the shiny tiled floor toward me. We open our arms for a big embrace. I let a tear run down my cheek. I've missed my dear friend.

Back at the apartment, Kim takes some time to freshen up while Kymani naps. I sit on our balcony with a cup of coffee and a croissant, looking out onto the busy street under construction. Soon Kim joins me with a beer in hand. We're in different time zones, and she is in vacation mode.

I feed off her energy and try pulling myself into a positive state. My best friend and I are in Europe together. Nadine would have wanted me to enjoy this.

Kim frowns over the yellow excavator digging a massive hole in the middle of the street, the old gray and white buildings that surround it, and the bustling crowds of people walking up and down the sidewalks. "This reminds me of Uganda. It's not how I pictured Europe at all."

"When we get into the heart of Barcelona, it has a different vibe," I say.

She shrugs it off, indicating that she wasn't wed to her preconceptions. This is good practice from a seasoned traveler. She knows that once you let go of your expectations, you'll be much more delighted by what's happening in the moment—and far less disappointed if things don't live up to the picture you've created in your mind.

Kim breaks out the itinerary on her phone, excited to talk about our upcoming week. "Did you get a babysitter for the wine tasting and the flamenco performance?"

"Yeah, it's all arranged. She's going to come by tomorrow for a few hours so we can do the Gaudi tour, too. I thought it prudent to test the waters." I get up to walk to the kitchen. I throw the rest of my coffee down the sink, open the fridge and grab a beer. I can't leave my friend hanging, drinking alone!

The week includes historical and architectural tours, but we also find time to shop, have long, lingering lunches, and seek out new happy hour spots.

Spain's central plazas are lined with cafés to sit for sangria or an espresso, ideal for happy hour. Many are equipped with playgrounds or grassy areas in which the kids can gather after school to play. Some days we're lucky and stumble upon a plaza with live music and a little dancing to go with it. It brings the community together in a large, semi-organized play date for the kids, and after-work cocktail for the adults. The parents happily chat with friends while the kids play fairly independently. The non-helicopter parenting is refreshing.

In the evenings, after Kymani goes to sleep, we lay out an assortment of tapas, pour wine, and commiserate. At thirty-six years old, Kim worries about finding the right partner in time to have children, and about her role in the failed relationships she's had since her divorce. She wants to finish her master's degree in social work to open up her career options but is feeling distracted and unmotivated. She struggles with her weight and wants to be more fit and lead a long, healthy life.

I share the good and the bad about being a parent to a newborn again after ten years. I tell her stories about our travels when we have struggled and places we loved.

We work our way through each subject, contemplating serious solutions, laughing at each other and life, crying about some situations and disagreeing to the point of arguing over others. It's nice to have someone beside me who knows me so well, and who loves me like family. She tells me exactly what she thinks, calls me out on my shit, and then gives me a playful smile like everything is going to be—and already is—just as it is supposed to be.

"I can't believe she's gone," I say, in tears once again at the shock of Nadine's passing. "She was everything I ever wanted in a mother-in-law. She was a close friend, a confidante, always helping us, and always there for us."

"She was an exceptional woman. I'm so glad you got to experience that kind of love," says Kim, her eyes wide and filled with compassion.

"Me too, I know, I am grateful, but it wasn't enough. Five years wasn't enough," I grab a tissue and try wiping away the sadness. "I hate that Kymani will never really know her. That he'll never get to experience how amazing she is."

"I'm so glad she got to meet Kymani," Kim says consolingly. "She left this world knowing that both Roland and Tricia are flourishing and are deeply loved by their partners and their children."

A tearful smile emerges from my pain-stricken face.

"Think of all the blossoming she got to witness," my friend continues. "In recent years she's seen Roland move up in his career, get his project management designation and his master's degree. She got to see your relationship grow and walk down the aisle at your wedding. She got to witness him being a dad to both Josephine and Kymani."

I give Kim a long, deep hug. She has dragged me out of the depressive swamp I've been wading in and propped me up in her lifeboat. We're not out of the murk yet, but we're at least on top of it, working our way through it together, making sure I don't get swallowed by the darkness of the waters and whatever lurks beneath.

✈

KIM GETS EXCITED ABOUT DOING touristy things that I find a bit cringeworthy. So here we are, with fake flowers in our hair and scarves wrapped around our shoulders like shawls, being taught how to punch our feet into the ground like flamenco dancers. Kim doesn't seem uncomfortable in the slightest as she swirls her arms around and stomps her feet with a wide smile on her face.

I shake off my embarrassment and my strong urge to sit down and watch. I try, for her, to get into it. For everything she does for me, the least I can do is indulge her with some enthusiasm instead of looking like I want the floor to swallow me up.

Kim does the same for me as we walk through the Museo Picasso. I read Kim's fake enthusiasm smile as easily as I read the Picasso quote out loud: "It took me four years to paint like Raphael, but a lifetime to paint like a child."

Despite our slight differences, we travel well together because we are both adventurous. We're happy to try new things, to embrace new cultures, and are even okay to take a few risks along the way. In past travels, we've been separated by motorcycle taxis in the Dominican Republic and lost in a forest in Québec while snowshoeing, thigh-deep in the thick white snow.

We have since grown up and learned how to travel without getting ourselves in as much trouble, but we still share that same fun-loving spirit. This year would not have been the same without her being a part of it, and she truly couldn't have come at a better time.

I don't hear much from Roland. He is busy spending time with his sister's family, with his friends, and taking care of what he can at the house and with his dad. When I reach Roland one night, he tells me they've decided to postpone Nadine's celebration of life until Josephine, Kymani, and I can fly home. This also gives friends and family from the various places she lived, from Barbados to across Canada, time to make arrangements. I am grateful. We will be home in two weeks.

✈

AFTER KIM LEAVES, AND BEFORE Josephine returns, I venture, with Kymani, to see Salvador Dali's Museum and house in Girona. It's a twelve-hour day including a van ride of over two hours outside Barcelona, which is a bit daunting. Despite the risks involved in a long solo parent–voyage, the rave reviews and my inner art enthusiast compel me to go.

I take a cab downtown early in the morning to avoid any delays and unnecessary stress. Despite arriving early, the tourist office is packed with people ready to take various daytrips. As always, the stroller attracts attention. Many people come over to introduce themselves, wanting to see the baby and comment on my bravery for being here. Kymani is his easygoing, happy self, and is charming his way through the crowd of people with his generous grin.

At the tourist-crammed Dali Museum I strap Kymani into a carrier as they do not allow strollers. He is happy and content, facing the world and taking in all the people and things around us, letting me enjoy the various eccentric exhibits and pieces. However, it's short-lived; after about an hour, Kymani is sick of it and starts to grumble and complain. I leave to go retrieve his stroller, content that I at least have plenty of time to change and feed him before getting back in the van.

Kymani plays and coos while the tour van drives us to Dali's residence. By the time we arrive, he has fallen asleep for his second nap. Our tour guide, a vibrant, petite, dark-haired woman, says she is happy to stay with the baby in the van if I want to go inside. She says the stroller won't work in there and he's much better off to wait with her.

I hesitate, and she insists. I thank her profusely for giving me an hour to myself to explore this iconic home. I look up and say thanks to Nadine for sending this generous tour guide my way, assuming she is playing a part in all this, taking care of us even still.

I'm greeted at the entranceway by a gigantic stuffed polar bear covered in costume jewelry. A stuffed owl glares at me with his permanent wild, yet dead fixed expression, dappled in a grid-patterned light from the lamp beside it. This is only the beginning. The house gets more interesting, eccentric, and straight-up weird, as I go. Dali's house is everything you think it would be and more, from taxidermy, to statuary, to a phallic-shaped swimming pool.

Kymani and I arrive back at our Airbnb late, well past his bedtime. As I place his sleeping head down in his bed, I thank him for being such a star. I glance back at him from the door. "Good night baby, I love you." He continues to impress and amaze me.

Today gives me a slight boost of confidence that I might make it across the Atlantic Ocean without major trauma and on my own with two kids. I look up again, searching for Nadine. "I think I might need your help on this one," I say out loud, hoping she can hear me.

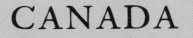

CANADA

Ed and Nadine Best

Home

10 months, 2 weeks old
November 2–18

"What we have once enjoyed deeply we can never lose.
All that we love deeply becomes a part of us."
—HELEN KELLER

FOUR FLIGHTS, TWO KIDS, AND ONE parent is not good math. However, Gravol and Netflix help balance out the equation. We arrive at Ed and Nadine's house in Victoria at 1 a.m. PST, after thirty-six hours of flying and layovers.

I'm caught by Roland's wide arms, which he wraps around me, taking me in for a kiss hello. There is a large bouquet of pink lilies on the table, to me from him. I can't believe he thought to do that for me at a time like this.

I glance at the chair where Nadine would have been waiting for me. It is empty and the house is quiet, void of her laughter and hearty welcome.

I've slept for less than two hours in the past twenty. I'm exhausted, but now, being back in this house and seeing Roland again, I say yes to his offer of a drink. In Nadine's honor, he pours us each a vodka on ice. I sit in Nadine's roomy brown

343

recliner and Roland sits in Ed's. The quiet lifelessness in the air is palpable. My eyes survey the room. I look at the pictures on the wall, the rug on the floor, her iPad on the table.

"I keep feeling like she's going to walk around the corner," I say. "It's hard to believe she's not here."

"I know, baby," Roland says consolingly, "I know." He tilts his head back and looks up at the living room ceiling, lets out a deep sigh, closes his eyes and lets a tear roll down his cheek. I haven't seen him cry since Kymani was born. He is heartbroken.

After a few moments of silence, I ask how he's feeling. I'm surprised by his answer, which is that he's largely at peace. I don't detect the anger I am experiencing. He is sad but expresses how glad he is that his mom is not suffering, how there's no way she would have tolerated being in a home, and how ready she was in the end. All this gives him the comfort he needs to deal with the pain. Roland's mind is a beautiful thing; he chooses to focus on the good, in even the hardest of situations.

Roland fills me in on the details of Nadine's celebration of life. The next week sounds hectic between lawyers, accountants, the funeral home, caterers, the church, his dad in the hospital, and people flying in.

✈

AS I DRIVE WITH JOSEPHINE TO VISIT Ed in the hospital, I'm surprised by my great sense of relief at being home. This week is hectic in that I have errands to run and people to meet, but I know the streets to drive down, I know how to interact with the cashiers, I know what restaurants to go to, including which ones are open late and which ones deliver. Everyone not only speaks English, but my specific cultural dialect. I know where to pick up my favorite groceries and can find diapers and formula effortlessly.

Even finding Ed's room in a hospital I'm unfamiliar with

is easy. I can read the signs and I know who and how to ask for help if I need it.

"Hi, Ed!" I say brightly, but not so loudly as to startle him or disturb his roommates.

Ed glances over at us with a smile, but his eyes are telling me he doesn't recognize who we are. "Hello dear," he says politely.

I knew his memory had been affected, but I wasn't expecting him to not know who we are. He doesn't attempt to get up from his chair. He's wearing some old sweatpants that need changing and a shirt that has seen better days. He is much more fragile and looks years older than the last time we saw him in the spring.

I lean in and give him a hug and a customary kiss on the cheek. "I'm Alana, your son Roland's wife," I say pointing to the family picture of the four of us hanging beside his bed. "This is your granddaughter Josephine," I say gesturing behind me.

"Hi, Granddad," Josephine says politely, looking at me for guidance. I move over so she can give him a hug hello.

"Hi there, Josephine," Ed says confidently, as if he were saying, *Of course it's you!*

Josephine and I grab a chair and sit beside him. He tells us he's doing fine, that he enjoys the food and no, there's nothing we can bring him. We find a deck of Uno and spend twenty minutes playing an unconventional game of cards with him as he makes up whatever rules he wants each time it's his turn. When a nurse comes around to tend to him, we give him our love and say goodbye.

"He's changed a lot," says Josephine as we walk out of the hospital. "What's wrong with him?"

We have tried to explain it to her already. However, it wasn't until she saw him that she began to grasp what is happening. I do my best to explain his condition and the plans for him to move to a care facility. She listens carefully, asking questions about why he can't go home and why he has changed and what type of care he needs. As I talk, I feel my own heart and mind wrapping themselves around the new reality: taking the pieces of information I had and trying to reconcile them with the actualities of what I've just seen. Readjusting my own expectations of the future.

✈

THE DAY OF NADINE'S CELEBRATION of life I wake up and spend fifteen minutes locked in a bathroom, needing a few minutes to myself before I tend to the kids. I carefully paint my nails her favorite color, purple. I put on light makeup, knowing it will be washed away by tears within minutes of entering the church. I find some of her gold dangly earrings and put them on, wanting even just a tiny part of her with me today.

The church overflows with people. Everyone stands and turns toward us with somber eyes as we take our seats at the front. Roland's best friend Sam, a professional opera singer, fills the room with his powerful voice. Tears stream down our faces and even Sam is overcome by emotion and cannot make it through the entire song.

Roland and his sister stand to speak. Roland inhales deeply and begins.

"There are so many things I would like to say to you, Mom. The shock and heavy sadness of knowing you're no longer physically here with us is hard and painful to wrap our heads around. Although your loving spirit will always be with us, and watching over us, it still hurts. It's hard knowing we'll never hear your calming voice, delightful laugh, and even your *stchoops* ever again. We can't believe you're gone.

"Over your seventy-six years, you touched a myriad of lives in the most wonderful ways. You were a magnet that pulled people in. Once they interacted with you (and heard that extremely contagious laugh of yours) that was it, they were sucked into the Nadine Best forcefield and wanted to remain in it forever. You would attract random strangers at the grocery stores, in shopping malls . . . everywhere. People always wanted to talk to you and be around you. It was an extraordinary gift you had, Mom: your positive energy was incredible. You would light up any room you stepped into. You loved all of your family and friends so very much, and they definitely felt that love from you.

"Mom, for our family, you have always been a special source of power. You gave us the strength and belief in ourselves that we could achieve anything we put our minds to. You were our rock. We could always lean on and count on you to support us. You were always there to help us in any way possible. You were the glue that kept the family together over the years.

"You had a rare ability to be kind and full of love but at the same time, firm and tough. It was an impressive balance. Everyone loved you immensely, but people also knew not to mess with you, because Mama Best did not play or put up with any crap. You always spoke your mind and lived your life to the fullest, with such joy, integrity, honesty, sense of humor, and an overflowing amount of love.

"Tricia and I have learned a lot from you over the years. You taught us the importance of fully loving and respecting ourselves. You showed us what it meant to be mentally strong. You made it clear we should live life with love in our hearts, and we should judge people by the content of their character, not by the color of their skin. Growing up, you made sure we understood the reality and truth around us. You told us we would always have to work twice as hard as the next person because of the color of our skin. You were the strongest woman we have ever known.

"We will always love you, Mom, and we miss you. May your beautiful soul rest in peace."

SOUTH AFRICA

*Alana and Josephine enter the Apartheid Museum
through the 'whites' entrance, while Roland and Kymani
enter through the 'Non-whites' entrance*

Johannesburg

11 months, 1 week old

November 20–30

———◆•◆———

"It is white people's responsibility to be less fragile;
people of color don't need to twist themselves into
knots trying to navigate us as painlessly as possible."

—ROBIN DiANGELO

AFTER THE CELEBRATION OF LIFE, we had a choice: to
wrap up the year and stay in Canada or finish this last part of
our journey. We know Nadine would have been proud to see
us finish the journey we started, to live the best life we can,
and so we cancelled two destinations, Malta and India. With
grieving hearts and tears in our eyes, we made our way to the
third and final stop on our yearlong adventure.

We are sure if any place can fill our hearts and calm our
souls, it's Africa.

We arrive in Johannesburg at nine in the evening, but by the
time we go through all the motions, we arrive at our Airbnb close
to midnight. It's pitch dark, and I am nervous because everyone
has put the fear of God into us about safety in South Africa.

The residential neighborhood is ghostly quiet. Electrified
barbed wire runs atop the walls of the compound around the

house. The large front gate opens, and we move the car quickly into the driveway before it shuts behind us.

A man in simple beige pants, runners, and an old gray golf shirt greets us at the front door. Jeffrey introduces himself as the domestic help, and responsible for keeping the pristine appearance of the residence. With the help of outdoor lighting, he proudly shows us the immaculately-landscaped yard. He then tells us how to operate the security system, the keys, and the alarms. It's a fortress of a home.

Inside the house, African masks line the high walls like artistic crown molding. Leather couches and chairs are per-fectly positioned around a coffee table holding books about travel, photography, and art.

The kitchen's stainless-steel glistens next to a thick wood-topped island. A door off the back glimpses into another room, starkly plain in contrast to the kitchen where Jeffrey does his daily washing and ironing. His quarters are in a small residence behind it, hidden from view. He will always be around, tending to our needs. The main bedroom is grand, equipped with a table and reading area.

Everyone is exhausted from the long journey, but not tired because of the time change. We force ourselves to try and sleep and successfully do for about five hours. Kymani is having the worst go of it and will take him five days to acclimatized to our new time zone.

Everyone seems to have an opinion about South Africa, and Joburg in particular. Most warned us about the crime, and few had positive things to say about the city, preferring the coastal beauty of Cape Town and the Garden Route. I listen but prefer to make up my own mind. I am excited for the city to reveal itself to us, to tell us its stories and show us its culture.

✈

WHEN I STARTED THIS JOURNEY, I thought I might fall in love with another place and want to move. However, the opposite happened. I fell in love with home. I have never felt so deeply rooted. I know I want to live, raise my kids, and enjoy my life with Roland in Victoria. We will always travel but we will return to Canada. Our heart belongs there.

To represent this sentiment, a North American Spruce tree is being tattooed on my back. Roland booked us appointments at the only professional tattoo parlor in Joburg, owned by Black South Africans. They have patiently transformed my vision into art, and the needle has just begun piercing the image into my back.

The tattooed tree's roots run deep past a horizon depicted with heartbeats of my children. Across the sky four sparrows fly, one for each of us, in homage to our adventures and the many nights we've spent watching these elegant little birds swoop across the landscape at sunset.

On Roland's back are two elephants, an adult and a baby, from a picture he took while we were on safari, during a previous trip in Kenya. It was important for him to represent Africa as the place that keeps calling him back. Josephine and Kymani's initials are written in hieroglyphics, in reference to Egypt, home to his favorite monuments from this year's trip. He also pays tribute to Mandela, with a famous portrait of his face and fist. Soweto, where we sit in our tattoo chairs, is the township where Mandela lived, and we are here during the year of the Mandela 100 celebration. After the many reactions to the color of Roland's skin, it feels fitting to have this tattoo done at the end of our journey.

Halfway through my four hours in the chair, I need a bathroom break. I ask Josephine if she wants to come with me. She stares at me, her cheeks turn red, but she doesn't say anything. I get in close and ask her what's wrong.

The shared bathrooms are outside the building in a court-yard. She is worried she will be the only white person. I tell her it's important for us to know how that feels. It's what Roland deals with every day back home. She looks over at him and nods in agreement.

I have to admit, it's more uncomfortable than I expected. I feel eyes on us from every angle. It doesn't feel threatening, but it is unnerving. Neither of us is used to standing out like this. We are attracting a lot of attention, and I'm sure not everyone is happy to see us here.

When the artist finishes his work, Kymani has fallen asleep in Roland's arms and Josephine has finished her book. I'm worried about being here after dark, but the artists and owner kindly escort us through the courtyard, helping us carry our diaper bag, Pack 'n Play, and stroller to our car.

A lot of people look our way as we walk by. I am grateful for the entourage. As soon as we get to the car, I jump in the passenger seat, figuring it's best to get my white skin out of sight as soon as possible. Roland tips the man who watched our car for us, and we wave goodbye to the artists.

With every turn and stop of the car on our way out of Soweto I get more nervous. No, I'm more than nervous, I am scared. I've never felt so painfully aware of my skin color before. I feel betrayed by it as it shines in the darkness of the night.

When we finally hit the highway back to our white, gated, and highly secure suburb, I sigh in relief. I am comfortable in my skin again. I feel safe.

Guilt pours over me as I note this reaction. Was I in any real danger? Why was I so scared? Was it warranted?

I sink into my seat and my eyes well up with tears. Am I the bad guy in my own story? *Am I being racist?*

The word brings up terrible images in my mind—of Klu Klux Klan members spewing hatred, of burning crosses and lynchings, of mangled bodies. Of men, women, and children being stolen, traded, beaten, raped, tortured, and forced into agonizing manual labor. Of babies being used as bait, crying on the muddy banks of alligator-infested swamps. Of dogs viciously snarling and biting civil rights protesters, of batons raining down on their backs in clouds of tear gas. Of civilians murdered by police, meant to protect them.

I am not that. Nor am I like the person who wrote the N-word across my husband's car, or the group of young adults pointing and laughing at him in Asia. I am not in the same category as these people. Therefore I can't be racist. Right?

I believe in equality and have always had strong, liberal, progressive views. I grew up with a mother who spent years fighting for women's rights and a decade writing the first multiculturalism legislation in Canada. My youth was spent in close connection with an adopted Cree grandmother and I actively learned Cree culture. I have attended powwows, sweats, and peace pipe ceremonies. My parents, wanting to expose us to a wide variety of cultures and religions, took us to churches, synagogues, and temples.

My best friend in elementary school was of Nigerian heritage and I've been friends with countless people of color. I go to diversity training seminars, I join protests, I watch TED Talks and documentaries, I listen to podcasts and read books and I talk to friends and family.

I have absolved myself of being racist because I believe myself to be an open-minded, loving, moral human who actively engages with a diverse range of people.

Plus, I think as I continue to count the ways I can distance myself from racism, *I married a Black man and had a child with him. I love this man, I love our child, and I am a decent person.*

Isn't that enough proof?

No, it's not.

I realize this as a tear streams down my red cheek. Because if the equation of absolution by association were legitimate, then there would be no misogyny. Everyone has a woman in their life—a mother, grandmother, friend, daughter, partner, sister, aunt, cousin, coworker . . . somebody. Being friends with, engaging with, or having a relationship with people who fall into a marginalized category does not stop a person from being a misogynist or a racist.

The car is quiet. Kymani sleeps in the backseat and Josephine is plugged into a show on my phone. I look at Roland and offer a small smile, not wanting him to bear witness to the tsunami of realizations crashing down in my mind, destroying my previous assumptions. He smiles back quickly before returning his attention to the highway.

I am riddled with guilt and pain. I want to hide. I want to pull the covers over my head and wrap myself back into the easy, comfortable, and privileged mindset I had occupied only moments ago.

Am I a racist? I still can't bear to answer the question, though I suspect it's because I know the answer, and I don't like it.

I look out the window and let the tears flow. My stomach churns and skinks along with my bruised ego. If someone saw my son and was scared because of the color of his skin, I would be devastated and angry. This is the response I had to someone else's child only minutes ago in Soweto.

When we turn the last street corner before the house, I wipe my tears. I don't want to burden Roland with all I am thinking.

With the children asleep and Roland occupied on the computer in the bedroom, I grab a glass of water from the kitchen and burrow into the dark leather couch in the living room.

Despite the hurt, I dig deeper. There are much bigger things at stake than my feelings and my ego—how do I expect the world to become different for my children if I, their mother, can't get over herself long enough to do the work necessary?

It is important for me to admit what I have done and where I have gone wrong. It's going to hurt and it's going to be uncomfortable, but recognizing my own prejudices is part of the process of taking responsibility.

I begin by making a mental list of racist thoughts and acts I have committed or witnessed without intervention:

1. In my youth I used racist terms including "Indian giver."
2. I grew up loving 90's hip-hop and have definitely said the N-word while singing songs.
3. I didn't confront a close relative who told me it was "okay to marry a Black man" though they never felt the need to give me permission to marry my previous, white husband.
4. If I see a group of young Black men together I am nervous about walking past them. I tell myself it's because I'm vulnerable as a woman, but the same level of fear is not there if I pass a group of young white men.

I continue with this until I slump into a depressive state. My back hurts from the fresh tattoo, and my head pounds from emotional overload.

I go to the ensuite bathroom and look in the mirror for a long while. Roland appears behind me and kisses my cheek. I lift my shirt over my head, and he removes the plastic protective wrap from my back and gently cleans it.

I slip into bed and let my body and mind rest.

✈

I GET UP EARLY THE NEXT MORNING with Kymani and let Roland and Josephine sleep in. My back feels raw and tight. My eyes are red-rimmed and puffy. I swallow some pain medication with a large glass of water before covering my anguish with makeup.

Playing with Kymani on the floor is heart-wrenching. He deserves better from me and from the world than what presently lies ahead for him. All people of color do. I cannot give in to a self-indulgent state of regret, guilt, and self-persecution. I worry that if I do, it will take over and this will be the end of my growth.

I put my emotions aside and look at my situation objectively.

Nobody is born racist. My prejudices have been taught and I need to actively engage in educating myself to reorient and rewire how I think and respond.

I have been snow-blind: overexposed to whiteness for so long that I've experienced a complete loss of objective sight. But this does not need to be my permanent state. I chose in the past to ignore the racism that was right in front of me and even inside of me. I made excuses for it, I shrugged it off, and in doing so I protected myself and others who are similarly well-meaningly guilty.

I have made mistakes, but I need to figure out how to change. And I cannot continue to expect Roland to teach me everything, as he has consistently done this year. That's not fair. I need to do my own research, so I can be a stronger ally and start to strategically dismantle the racism embedded in our social systems, wherever and however I can.

South Africa's complex and difficult racial history makes it an ideal place to start my re-education.

This country has come out of a nightmare, and within the past twenty-five years, it has rebuilt a nation. It's not perfect, but the rate of progress is impressive. When Roland and Josephine wake up, we agree to spend a number of days dedicated to visiting historical sites and museums that will help us better understand the history of the deeply racist and segregated times of apartheid. In the evenings I watch documentaries and read articles in a way I didn't before. My heart and mind are open. I drink it all in, like someone who has crossed the desert and discovered an oasis.

✈

TODAY, WE MEET OUR TOUR GUIDE at the Hector Pieterson Memorial. Hector was twelve when he was shot, in 1976, during a peaceful protest. He became famous when a journalist took a picture of a boy carrying his limp body, his sister running beside him. It was published all over the world and became a symbol of the uprising.

"I was scared," the woman standing in front of us says in an even tone, the passion in her voice worn away with the countless times she has re-told this story, like a shard of glass tossed in the tides and smashed by the sand over and over until it's smooth and glazed, beach glass.

Our guide continues, "I saw blood coming out of the side of his mouth. I kept telling the man carrying him, 'I am his sister, what are you doing with him, where are you taking him?' But the man kept running with my brother in his arms, not answering any of my questions. I ran beside them."

I look over to the iconic photograph blown up beside us. I can't believe it. Is the woman standing in front of me really Antoinette, Hector's sister, the sister in the photograph? I look at Roland to gauge his expression, but he is focused on her story.

"When the man finally said, 'He is dead,' I was torn in two. He was so young, too young to even really understand what was going on. How was he now dead?"

It is her.

After Antoinette finishes telling the story of the day that changed her entire life, she leads us to the museum named after her brother. She has dedicated her life since that fateful day to ensuring that his story lives on. She has been a keynote speaker at conferences around the world, and when she is home, she is a freelance tour guide.

She shows us the museum exhibits, recounting honestly and openly the events leading up to the march, and the outcomes of that fateful day. The tragedy of her brother's unnecessary death created a global outcry. People from around the world mourned with Antoinette and her family, demanding change. Although it took years, Hector's death was a pivotal turning point in South Africa's fight for equality. Antoinette feels that her brother's death was not in vain.

I can't help but feel angry, hurt, and ashamed as she tells us about the trials she and her fellow South Africans have been through. I wish the world had done more to help, to make things right. With every explanation and story she tells, I see how much she has endured in her life. She has witnessed this country transform. Her life is an inspiring tale of courage, sacrifice, and love.

"Many people died," she says, tilting her head to the sky. "Innocent people. People died in worse ways than my brother, tortured for days before being executed. Others had to live through torment, imprisoned, like Madiba." She stops and looks at us to see if we understand who she is talking about, using Nelson Mandela's clan name. We nod, urging her to continue.

"The symbol of apartheid could have been any of those people," she says. "My brother just happened to die in front of a journalist."

Her modesty doesn't stop me from putting her brother in my mental book of heroes, right beside Nelson Mandela and Desmond Tutu. But I understand her desire to convey how many unsung heroes contributed to the cause. Their names should be in my hero book too. The changes made by this country were accomplished through countless small and monumental tasks by many, many people.

Antoinette rides in the passenger seat of our rental car as we drive to the former residences of Nelson Mandela and Desmond Tutu. On our way, she points to the school she attended during the time of the demonstration in 1976. She takes us through the streets the students marched down, and to the intersection where her brother was shot. It's hard to imagine how these quiet streets were once the scenes of such a horrific event.

The honor of being toured around all day by Antoinette is just sinking in by the time we drive her home at the end of the day. It is deeply touching and meaningful to hear from someone who has lived through the apartheid, the revolution, and the aftermath. The lack of animosity and amount of forgiveness she shows is admirable. She tells us that it's only with this love-forward attitude that the nation can rebuild. Without someone deciding to stop the hateful cycle, the fighting never ends; it simply re-shapes itself into an ever-bigger beast that will consume everything in its path.

✈

WE DON'T WANT TO SPEND ALL our time in Joburg learning from the past; we also want to celebrate what it has to offer today. We take a graffiti tour, enjoying the local street art and meeting artists who are passionate about their city, and visit a number of markets, buying a few pieces to take home with us.

Today, we're at a trendy food market. We enter what looks like a large warehouse where the light hum of a busy crowd and the spicy smell of paella frying fills the air. Vendors line the perimeter walls selling an assortment of savory foods, sweet desserts, and tantalizing drinks.

The shared tables in the center are packed with friends and families, elbow to elbow, delving into the alluring food, drinks, and people-watching. The young, racially diverse patrons are glamorous in their trendy brunch attire.

It's a tiny exemplar of Mandela's dream of a rainbow nation: people of many different races coming together on a Sunday afternoon to share food and laugh with friends and loved ones. Not one skin color dominates the scene and no specific race serves the food or eats the food. I smile, taking it in, hoping this vibe spreads through businesses, across social classes, and throughout neighborhoods.

"I love Joburg," I say as I drive us home.

"Me too," Roland smiles. "There's a great energy here. A resilient, lively spirit."

"It has everything I love as a tourist: lovely people, beautiful art, rich history, interesting neighborhoods, and local authenticity. I'll hold a fond place in my heart for Joburg."

"I'd love to return one day and see how it continues to transform. You know what's weird, though? I expected to see a lot more biracial couples. There's much more integration than there was, I'm sure, but there's a lot of segregation still."

"Yeah, like the white suburbs we are staying in versus Soweto . . ."

"My stomach hurts," Josephine interrupts from the backseat. I adjust my rearview mirror to see if I can get a look at her.

"Are you okay, sweetie?" Roland asks, turning to face her.

There's a pause. Then I hear the unmistakable sound of vomit spewing out of her mouth. I turn to Roland. He looks like he is witnessing a real-life scene from *The Exorcist* as white, beige, and pink chunks hit the side of his face and the front dashboard. Little pings of it hit the back of my head.

"Oh my," Roland says. "Jo, are you okay? Babe, you need to give us some warning and cover your mouth. Wow, this is a lot. Are you okay?"

Jo isn't talking; the silence is interrupted with some heaving before another audible flow escapes from her wrenching stomach.

"What should I do?" I ask Roland, trying to keep focused on the busy highway.

"You have to pull over. Kymani is covered in vomit. It's everywhere."

Parked on the side of the highway, I take the kids out of the car. We use an entire package of baby wipes to scrape the chunks off the inside-ceiling and get the liquid out of the cracks in the seats.

I make a habit of always having a change of clothes for Kymani and me everywhere we go, just in case. Josephine tries her best to hide between the car door, the car, and me holding up a baby blanket as she changes into my clothes. She looks pale and gray, her eyes red from tears, and her hair is high-lighted with greasy streaks from the vomit. I find some Pepto tablets in my purse and give them to her. I wipe her eyes and her hair, stroking her gently and hugging her long and deep, though she smells like a rancid strawberry shake.

Kymani spots a giraffe on safari

Kruger National Park

11 months, two weeks old
November 30–December 7

———◆•◆———

"The eye never forgets what the heart has seen."
—African Proverb

THE ELEPHANTS STAMPEDE FORWARD, frightened. Dust fills the hot dry air as the herd runs with surprising speed across the road in front of us roaring a loud symphony of trumpets as they lift their trunks and flap their ears. A mom looks down at her calf, ensuring it's close by, and then turns her attention behind her to the road. They trumpet again, shaking their heads as they move off quickly.

"What has them so scared?" Josephine asks with a high-pitched, frightened voice. She leans forward from the backseat of our (thoroughly cleaned) rental vehicle so her face is beside ours as we all stare out the front windshield. It's Josephine's eleventh birthday this week, and we've been celebrating it with self-guided and professionally guided safari tours. Today, we are in our own car at the famous Kruger National Park.

"I should have bought that extra car insurance," I joke, trying to break the tension. Roland and Josephine ignore me, continuing to scan the scene for more clues as to what's going on. Kymani coos with excitement in his car seat. I swallow nervously, acutely aware that we are in their park, on the animals' turf, and things could quickly go sideways.

"It's the rangers, look." Roland is pointing to a green Jeep speeding toward us on the dirt road. In it are six rangers armed with high-power rifles.

"Why are they scared of them? Aren't they supposed to protect the animals?" Asks Josephine, confused and scared.

"Maybe they're scared of the guns, or maybe they're startled by how fast the Jeep is moving," I suggest, but I'm unsure myself why these intelligent creatures would be petrified of the National Park guards.

South Africa has a serious poaching problem. Rhinos have been especially targeted for their horns, which are sold predominantly in Asian countries where they use them in traditional Chinese medicine and as status symbols displaying success and wealth.

"Is that car driving into the elephants' path?" Roland is pointing to a small blue car with tourists inside. They're taking pictures of the herd, which is headed straight toward them.

"The elephant is trying to warn him, what is he doing?" Josephine's insight amazes me, especially when it comes to her beloved animals. "That elephant is clearly still upset, she will charge!" she shrieks, pointing wide-eyed at the naive tourists.

"I honestly can't watch this," I say. "Let's get out of here. I don't want to be stuck in an elephant's path should they decide to come back this way." I lurch the car around and down the dirt road.

We arrived at the park when it opened at 6:30 a.m. and do not plan on leaving until supper. Roland and I take turns driving the car while the other navigates. Kymani sits in his car seat next to Josephine in the back. Together, we squeal with excitement every time we encounter giraffes, zebras, hippopotamuses, crocodiles, warthogs, and various antelope.

In the week we have explored this vast park, luck has been on our side. We've seen four of the Big Five: water buffalos by the watering holes and traveling together in large herds; elephants walking through the bushes, crossing the roads, and drinking down by the water; a large lion pride lazily warming themselves in the sun, napping away the morning; and, a leopard high in a tree, sleeping next to his kill, which dangled from the branches.

The only Big Five animal we haven't yet seen is a rhino. It was the same when we visited Kenya, four years previous: we saw lots of wild animals, but no rhinos.

Today is our last day on safari and we have been searching for rhinos for six hours. We make a pit stop for lunch at one of the camps, where we find a sightseeing board marked with the animals that have been spotted today by other tourists. Due to the poaching issues, postings of rhino sightings are prohibited. We put our findings on the map and talk to other guides and tourists about their encounters. Nobody has seen any rhinos today.

I wipe the dust from my sunglasses and rewrap my hair in a stiff scarf that keeps the sand and dust at bay. Roland pushes Kymani in his stroller and Josephine grabs my hand as we walk to the gift shop. Inside, Josephine finds some bracelets and shows them to me, which is her way of asking if she can have one. The proceeds go toward anti rhino–poaching efforts.

"Maybe they'll give us good luck," she says. "Remember when we bought the lion stuffy, and we saw a lion pride right after? Maybe it will happen again."

"Okay, sure. Let's give it a shot." Either way, I'm willing to put five dollars toward a good cause. "We need all the luck we can get."

At lunch, we pull out the maps and guidebooks and strategize our route for the afternoon.

"We haven't been here yet," I say, indicating a road that runs along the eastern side of the park. "From here we could follow the road to the south gate. We'd get there before it closes at four-thirty, but we'd have an almost two-hour drive from the gate back to our place." I look at Roland and Josephine to see if they're willing to commit to the long day.

Roland nods, "Sure."

"Okay," Jo agrees. "Where are we going to eat supper though?" I snicker; kids' priorities are so different to ours.

"Why don't we pick up some snacks at the shop here to keep us going through the afternoon, and we'll make supper when we get back home. We have frozen pizzas at the house. Does that work?"

Jo smiles in satisfaction.

We set out for the afternoon, feeling like real explorers. Kymani has his blue jungle hat on. Josephine has binoculars in one hand and her animal field guide in the other. Roland has our bags of snacks and drinks. I have our trusty maps, a guidebook, and a plan.

We drive slowly, eyes peeled for signs of wildlife. A group of cars is gathered ahead of us, pulled over to the side of the road: a sure sign of something interesting. We wait our turn behind the last car, looking around to see what the fuss is about.

"Oh wow, it's a huge pride of lions!" Roland says, straining his neck to look over the cars in front of him.

We make our way to the front of the line and can't believe how close they are to us. A few feet off the side of the road, a half-dozen female lions and a large male are lying under the trees. Once in a while one of them will extend a leg and flex its paw, then lift its head lazily with half-opened eyes to survey the cars before closing them again.

An hour later, we get out at a lookout point over a river to stretch our legs. I take in a long inhale of the dry, hot, African air as we walk onto the gated veranda. An elephant is whisking water from its trunk onto its back in the river below. Close by, a hippopotamus lingers near the surface of the water. Kingfishers fly by, showing off their flashy blue wings.

Behind us, a family of warthogs goes trotting by, tails propped high in the air. "Pumba!" Josephine exclaims as she watches them go by.

This couldn't get any more amazing.

We drive along a stretch of road with little traffic. The dry, semi-arid landscape has low bushes and few trees, making it easy to scan for wildlife, however it has been scarce. Suddenly, the landscape changes. Large bushes appear as if from nowhere. They're thick, and it's hard to see through them so I slow down. Roland is in the backseat keeping a lookout while also entertaining Kymani. Josephine has given up and is reading her wildlife book.

I hit the brakes and reverse. "I think I saw something." Everyone jumps to attention, faces an inch from the glass, eyes scanning back and forth. "Right there, do you see it? Is it a rhino?"

A big mammal makes its way through the bushes, walking parallel to the road with another smaller one behind it. I'm looking for a horn to confirm what I'm seeing, but the bush is thick. Then they come into a small clearing. Fifteen feet in front of us is an adult rhino and its calf.

We erupt into cheers, clapping and giving each other high-fives before quieting back down to watch.

Roland pulls his camera out and is snapping pictures rapidly. I inch the car forward to an advantageous angle and take a video as the rhinos walk by. There are *two* adults and a calf making their way triumphantly through the bush. Although we have seen them in *National Geographic* magazines, in documentaries, and at the zoo, there is nothing like seeing these animals in the wild.

The sky shifts, dark clouds cover the sun, and it starts pouring rain. The animals disappear when the rain starts, and we have accomplished our goal of seeing the Big Five, so we take the most direct road out of the park. Lightning flashes in a long vertical streak far in front of us, followed by the loud clatter of thunder. We stop on a bridge to take in the lightning storm erupting against the African landscape.

"Before we go into the house, do you want to go see the hippos?" I ask. The resort has a hippo sanctuary and a lookout point. They should be coming out of the water soon, getting ready to graze in the evening.

"Yes!" Josephine exclaims from the passenger seat.

Roland agrees with a nod as he continues to coo and play with Kymani. As I leave the park, I'm careful to watch for oncoming traffic from the highway we merge onto. I see an opening and accelerate hard to insure a seamless integration. Lights flash behind me and a siren sounds. Police.

Shit.

I pull over slowly, instructing Josephine to grab the registration from the glove box and Roland to get my international driver's license from my backpack on the floor of the backseat.

A tall, muscular Black officer saunters confidently up to my window.

I scramble in the glove box to find the registration Josephine can't locate. I'm a little flustered—but is it genuine, or the well-rehearsed scene I perform semi-subconsciously whenever I have an encounter with the police? The truth is, I know if I am sweet, kind, and slightly frazzled there's a high chance of me walking away without a ticket.

"Hi!" I say with a charming smile.

He frowns, then looks at the other passengers in the car. Shit, already this is not going well; he's looking at me like I'm an annoying wad of gum stuck to the bottom of his shoe. When he sees Roland, he perks up and asks him something in what I assume is Zulu.

"Good evening officer," Roland responds in an even, respectful voice. "Sorry, we are from Canada, we only speak English."

Roland has his hands visible on his lap. This is one of the

rules he learned growing up from his parents when they gave him the talk about how to conduct himself around the police. He was told to one, make sure your hands are visible at all times, two, speak calmly, politely, and respectfully to the officer, three, do not under any circumstance get into a disagreement with the officer, four, do not make any sudden movements, and five, if you need to get something, ask permission first.

"I have my license and registration," I offer in a kind voice with a slight quiver.

The officer ignores me and continues talking to Roland. "Where are you going?"

"We are coming from Kruger National Park, and we are on our way to our accommodations in Hazyview."

"Who are they?" The officer asks, gesturing to Josephine, Kymani, and I. "What is your relation?"

"This is my wife, and these are my children."

The officer looks at Josephine's barely tanned white skin and light brown hair, streaked blond with the sun.

The officer looks confused and tries again. "Are you all right sir, is everything okay?"

"Yes officer, I am fine," Roland says, a bit surprised. "We are all from Canada, we are a family. We are heading back to our villa."

"Do you know why I pulled you over?" He continues to address Roland. Shouldn't he be asking the driver this question?

"No officer."

"She ran a stop sign," he says, gesturing to me but continuing to look Roland in the eyes.

"I apologize, sir."

"There is a fine for this. Do you have any cash?"

"No sir, we do not. Is it possible for us to pay the ticket online, or at the station tomorrow?"

"Yes, you can pay at the station tomorrow," he says writing in his notebook.

I can't remember the last time I actually got a ticket. I'm always let off with a warning. As a white woman, *my* biggest fear when pulled over by the police: I get the traffic ticket I likely deserve.

The officer and Roland continue to chat. I'm not even listening to what they're saying anymore; I'm annoyed about getting the ticket.

". . . you know what sir," the officer says to Roland, "I am going to let you off with a warning this time. In the future, be careful to obey all street signs."

"Yes sir, we will. Thank you, sir. Have a great day," Roland replies.

The officer nods his head to Roland and walks away. I carefully roll up the window all the way before I speak.

"What just happened?"

"I think, for the first time in history, my skin color was helpful in dealing with the police."

I try not to laugh, but a grunt sneaks out. I start the car, turn on my signal light, and carefully merge into traffic. I am extra cautious the rest of the way back to the villa.

We arrive at the hippo sanctuary, within the compounds of the villa, as the sun sets.

I take Kymani in my arms and shelter us from the rain under my umbrella. We walk briskly across the resort's golf course to the main lookout point, where a thatched roof protects the perfect vantage point, facing the water. The river is filled with hippopotamuses, all making their way toward the short sandy shoreline. They communicate with each other in grumbling and gurgling calls, and by blowing bubbles under the surface of the water. One large hippo opens its mouth impossibly wide and slams it shut on the water.

The gray, cloudy sky releases rain over the river. We squint to see the hippos in the dimness; flashes of lightning break the darkness for fleeting moments, giving us glimpses of the massive animals. Slowly, the first hippo hefts itself out of the water onto the sandy bank, climbing leisurely but effortlessly into the bush by way of a well-trod path. One by one, they heave themselves out of the water and follow the trail. I watch in amazement.

Kymani's one-year-old birthday shot
with the penguins at Boulders Beach

Cape Town

1 year old

December 13

———●·●———

"New beginnings are often disguised as painful endings"

—LAO TZU

AFRICAN PENGUINS LAZE ON the beach and between the rocks at Boulders Beach. We watch them dive into the water like mini-torpedoes, fast and efficient. It's Kymani's first birthday. If we were back in Canada, we would have a smash cake and invite friends and family over to celebrate. We would decorate with streamers and balloons and people would buy him a bundle of toys. A small part of me misses these traditional normalcies.

Josephine returns from exploring the boulders along the shoreline, jumping up and down and waving at me excitedly. "Mom, Roland, you have to come see this, there are a *ton* of penguins!"

I cover up with a rash guard to protect my tattoo from the sun and crawl through the tunnel in the rocks behind her. Roland takes Kymani out of the carrier, and we pass him to each other as we climb up and down the boulders. Kymani splashes with glee as we wade through the ocean, and then a small opening between the boulders appears, revealing a spotless beach filled with penguins laying in the sun.

We sit Kymani carefully on the sand next to his ONE-YEAR-OLD sign to snap a picture of him with the penguins in the background. Some of them are sleek, while others are still molting, with funny patches of fluffy feathers sticking out in random patterns.

Josephine and I sing "Baby Shark" to get Kymani to smile. The catchy tune along with our exaggerated expressions and hand gestures get him going every time. Roland snaps several pictures before giving us the thumbs-up, telling us he's got it. The last monthly birthday picture is complete!

There are hundreds of penguins gathered on a rock not far from us. We sit on the beach watching them dip into the ocean, swim by us, and bound out of the water. The sun is warm but not too hot, and a cool breeze is blowing off the water. There's no cake or gifts, but it doesn't matter. This is the coolest first birthday ever.

✈

JOSEPHINE, WE'VE DECIDED, IS OLD enough and mature enough to watch her brother for a few hours in the morning. She has been with us every day all day for the past six months, helping us make bottles, change diapers, and entertain him. She's agreed to take care of him while we go on an early-morning, shark cage diving adventure. I am not totally sure about it, sharks kind of freak me out. However, this is a must-do for Roland, so I rally.

We leave the house early in the morning with a dozen other tourists in a small two-decker speedboat. It's windy and cold, so Roland and I huddle in our sweaters in the boat's cabin. I'm not one to get seasick, but the small boat is bouncing up and down heavily and I'm not feeling awesome. My stomach is in knots as we splash over the waves. Roland hands me a juice box and an empathetic look. The drink makes me feel instantly better.

"Come outside," Roland encourages. "Some fresh air might help."

Most of the other tourists are on the top deck, taking in the view and enjoying the sun. Roland sits me on a small bench on the lower deck at the back of the boat. I close my eyes and take a deep breath. I let the cool ocean air fill my lungs. I open my eyes and continue to concentrate meditatively on my breath.

We arrive at the shark-infested bay and the boat slows down. *Thank goodness,* I think, closing my eyes and taking a few more deep breaths, glad to be still, even if we are surrounded by sharks. My eyes jut open at the stinging stench—a crewmember is smashing fish guts in a bucket and mixing it with seawater. He pours the bloody mixture overboard slowly as the boat trawls through the ocean.

"That smell is going to make me throw up," I say to Roland, holding my breath as I scurry back into the cabin.

After thirty minutes with no action, the captain explains that seeing sharks here has been a challenge recently. The sharks have been attacked by orcas, which the crew believes has made them move on. Shark finning has also played a catastrophic role in the depletion of shark populations. The sickening practice entails cutting off the sharks' fins and leaving them in the ocean to drown or die of starvation because they are then unable to move. The shark fins are sold to make shark fin soup, a Chinese delicacy once served to royalty and nobility and now sought after as a symbol of wealth and status.

An hour passes and I'm worried we might be out of luck, though the crew doesn't stop trying. "Fifteen more minutes," the captain declares, "then we'll have to go back. I'm sorry. There's another group waiting to come out."

Fifteen minutes later, I claim a seat outside and prepare myself with layers of clothes, water, and juice, for the gut-wrenching ride back.

"Shark!" one of the crew yells, pointing into the water beyond the back of the boat. The entire crew races around, prepping the cage, pouring more fish guts into the water, and grabbing a giant tuna head attached to a rope which they splash in the water.

Roland strips off his clothes, getting ready to jump into the cage with three fellow enthusiasts.

"When I tell you to go down, go under the water and you'll see the shark swim by," a crewmember tells them.

I rush to the top deck to take pictures and videos as Roland is lowered into the cage, ready to watch the shark from the water. He waves up at me excitedly.

It's a small great white shark, only a child. The shark is young enough (and ignorant enough) to be curious about the boat and come see what's going on. A crewmember splashes the tuna head in the water, and the shark bounds out of the water to try and catch it, circling the cage and the side of the boat, its fin grazing the surface of the water. He is a magnificent and menacing-looking creature, and our proximity and his age make us fonder of him than I would ever have anticipated.

THE FOLLOWING DAY WE HAVE A boat ride planned for Robben Island, which held Nelson Mandela prisoner for eighteen years. The thought of getting on another boat makes me instantly queasy. It's much less windy today than yesterday, and I imagine the ferry is much bigger and more stable, so I persevere and load my bag with extra water, juice, and snacks to help ease my stomach if it decides to get fussy.

The boat ride is smooth, and I feel relatively well on our

way there, though I'm still feeling a bit off. I must have caught a bug on the plane from Joburg to Cape Town and do my best to avoid sharing it with Josephine, Kymani, and Roland.

By the time we get back to Cape Town I'm still not feeling great, but I'm starving. We find a local pub, and I order the biggest thing I see on the menu, a giant burger and fries. Roland's calamari and shrimp dish arrives and the smell and look of it is revolting.

What is going on with me? Then, in a flash, it all comes together.

✈

THE TWENTY FOOT–HIGH, FLOOR-to-ceiling windows of our penthouse suite look over Cape Town and the famous Table Mountain. A cold wind is blowing through the city, but we are comfortably perched on the patio, at the raw-wood table, covered with big, knitted blankets and seated on soft outdoor pillows.

Kymani is sleeping and Josephine is watching a documentary in the living room.

Roland pours two glasses of champagne and hands me one. My stomach is queasy, and a little anxious. *I need to tell Roland.* The clouds roll off the top of the mountain and cascade into the pink and purple sky.

"Cheers, to another glorious day in Africa!" Roland smiles and clinks my glass before returning his gaze to the stunning view.

I haven't been myself lately, tired and grumpy. He's going to notice something isn't right if I don't tell him. I'm not worried, just nervous. I want it to be the right time, the right moment. It will be a relief to say it out loud; I won't feel like I have to soldier through it on my own any longer.

"This has been my favorite place of the year," Roland sighs, taking in the view. "I love South Africa."

"It has been incredible," I say, chickening out and not saying what I really want to say. *Stop overthinking it and tell him.*

"It's the wildlife, the culture, the history, everything."

"Plus the food scene in Cape Town doesn't hurt," I agree. *You're stalling!*

No, I'm just not interrupting the current conversation.

I roll my eyes. *Great, now I'm arguing with myself.*

"Right? That seafood restaurant—that burger joint in the garage—and that coffee shop, that was awesome."

Okay, enough is enough. "Baby," I say in a tone that means I have something I need to talk about.

"What's up?" he says looking at me.

"I have one more toast to make." We lift our glasses. I pause. He patiently waits for me. I take a deep breath. I feel like I'm going to throw up. "We're having another baby."

"Oh! What!?" He puts down his glass to give me a giant hug. He pulls back and puts his hands on my shoulders and looks at me. He's ecstatic. "Are you sure? How long have you known?"

"I'm over a week late, I'm never that late, but it's not just that. I can feel it. I'm tired and nauseous all the time. Some smells are completely revolting, my patience is short, and I have to make a conscious effort to not be grumpy. I'm a hundred percent sure."

He picks up his glass again and we toast. We hug, kiss, and talk about the future.

AFTERWORD

"I am not the same having seen the moon shine on the other side of the world."

—Mary Anne Radmacher Hershey

IF IT IS TRUE THAT WE ARE ABLE to look down from heaven with the opportunity to choose our parents, Nadine would have been instrumental in our baby girl's decision. In the brief month between Nadine being lifted up and our baby girl descending, they would have talked, shared stories, laughed, and fallen in love. It would have been Nadine who convinced her we were the ones. And our baby girl, seeing Nadine's spirit in us, surely chose to help mend our fragmented hearts and souls, still hurting with Nadine's passing.

We had a family tradition, with Nadine, to plant flowers every spring. Nadine sending down our daughter tells us that even though she's gone, she's still planting flowers with us. We named our precious baby girl Sydahlia. The dahlia flower symbolizes diversity, grace, and the inner strength to stand up for one's values. Her middle name is Nadine, in honor of her grandmother's memory.

This was the most incredible year, but it has also been heartbreaking and challenging. We met with so much kindness

Sydahlia Nadine Standish Best
Photo credit: Lindsay, Tails and Wings Photography

and experienced a disappointing amount of racial and gender-based prejudice. We discovered greater depths of inner strength, and I awoke to my own prejudices. We shared breathtaking experiences and quality time, and were reminded, with Ed's stroke and Nadine's passing, that time is not guaranteed. We will not always have these beautiful days to share with each other.

Sydahlia brings us renewed love and hope in the way only children can. We are delighted that she came to us on our trip, and happy to return home, a family, complete.

Roland and Alana with giraffes in Uganda

NOTE TO THE READER

———•—

"What counts in life is not the mere fact that we have lived. It is what difference we have made to the lives of others that will determine the significance of the life we lead."

—NELSON MANDELA

THE PAGES YOU HAVE JUST FINISHED reading have captured a year that changed our lives forever.

I am Roland Best, partner of this book's author, Alana Best. Even though I'm introducing myself for the first time, it feels like you know a lot about me and my family. I was blessed to have been raised by the most incredible mom, pops, and big sister (Trishy). They loved me unconditionally, constantly supporting and encouraging me, which helped build my strength, confidence, and resilience. They fostered my incredible pride in being Black, and as a result, I have always loved my beautiful dark skin.

In my adulthood, I thought I was doing my part in the fight against racism and building awareness where I could. But early on during our 2018 adventure, I realized I was not doing enough, even in my own home. This was evident when I realized the racist occurrences we encountered were surprising for Alana—when it became clear that she didn't realize the extent of racism and how painful and far-reaching it was.

I'm used to racist treatment. I expect it at airports, with their "random" security checks. For me, it is a regular and normal occurrence for security guards to follow me in stores, museums, and art galleries. However, this year of travel put me in new situations which, in turn, offered me new ways of experiencing racism. Beyond being on the receiving end of intense stares, I would also be pointed and laughed at. This level of racism, so overt, was something I was unaccustomed to.

The quantity and frequency of racist acts we experienced during our travels helped Alana understand the extent to which racism exists, and also how real and powerful her white privilege is. She witnessed, constantly, the differences between how she and I were treated, strictly based on the color of our skin. These experience-based lessons were impactful. It is important for all white North Americans to acknowledge the realities of racism—but it is even more crucial that Alana gain this understanding because she is raising Black children.

When we returned home from our 2018 journey, there was an intense fire burning inside both me and Alana. We didn't have a specific plan, but we knew we needed to do a lot more to help build awareness and do all we could to help fight racism. Then, as if the universe hadn't already been clear enough, in 2019 someone wrote the N-word in two places on my car in massive letters. Seeing those words written across my car, which was sitting right in front of my house, was extremely painful—especially because I had my sixteen-month-old son, Kymani, in my arms. It set in motion my new direction and life mission and intensified my fire to make changes. The individual(s) who wrote on my car have no clue the power they gave me. My "Car Story" is one I frequently share to educate those who don't have to face racism firsthand. It demonstrates the pain of racism, and the fact that it happens in your community, to people you know and care about.

After the car incident I began speaking out about my truths

and lived experiences to amplify the voices of racialized people. I focused on building awareness and creating important and difficult conversations. I have done this on every platform possible—blog posts at my work, numerous podcasts, and panels on webinars and at events. I also teamed up with a colleague to cocreate the Black, Indigenous, People of Colour (BIPOC) Employee Resource Group (ERG) for the BC Government, which now has more than 300 members. This provides a safe space for BIPOC government workers to come together. I moved into an Anti-Racism Manager position and created anti-racism training. Following that role, I moved into an Executive Director, Multiculturalism, and Anti-Racism position, in which I was part of the team that helped shape North America's first Anti-Racism Data Act (ARDA) and am currently leading work on a broader Anti-Racism Act. This legislation will create the strategy and action required to address and dismantle the systemic racism that is identified through ARDA. Along with those two bills, my incredible team and I lead multiculturalism and anti-racism grants and awards programs to help support and celebrate those that are doing great anti-racism work in their communities.

Alana, fueled by the experiences of our year of travels and supported by the countless books she has read, courses she has taken, and talks she has attended since, also uses her voice at every opportunity she gets. She acts as a strong ally when racialized people don't have a voice at the decision-making table or in the room of power. Alana worked on modernizing policies to change BC's Police Act after the George Floyd murder. More recently, she has created two senior-level roles at her organization that are fully dedicated to equity, diversity, and inclusion work. She sponsors large events and fosters important conversations in boardrooms. She continuously educates herself and builds awareness among her network on racism and white privilege. I am incredibly proud of the

courage and stamina it took Alana to lay bare, in full vulnerability, her learnings and journey with all of you in this novel.

Our dedication to anti-racism initiatives started here, from
the powerful experiences that we shared during our epic year
of traveling in 2018.

I hope our story sparks your soul and ignites action
within you. Combating racism can feel like an impossible,
overwhelming task—but like a pebble tossed in a pond, each
anti-racism action can create a ripple effect among family,
friends, colleagues, and strangers. Every small action can grow
into something bigger, building more awareness and creating
change that makes a real difference in this world.

ACKNOWLEDGMENTS

———————◆•◆———————

THIS NOVEL WAS FIVE YEARS in the making. Like a child, it was shaped, supported, and ultimately raised by a loving community.

My warmth and light, Roland Best. First, Thank you for documenting our adventure through your stunning photography, of which helped me construct this memoir. You are the reason this book exists. Thank you for feeding my adventurous soul, appreciating my intellectual pursuits, and supporting my creative endeavors all while making me feel like the most important, strong, and talented person in the world. You filled my heart, which gave me the resilience I needed to publish our story. I never knew life or love could be this grand, thank you for our wonderful life and incredible family. I'm so fortunate to be able to adventure through life with the likes of you, I can't wait for our next chapter.

Josephine, thank you for helping to inspire this trip and for constantly making me a better person. Roland and I love and appreciate your flexibility, help and understanding as our family has changed and grown. Thanks for being such a fun, brilliant and entertaining travel partner. You made us laugh frequently and kept our spirits light. We appreciate your old soul, your natural introspective nature, your thoughtfulness of others and your sense of humor. You make traveling with children easy—thank you for being you.

Kymani, the moment I met you, I fell in love with you and have been captivated ever since. Without you, this adventure would have never been the same. You inspired us to travel and have in turn motivated so many others to take their own journeys. Your beautiful smile and easygoing nature made this year fun, rewarding and joyful. You had everyone we encountered on this journey singing your praises. I hope you continue to enchant, inspire, and motivate people well into your future, the way you did us, and all the people you met along the way.

Sydahlia, you are a precious gift to us. You came into our world at the exact time we needed you most. Thanks for being a gem of a child and for completing this big, beautiful family of ours. I have no doubt your fiery yet caring, and fierce yet kind spirit will have us continually amazed as you grow. We look forward to future adventures with you (thanks in advance for your support in these constant endeavors). I am honored to be your mom and grateful for the wealth of joy, love, and energy you bring to our lives every day.

My parents showed me how to take life by the hand on a perfect summer day and run off the dock into the crisp, clear Canadian lake. They showed me the meaning of life right from the start by teaching me how to live a full life through enjoying the work as much as the play and taking pleasure in the simple things as much as the extravagant ones.

My father, Aurèle Morrissette, did not live to see this book printed, but he was one of the first to read an early draft. Thank you for championing my every move and for always believing in me. My heart aches that I am not celebrating this moment with you. Thank you for your endless support and for showing me what unconditional love is.

Mom, thank you for instilling in me a deep intellectual curiosity, for teaching me how a woman should be treated in all aspects of her life, and demonstrating that unrealistic goals ~~can~~ will be accomplished with determination, fight, and passion. I'm so grateful to have been raised in Saskatchewan under those enormous, wild skies. It taught me how to work hard, be humble, help your neighbor, be generous with whatever you can offer and always be kind.

Miguel Morrissette, my big brother, who always managed to find that right balance between loving me and calling me out on my shit, for believing in me and telling me what I was doing wasn't enough. You have always pushed me and keep raising the bar. Billie-Jo Morrissette, my sister-in-law, thank you for believing that I could write this book, and that my voice and these stories were worthy of the printed page.

Charlotte Schriml, my spark of a sister. Nobody knows me the way that you do, and I am forever grateful that you always use that bond to ground me, or lift me up, exactly when I need it. You are what keeps our family together, in a loving and compassionate state. I am forever grateful for the energy you have made to support our relationships and us as individuals. Ben Schriml, my brother-in-law, thank you for the many times you held down the fort and gave us the gift of sister time including our Greece adventure.

Katherine McCannel, my beloved baby sister. Your creative, thoughtful, hilarious, and brilliant being frequently has me in awe. You're gentle, kind nature is exactly what this family needs, especially me. Thank you for sticking with me through the ups and downs. Colin McCannell, my brother-in-law, thank you for being an early supporter of my writing venture, for reading the way-to-long first draft and providing such kind, considerate and supportive feedback.

Nadine, your force was so powerful it will echo in the hearts of our family for generations to come. We miss you every day. Ed, Tricia, Brian, Jamal and Jalen—your kindness, warmth, generous spirits and loving nature has had a profound impact on my life, and I am forever grateful that I and our children get to be a part of this exceptional family.

Kim, Kristine, and Rachelle—you are my closest and dearest friends and have been in my corner for as long as I can remember. Thank you for always acting as if this book was already a done deal long before it was and instilling that undeniable belief that it would be accomplished. It helped me stay strong and keep fighting. Kim—my best friend, my fellow adventurer, my rock. The love and friendship we share runs deep like sisters and I am grateful to have such an incredibly vibrant and caring soul in my life. Thank you for swooping into my life in Spain when I needed you the most. You are always there for me, whether it is to drag me out of a dark space or throw confetti in the air in celebration of life's awesomeness.

Emma, my gracious, kind, elegant and kick-ass friend. Like two-stepping and swirling on a dancefloor, you whisk me away and brighten up my life. Thank you for knowing exactly when to ask about 'how the book is going' and knowing when not to, and for being the first to put up your hand and volunteer to help do a book launch. You're the unicorn, my friend—I'm so grateful to be in your orbit.

Yvonne Bloom took my unwieldy, lengthy splattering of words and shaped it into some semblance of a real novel . . . twice. Thank you. Beyond being an editor, Yvonne was also my instructor and adviser throughout the process—thank you for always giving me great advice and helping whenever I reached out.

Kate Juniper took my scrappy manuscript and turned it into a polished piece of work. She encouraged me to be bold and write in the raw vulnerability needed for this story to reach into reader's hearts and squeeze the hurt until their brains yield to reflection and change.

Brooke Warner, and the She Writes Press team—thanks for allowing a wider variety of voices to be heard through publishing. The community you have built was invaluable in getting me through this process. Thank you for your professionalism, candor, and transparency.

I want to express my gratitude to all those who have come before me, that made me believe our adventure and this book was possible. Traveling the world for a year and then authoring this book is a product of hundreds of thousands of people that have built the waves of change throughout generations. I stand on your shoulders. In return, I aim to stand tall, reach my hands out to those beside me, and lift up those who will come after me.

Thank you, readers, for taking the time and energy to read this book. I hope it has stirred something inside of you and that you will turn that churn into action and make your life better along with all those of whom we share this world with.

ABOUT THE AUTHOR

ALANA BEST grew up with her parents, two younger sisters, and older brother on the traditional lands of the Treaty 4 Territory, the original lands of the Cree, Saulteaux, Dakota, Nakota, Lakota, and the homeland of the Métis, also known as Regina, Saskatchewan. As a travel enthusiast, Alana is passionate about being a global citizen, encouraging wanderlust, and living a full life. She believes travel helps create tolerance, understanding, and empathy. She and her husband, Roland, have the pleasure of working and living on the traditional, unceded territory of the ləkʷəŋən peoples, with their three incredible children. She and her family love their home in Victoria, British Columbia, and will never stop exploring.

Author photo © Ryan Enright

SELECTED TITLES FROM SHE WRITES PRESS

She Writes Press is an independent publishing company founded to serve women writers everywhere. Visit us at www.shewritespress.com.

Bowing to Elephants: Tales of a Travel Junkie by Mag Dimond. $16.95, 978-1-63152-596-4. Mag Dimond, an unloved girl from San Francisco, becomes a travel junkie to avoid the fate of her narcissistic, alcoholic mother—but everywhere she goes, she's haunted by memories of her mother's neglect, and by a hunger to find out who she is, until she finds peace and her authentic self in the refuge of Buddhist practice.

Brave(ish): A Memoir of a Recovering Perfectionist by Margaret Davis Ghielmetti. $16.95, 978-1-63152-747-0. An intrepid traveler sets off at forty to live the expatriate dream overseas—only to discover that she has no idea how to live even her own life. Part travelogue and part transformation tale, Ghielmetti's memoir, narrated with humor and warmth, proves that it's never too late to reconnect with our authentic selves—if we dare to put our own lives first at last.

Gone: A Memoir of Love, Body, and Taking Back My Life by Linda K. Olson. $16.95, 978-1-63152-789-0. When Linda Olson became a triple amputee at twenty-nine, her husband declared, "I didn't marry your arms and your legs." This is the inspiring memoir of how they chose not to be victims and went on to succeed in careers as physicians, become parents, and travel the world.

No Spring Chicken: Stories and Advice from a Wild Handicapper on Aging and Disability by Francine Falk-Allen. $16.95, 978-1-64742-120-5. A companion to Falk-Allen's memoir *Not a Poster Child*, this handbook deftly and humorously shares tips and stories about disability-oriented travel, how to "be with" and adapt to a handicapped or aging person, and simple assistive health care we can employ in order to live our best and longest lives.

Reclaiming Home: Diary of a Journey Through Post-Apartheid South Africa by Lesego Malepe. $16.95, 978-1-63152-332-8. Malepe documents her travels in South Africa in 2004, the 10th anniversary of South Africa's democracy—a sprawling, revealing journey that illuminates the ways South Africa has changed, and the ways it has remained the same, since the end of apartheid.

Rudy's Rules for Travel: Life Lessons from Around the Globe by Mary K. Jensen. $16.95, 978-1-63152-322-9. Circle the twentieth-century globe with risk-taking, frugal Rudy and his spouse Mary, a catastrophic thinker seeking comfort. When this marriage of opposites goes traveling, their engaging stories combine laugh-out-loud humor with poignant lessons from the odyssey of a World War II veteran.